LONDON RESTAURANT GUIDE

Nicholson

An Imprint of HarperCollins*Publishers*

A Nicholson Guide

© Nicholson 1994

First published 1975
10th edition 1994

Illustrations © Charlotte Wess with the exception
of those on pages 5, 112, 132 by Claire Littlejohn

London street maps
© Nicholson, generated from the
Bartholomew London Digital Database

London Underground Map by
permission of London Regional Transport
LRT Registered User No 94/1496

All other maps
© Nicholson

Nicholson
HarperCollins*Publishers*
77-85 Fulham Palace Road
Hammersmith
London W6 8JB

Produced by HarperCollins, Hong Kong

ISBN 0 7028 2295 7

75/10/1410

CONTENTS

INTRODUCTION

This guide is invaluable to both London's residents and visitors, offering a selection of over 750 restaurants from the thousands that are to be found in the capital. They are divided by nationality and theme to make it easy to find exactly what you want. The guide covers every aspect of eating out in London, from classic cuisine in elegant surroundings to an inexpensive supper or pub meal. There are sections on vegetarian restaurants, those which cater specifically for children, restaurants for parties and some rather unusual places to eat. There is also a section on brasseries and cafés, many of which stay open all day offering good food and drink whether you are looking for a light brunch or a three-course meal.

SYMBOLS AND ABBREVIATIONS

B – Breakfast
L – Lunch
D – Dinner
Open to. . . – Last orders
(Reserve) – Advisable to reserve
(M) – Membership required

Average cost of a meal for one inclusive of VAT (and service where applicable) but without wine:
£   – £10.00 and under
££   – £10.00-£20.00
£££ – £20.00-£30.00
£££+ – £30.00 and over

Credit cards:
A   – Access/Master Card/Eurocard
Ax – American Express
Dc – Diners Club
V   – Visa/Barclaycard

Whilst we make every effort to be accurate in the guide, opening times, specialities and even management can change overnight so it is always worthwhile phoning in advance.

> **Restaurant Services** is a free telephone consultancy service offering up-to-the-minute information and advice on London's restaurants. They will also make a reservation for you if you wish. Their telephone number is **081-888 8080**, and they are open *09.00-20.00 Mon-Fri.*

AFRICAN & CARIBBEAN

AFRICAN and Caribbean cooking is influenced by Indian, Chinese and European cuisines and varies from island to island and country to country. A wide range of exotic ingredients is used and food tends to be spicy and filling. Great use is made of fruit and vegetables such as avocados, coconuts, mangoes and guavas. Pickled and salted cod, chicken and pork form the basis of casseroles flavoured with chilli peppers and fruits. Fish and seafood are also popular dishes, and are frequently barbecued.

Afric-Carib
1 Stroud Green Rd N4. 071-263 7440. Restaurant specialising in authentic, spicy Nigerian dishes: pepper soup, chicken, beef or fish served with yams, plantain and West Indian rice and peas. Relaxed atmosphere encouraged by abundant quantities of palm wine and African music. *LD open to 23.00.* A.Ax.Dc.V. ££

Brixtonian 18 C2
11 Dorrell Pl, off Nursery Rd SW9. 071-978 8870. Wooden floors and white linen table cloths give this French Caribbean restaurant a colonial feel. Each month the menu features specialities from a different island. Salmon en croute, stuffed paw paw and Creole stewed shark are amongst the dishes featured. Huge selection of rum. *LD open to 24.00 Mon-Wed, to 01.00 Thur-Sat, to 23.00 Sun. Closed L Sun & LD Mon.* A.Ax.V. ££

Brixtonian Backayard   7 B5
4 Neal's Yard, off Shorts Gdns WC2. 071-240 2769. A cool colonial restaurant upstairs and a shanty-town-style bar downstairs. The menu is inspired by the West Indies; sweet potato and salmon patties, chicken Columbo and fried snapper with red bean sauce. *LD open to 24.00 Mon-Sat. Closed D Sun.* A.Ax.V. ££

The Calabash   11 B1
38 King St WC2. 071-836 1976. This restaurant in the basement of the Africa Centre is a popular meeting place for London's African population. Masks, head-dresses and African textiles adorn the walls. Tasty selection of regional dishes such as beef with green bananas and coconut cream, chicken groundnut stew, couscous, blackeyed beans and grey mullet. North African beer and wine. Bands play upstairs *at weekends. LD open to 22.30. Closed L Sat & LD Sun.* A.Ax.Dc.V. ££

Cottons Rhum Shop, Bar & Restaurant   2 D4
55 Chalk Farm Rd NW1. 071-482 1096. Trendy cocktail bar and split-level restaurant where you can sample Caribbean home cooking; hot peppered prawns, rasta pasta with ackee and avocado, and wonderful puddings. Rum punches, reggae music and a resident parrot! *LD open to 23.45, to 22.45 Sun.* A.V. ££

Cuba   9 E3
11-13 Kensington High St W8. 071-938 4137. This is a relaxed and friendly place to discover Cuban cuisine. You can enjoy tapas dishes with your pre-dinner rum cocktail, then sit down to Cuban meatloaf or shredded beef Creole. Finish with a strong Cuban coffee. *D open to 02.00, to 23.30 Sun.* No credit cards. ££

Plantation Inn
337-339 High Rd E11. 081-558 6210. A ray of Caribbean sunshine, with pictures of islands adorning the walls and plenty of plant life. Friendly atmosphere, slick service and adventurous Caribbean cuisine. Red bean soup, chicken gumbo montego, lobster with coconut sauce. Rum punches and Jamaican cocktails. *LD open to 23.00, to 24.00 Sat.* A.Ax.Dc.V. ££

A Taste of Africa   15 D3
50 Brixton Rd SW9. 071-587 0343. A very popular West African restaurant offering a wide range of Nigerian and Ghanaian specialities. The egusi meat dishes (stew made with oxtail, cow's foot, chicken, beef, pounded yam and okra) are particularly good. Nigerian beers. *LD open to 24.00. Closed L Sun.* Ax. £

AMERICAN

AMERICAN restaurants in London are changing to include a wider variety of cooking styles. Alongside typical fare of burgers, ribs and Tex-Mex dishes, you can sample Cajun and Creole cooking which comes from around New Orleans in the USA's deep south. This type of cuisine is a blend of French, Spanish, African and Caribbean styles and dishes come 'blackened' after being coated with spicy marinades and then cooked rapidly in very hot oil. Californian cooking is an eclectic mix of influences; variations on Mexican fare result in unusual dishes such as crabmeat tortilla and corn mesa blinis with salsa verde. Pasta and fish dishes are also common.

Big Easy   13 G2
332-334 King's Rd SW3. 071-352 4071. An American 'crab shack' offering crab claws in various sauces, barbecued shrimps and even crab fritters. Also burgers, ribs and chicken. Live music *every night* ranging from jazz and folk to country and western. *LD open to 24.00, to 00.30 Fri & Sat.* A.V. ££

Boardwalk   6 G5
18 Greek St W1. 071-287 2051. Arranged over three floors this Soho restaurant has a menu influenced by the Deep South. Huge portions of ribs, swordfish, seafood gumbo and jambalaya. Surf 'n' Turf (steak and lobster) is one of their specialities. American-style puddings.

Bar; disco *at weekends. LD open to 01.00 Mon-Thur, to 02.00 Fri & Sat. Closed Sun.* A.V. ££

Chicago Rib Shack   10 C3
1 Raphael St SW7. 071-581 5595. Following in the tradition of his Chicago pizza restaurant (see under *Italian*), Bob Payton's cavernous rib shack has a lively atmosphere and American-style service. Wood-smoked barbecued meats with salads and trimmings are the mainstays. Plus steaks, ribs, chicken, turkey sandwich, onion loaf. Cheesecake, pecan pie and American ice-cream to follow. Non-smoking section. *LD open to 23.45, to 23.00 Sun.* A.V. ££

Christopher's   11 C1
18 Wellington St WC2. 071-240 4222. The entrance hall, curving staircase and domed ceiling provide a dramatic interior to this elegant, new style of American restaurant. An east-coast steak and lobster house serving up New York strip steak or Maine lobster (both imported from the US), grills of beef, lamb and chicken, Caesar salad. Vegetarian dishes. *LD open to 23.00. Closed D Sun.* A.Ax.Dc.V. £££

The Criterion   10 G1
Piccadilly Circus W1. 071-925 0909. This impressive art deco dining hall is worth visiting just for the opulent surroundings. The cuisine is Cal-Ital, a blend of American and Italian food. Dishes include grilled chicken with bruschetta, Caesar salad, and sticky toffee pudding to follow. *LD open to 23.30. Closed Sun & B.hol Mon.* A.Ax.Dc.V. ££

Ed's Easy Diner
12 Moor St off Old Compton Street W1. 071-   6 G5
439 1955.
362 King's Rd SW3. 071-352 1956.   14 B1
335 Fulham Rd SW10. 071-352 1952.   13 G1
16 Hampstead High St NW3. 071-431 1958.   1 F1
Lively '50s and '60s-style diner with counter-top juke-boxes and swivel stools round a circular bar. Burgers, hot dogs, cheese fries, malts, milkshakes and US beers. *LD open to 24.00, to 01.00 Fri & Sat.* No credit cards. £

Fatboy's Diner   11 B1
21-22 Maiden Lane WC2. 071-240 1902. An authentic 1940s American dining carriage which has been transported across the Atlantic. Lively and noisy with friendly staff and a brisk turnover. Huge burgers and hot dogs,

ice-cream floats. *LD open to 24.00, to 22.30 Sun.* No credit cards. £

Hard Rock Café 10 D2
150 Old Park Lane W1. 071-629 0382. Ever-popular hamburger joint identifiable by the long queues outside. Houses one of the largest collections of American memorabilia in the world. Burgers and steaks are excellent; other favourites include barbecued pork ribs, BLT and roast beef sandwich. Vegetarian menu. Non-stop blaring rock music. Cocktails. *LD open to 00.15, to 00.45 Fri & Sat.* No credit cards. ££

Henry J. Bean's (But His Friends All Call Him Hank) Bar & Grill
195-197 King's Rd SW3. 071-352 9255.	**14 B1**
490 Fulham Rd SW6. 071-381 5005.	**13 D3**
54 Abingdon Rd W8. 071-937 3339.	**9 D4**

Another successful Bob Payton venture modelled on a typical American bar/grill. High stools and 1950s American memorabilia on the walls. Burgers, hot dogs, fried chicken, nachos, potato skins. Barbecues in the garden at the SW3 branch *in summer. LD open to 23.00. Closed D Sun.* A.Ax.V. £

Joe Allen 11 B1
13 Exeter St WC2. 071-836 0651. In a converted ware-house in Covent Garden, the London 'Joe Allen' follows the pattern of its New York and Paris counterparts. Checked tablecloths, brick walls hung with theatre posters and photos. First-rate cocktail bar. Menu is changed twice daily; includes dishes from California and the south-west plus steaks, shrimps, chilli, delicious spinach salad. Brownies or pecan pie to follow. *LD (Reserve) open to 00.45, to 24.00 Sun.* No credit cards. ££

Johnny Rockets 13 G1
140 Fulham Rd SW10. 071-370 2794. A British branch of an LA institution, this is a lively, noisy American diner with chrome counters and Seeburg dime jukebox-es. Burgers, fries, shakes, malts, even peanut butter and jello sandwiches. Very friendly staff. No smoking. *LD open to 24.00 Mon-Sun.* No credit cards. £

Maxwell's
9 James St off Floral St WC2. 071-836 0303.	**7 B6**
76 Heath St NW3. 071-794 5450.	

This well-established hamburger joint attracts a young clientelé drawn to the lively atmosphere, loud rock music and good selection of cocktails. Burgers, steaks, ribs and salads, plus Cajun and Tex-Mex dishes. Delicious desserts. The NW3 branch has a garden for outdoor summer eating. *LD open to 24.00, to 01.00 Fri & Sat.* A.V. ££

Old Orleans

29-31 Wellington St WC2. 071-497 2433.   **11 C1**
64 Heath St NW3. 071-794 0122.
26-42 Bond St W5. 081-579 7413.
Huge, lively and bustling, designed to re-create the feel of New Orleans. Huge portions of Deep South food; seafood gumbo, blackened red snapper, Deep South ribs. American and Mexican beers, plus expertly-mixed cocktails from the bar. *LD open to 23.00.* A.Ax.Dc.V. ££

Parsons   13 E3

311 Fulham Rd SW10. 071-352 0651. One of the first American-style restaurants in London. Parsons is relaxed, informal and always busy – there are no bookings so expect to queue. Burgers, ribs, pies, pasta, chargrilled salmon and tuna steaks. Rich and delicious desserts. *LD (no reservations) open to 00.30.* A.Ax.Dc.V. ££

Planet Hollywood   10 G1

13 Coventry St W1. 071-287 1000. The biggest restaurant in Europe, packed with movie memorabilia, and a three-dimensional diorama of its celebrity backers, Arnold Schwarzenegger, Sylvester Stallone and Bruce Willis. Huge portions of burgers, ribs, swordfish, pizza and pasta, plus Mexican dishes and a wide range of desserts. Bar area. Memorabilia shop next door in the Trocadero Centre. *LD (no reservations) open to 01.00.* A.Ax.Dc.V. ££

Rock Garden   7 B6

6-7 The Piazza, Covent Garden WC2. 071-240 3961. Ground and first floor restaurant, often packed, especially the outdoor tables in summer. Relaxed and friendly atmosphere. Live music. Framed pictures of rock bands adorn the walls. Ribs, burgers, steaks, salads. Delicious hot fudge chocolate cake to follow. Live bands and DJs in the converted banana warehouse below. *LD open to 24.00, to 01.00 Fri & Sat.* A.Ax.V. £

Rock Island Diner   10 G1

2nd Floor, London Pavilion, Piccadilly Circus W1. 071-287 5500. All-American '50s and '60s diner overlooking Piccadilly Circus. Above the bar is a 1954 Chevy, and bobby-soxed waiters and waitresses dance to music played by the resident DJ. It even has its own radio station, WRID, which plays '50s and '60s hits. Burgers, ribs, steaks, chilli, salads and American-style sandwiches. Mouth-watering chocolate brownies with hot fudge sauce and ice-cream. Good range of beers and cocktails. Children's menu. *LD open to 23.30, to 22.30 Sun.* A.Ax.Dc.V. £

TGI Friday's

6 Bedford St WC2. 071-379 0585. **7 B6**
29 Coventry St W1. 071-839 6262. **10 G1**
Part of a large American family restaurant chain. Loud and lively and always busy. Burgers, steaks, pasta, south-western and Cajun specialities. Delicious desserts. Over 600 cocktails! *LD (no reservations) open to 23.30, to 23.00 Sun.* A.Ax.V. ££

BRITISH

TRADITIONAL ENGLISH

IT is the quality of the ingredients in British cooking that makes for good food – fresh meat and vegetables, salmon and game. The following restaurants either specialise in British cuisine or have a selection of British classics on the menu, ranging from bangers and mash to pheasant and walnut pie. Surroundings can be cheap and cheerful or elegant and expensive. Many pubs serve traditional English lunches. See under *Pub restaurants.*

Baker & Oven **6 D1**

10 Paddington St W1. 071-935 5088. This traditional cellar restaurant offers a selection of sound, simple food in generous quantities; pies, chops, roasts, pheasant (in

season). Hot bread is served from the original ovens of the Victorian bakery. Specially selected wines are served in ceramic jugs. *LD (Reserve) open to 22.30. Closed L Sat & LD Sun.* Ax.V. ££

Betjeman's   7 E4
44 Cloth Fair EC1. 071-796 4981. This English restaurant and wine bar is housed in the Jacobean home of former Poet Laureate, John Betjeman; framed originals of his letters and poems hang on the walls. Try the game stew, Aberdeen Angus sirloin, Scottish smoked salmon or wild boar pie. Wide selection of British cheeses. *LD open to 22.00. Closed Sat & Sun.* A.Ax.V. ££

Boswell's   9 F5
239 Old Brompton Rd SW5. 071-373 3502. Cosy, wood-panelled, traditional restaurant. Try Devon crab soup with cream and brandy, grilled Scottish wild salmon and beef Wellington. Finish with Lord Mayor's trifle. *D (Reserve) open to 23.30.* A.Ax.Dc.V. £££

Buchan's   14 B4
62-64 Battersea Bridge Rd SW11. 071-228 0888. Named after the Scottish author John Buchan *(The Thirty-Nine Steps),* this attractive restaurant has a weekly-changing menu which features Scottish produce cooked in a French style. Start with haggis bathed in claret, then try cassoulet of pheasant with whisky and chestnuts or Scottish cod fishcake with prawn sauce. Selection of Scottish and French cheeses. Fine selection of 39 wines and 39 malt whiskies. *LD open to 22.45, to 22.00 Sun. Closed L Sat.* A.Ax.Dc.V. ££

Chimes of Pimlico   10 F5
26 Churton St SW1. 071-821 7456. A charming restaurant serving pies in various forms. Try pheasant, orange and walnut pie, Gloucestershire lamb pie, or farmhouse sausage hot pot. Informal atmosphere and friendly service. English country wines and a variety of ciders. Other branch at 91 High St, Wimbledon SW19. 081-946 2471. *LD open to 22.15.* A.Ax.V. ££

F. Cooke & Sons   4 C3
41 Kingsland High St E8. 071-254 2878. Described as 'the Savoy Grill of the eel and pie houses', this East End restaurant is owned and run by brothers Fred and Chris Cooke whose family have been in the business since 1862. Small but specialised menu includes stewed or jellied eels, minced steak and kidney pie, and desserts such

as blackcurrant and apple pie. Unlicensed. *LD open to 19.00 Mon, to 19.45 Tue & Wed, to 20.00 Thur, to 21.45 Fri & Sat. Closed Sun.* No credit cards. £

Dorchester Grill Room   10 D2
The Dorchester, 55 Park Lane W1. 071-629 8888. Outstanding cuisine in the magnificent surroundings of the Spanish-style baronial Grill Room. Fine traditional English dishes, delicious roasts from the trolley. Faultless service in this very classy restaurant. Set menu available. *LD (Reserve) open to 23.00.* A.Ax.Dc.V. £££+

The English House   10 C5
3 Milner St SW3. 071-584 3002. Charming dining room in a private house. Antique chairs, expensive chintz wall fabrics, brass based plates laid on quilted tablecloths and cream table linen. The menu changes every two months – chicken and almond salad with mango, fillet of venison with blackberry and apple sauce, home-made orange and cinnamon ice-cream. Specially selected wines. Private rooms available. *LD (Reserve) open to 23.30, to 22.00 Sun.* A.Ax.Dc.V. £££+

Farringdon's   7 E5
41 Farringdon St EC4. 071-236 3663. Dine 'underneath the arches' in the candlelit vaults of Holburn Viaduct. Queen Victoria opened them in 1869, and the style of the place hasn't really changed since. Hot mussels, Holburn halibut, beef Wellington, port-fed Stilton and various desserts. Extensive wine list. Upstairs houses a bistro/bar. *LD (Reserve) open to 23.00. Closed L Sat & LD Sun.* A.Ax.Dc.V. £££

George & Vulture   7 G5
3 Castle Court, off Cornhill EC3. 071-626 9710. Built in 1170 and restored after the Great Fire, this ancient hostelry was one of Dickens' haunts; part of the *Pickwick Papers* was written here and his great-grand-son uses a private dining room in the restaurant. Traditional English fare like Dover sole, roast beef, liver and bacon, sherry trifle. *L (Reserve for large parties) open to 14.45. Closed Sat & Sun.* A.Ax.Dc.V. ££

Green's Restaurant & Oyster Bar
36 Duke St SW1. 071 930 4566   10 F2
Marsham Ct, Marsham St SW1. 071-834 9552.   11 A4
Elegant, club-like restaurant and oyster bar. Menu changes daily; oysters in season, smoked eel, salmon fishcakes, steak and kidney pie. To finish – jam

roly-poly, Bakewell tart or spotted dick. Extensive wine list. *LD (Reserve) open to 23.00. Closed D Sun.* A.Ax.Dc.V. £££

Lindsay House   6 G6
21 Romilly St W1. 071-439 0450. You must ring the doorbell of this 17thC town house to gain entry, but don't be put off – the staff are pleasant and efficient and the decor is splendid. The dining rooms are furnished with rich draperies and traditional paintings. Superb cuisine; the grilled breast of duckling in orange preserve is exquisite. *LD (Reserve) open to 24.00, to 22.00 Sun.* A.Ax.Dc.V. £££+

Maggie Jones   9 E3
6 Old Court Pl, Kensington Church St W8. 071-937 6462. Hearty, traditional English fare in this cosy restaurant reminiscent of a farmhouse kitchen. Boiled beef and dumplings, rack of lamb, baked mackerel with gooseberries, steak and mango casserole, game when in season. Crisp, fresh vegetables. Sherry trifle, chocolate and banana pots. Cheaper set meals also available. *LD (Reserve) open to 23.30.* A.Ax.Dc.V. ££

Porters   7 B6
17 Henrietta St WC2. 071-836 6466. Well-established theme restaurant specialising in pies: try Billingsgate, lamb and apricot, traditional fish pie or turkey and chestnut. Excellent steamed and baked puddings. Traditional Sunday lunch. Real ale, English wine, cock-tails. Friendly service. *LD open to 23.30, to 22.30 Sun.* A.Ax.V. ££

Printer's Pie   7 D5
60 Fleet St EC4. 071-353 8861. Simple English dishes in a pleasant setting at this traditional eating house. Victorian wallpaper, old English pictures and prints. Grills, pies, fish, steak and kidney pudding. Traditional desserts. Extensive beer and wine list. *LD (Reserve L) open to 22.00. Closed Sat & Sun.* A.Ax.Dc.V. ££

Quality Chop House   7 D3
94 Farringdon Rd EC1. 071-837 5093. A lovingly preserved 'working-class caff' where labourers came to eat for over a hundred years. Now serves enormous portions of traditional English fare like sausage and mash and corned beef hash, plus some European dishes. Always busy and lively – seating is at tables of six. *LD*

(Reserve) open to 24.00, to 23.30 Sun. Closed L Sat.
No credit cards. ££

Rules 7 B6
35 Maiden Lane WC2. 071-836 5314. Almost 200
years old, this is a splendidly preserved eating house
rich in associations – Dickens, Thackeray, Edward VII
and Lillie Langtry all dined here. An immense collection
of pictures, prints, cartoons and playbills adorn the
walls. Speciality of the house is game which comes from
Rules' estate in the Pennines; also traditional dishes like
jugged hare, Guinness casserole and steak and kidney
pudding. Delicious desserts. *LD (Reserve) open to
24.00.* A.Ax.V. £££

The Savoy Grill 11 C1
The Savoy Hotel, Strand WC2. 071-836 4343. Elegant
wood-panelled dining room in this world-famous hotel.
Classic English and French cooking and a well-deserved
reputation for impeccable service. Magnificent dessert
trolley. Fine wine list. *LD (Reserve) open to 23.15.
Closed L Sat & LD Sun.* A.Ax.Dc.V. £££+

Simpson's-in-the-Strand 11 B1
100 Strand WC2. 071-836 9112. This sumptuous
Edwardian dining room is an English institution.
Remarkable for the excellence of its roasts; choose large
carvings from enormous joints of beef and lamb. Also
smoked salmon, Dover sole or saddle of mutton.
Delicious treacle roll, spotted dick and bread and butter
pudding. Fine wines and vintage port. Booking and
correct dress essential. *LD (Reserve) open to 23.00, to
21.00 Sun.* A.Ax.Dc.V. £££

Throgmorton Restaurants 7 G5
27a Throgmorton St EC2. 071-588 5165. A very friendly,
club-like atmosphere pervades this City establishment.
Three underground restaurants specialising in traditional
British food – grills and steaks in the Long and Short
Rooms and roasts in the Oak Room. *L (Reserve) open
to 15.00. Closed Sat & Sun.* A.Ax.Dc.V. ££

Veronica's 5 D5
3 Hereford Rd W2. 071-229 5079. The menu at this
homely British restaurant concentrates on nationwide
recipes and is historically themed, offering dishes from
different periods. Dishes could include watersouchy
which is a medieval stew filled with seafood, or duck 'n'
spinage. Everything on the menu is healthy, with low

fat, high fibre and vegan dishes clearly marked. Excellent British cheese board. *LD (Reserve) open to 23.30.* A.Ax.Dc.V. £££

Waltons　　　　　　　　　　　　　　　　**10 B5**
121 Walton St SW3. 071-584 0204. Sumptuous decor and ambitious menus featuring both traditional English and international dishes. Smoked salmon, fois gras, seafood sausage with mushrooms. For dessert, passion fruit mousse or strawberry pavlova. Menus change regularly and there are good-value set menus. Smooth service and a notable wine list. *LD (Reserve) open to 23.30, to 22.00 Sun.* A.Ax.Dc.V. £££+

Wiltons　　　　　　　　　　　　　　　　**10 F2**
55 Jermyn St SW1. 071-629 9955. This 250-year-old restaurant has a reputation for outstanding traditional English cooking. An excellent selection of seafood; baby lobsters, crabs, salmon, halibut, sole and turbot. Also grills and game. Classic desserts such as apple tart or sherry trifle. Fine wine list. *LD (Reserve) open to 22.30. Closed L Sat & LD Sun.* A.Ax.Dc.V. £££+

CARVERIES

OFFER good value set-price meals in a pleasant, informal atmosphere. Carve for yourself, or be served by the chef from enormous succulent joints of beef, pork or lamb. A choice of simple starters and desserts is normally included in the price.

Betjeman Carving Restaurant, Charing　　**11 B1**
Cross Hotel
Strand WC2. 071-839 7282. *LD open to 22.30, to 22.00 Sun.* A.Ax.Dc.V. ££

Bowlers Restaurant, Great Eastern Hotel　　**8 B4**
Liverpool St EC2. 071-283 4363. *LD open to 22.00, to 21.30 Sat & Sun.* A.Ax.Dc.V. ££

The Carvery at the Hotel Rembrandt　　　**10 B5**
Thurloe Pl SW7. 071-589 8100. *LD open to 22.00.* A.Ax.Dc.V. ££

The Carvery, Strand Palace Hotel　　　　**11 B1**
Strand WC2. 071-836 8080. *LD open to 22.00, to 21.00 Sun.* A.Ax.Dc.V. ££

Hotel Russell Carvery Restaurant　　　　**7 B4**
Russell Sq WC1. 071-837 6470. *LD open to 22.00. Closed L Sat.* A.Ax.Dc.V. ££

Searcy's Brasserie, Barbican Centre　　　**7 F4**
Silk St EC2. 071-588 3008. *LD Last orders half an hour after last performance.* A.Ax.Dc.V. £££

Tower Thistle Hotel 12 C1
St Katharine's Way, off East Smithfield E1. 071-481
2575. *LD open to 22.30 Fri, to 24.00 Sat.* A.Ax.Dc.V.
££

MODERN BRITISH

T HIS is a constantly evolving cuisine relying on innovative chefs to create dishes with a modern outlook.
Traditional ingredients are used with Oriental and
Mediterranean influences.

French House Dining Room 6 G5
49 Dean St W1. 071-437 2477. Small, first-floor restaurant above the French House pub in Soho. The daily-changing menu may include such delights as guinea
fowl in red wine, lamb and barley stew, or grilled
pigeon with leeks. Jovial atmosphere and friendly
service. *LD (Reserve) open to 23.30. Closed Sun.*
A.Ax.Dc.V. ££

The Greenhouse 10 E2
27a Hays Mews W1. 071-499 3331. Comfortable
atmosphere with lush green plants which give a light
and summery effect. Service is efficient and friendly. For
starters try braised oxtail, grilled calf's liver. Continue
with fillet of smoked haddock with welsh rarebit. For
dessert bread and butter pudding, steamed sponge.
Limited wine list. *LD (Reserve) open to 23.00. Closed L
Sat.* A.Ax.Dc.V. £££

Hilaire 9 F5
68 Old Brompton Rd SW7. 071-584 8993. Smart South
Kensington restaurant serving classic English cuisine
with some European influences. Frequently-changing
menu may include turbot with mustard sauce, confit of
duck with Puy lentils, loin of Welsh lamb. Set menus.
LD (Reserve) open to 23.30. Closed L Sat & LD Sun.
A.Ax.Dc.V. £££+

Leith's 9 C1
92 Kensington Park Rd W11. 071-229 4481. A charming restaurant in a converted Victorian house run by
Prue Leith, well known for her inventive cuisine. The
seasonal menu ranges from old Beeton recipes to classic
French cooking. Excellent dessert trolley and a good
selection of British cheeses. *D (Reserve) open to 23.30.*
A.Ax.Dc.V. £££+

Ransome's Dock Restaurant 14 B3
35-37 Parkgate Rd SW11. 071-223 1611. Located within

a riverside development in Battersea, this bustling restaurant offers contemporary British cooking in a modern, informal setting. Artichokes and walnut salad, saddle of lamb with spinach, tomato and olive salsa. For dessert, caramelised rice pudding with poached nectarines, hot prune soufflé with hot Armagnac sauce. Menu changes monthly, seafood menu changes daily. Modern jazz background music. Dockside terrace with seating outside. Innovative wine list. *LD (Reserve) open to 23.00. Closed D Sun.* A.Ax.Dc.V. ££

Restaurant & Arts Bar   6 D5
Jason Court, 76 Wigmore St W1. 071-224 2992. Softly-lit basement restaurant with an interior inspired by Monte Casino Abbey in Italy. Fine modern British cuisine; confit of duck, fillet of pork with prunes and Armagnac, hot goat's cheese with cranberry sauce. Delicious desserts and a nationwide variety of cheeses. Good wine list. Assorted live music *every day* – also poetry readings and exhibitions. *LD (Reserve) open to 23.00.* A.Ax.Dc.V. £££

Smith's Restaurant   7 B5
25 Neal St WC2. 071-379 0310. A simple, spacious restaurant in the basement of Smith's Art Galleries. Specialises in modern British cuisine; avocado, bacon and spinach salad, portwine sausages with tomatoes and mashed potatoes, roast artichoke and asparagus tart. *LD (Reserve) open to 23.30. Closed L Sat & LD Sun.* A.Ax.Dc.V. ££

The Square   10 F2
32 King St SW1. 071-839 8787. Inventive cuisine in elegant surroundings at this large, smart restaurant. Grilled venison, breast of guinea fowl, oysters cooked with lemon grass and lime leaves. Fine wine list. *LD (Reserve) open to 23.45. Closed L Sat & LD Sun.* A.Ax.Dc.V. £££

Turner's   10 B5
87-89 Walton St SW3. 071-584 6711. A small restaurant in stylish surroundings with a relaxed and intimate atmosphere. The chef, Brian Turner, is frequently seen front of house. Excellent modern British cuisine; breast of duck roast with Thai spices, grilled venison, rack of lamb. Classic English desserts. *LD (Reserve) open to 23.00, to 22.30 Sun. Closed L Sat.* A.Ax.Dc.V. £££+

CENTRAL EUROPEAN

THE following section covers the cuisines of Austria, Germany and Switzerland. Menus tend to be mainly meat-based, but you will also find cheeses and vegetables. Desserts are normally cream-laden puddings or delicious cakes and pastries.

Austrians love dumplings and put them in most of their dishes. Known as knoedels, they can be mixed with bread, cheese and potatoes and are a perfect accompaniment to soups. Wienerschnitzel (veal covered in breadcrumbs and fried) and red cabbage is a typical Austrian meal.

Sausages, red cabbage and sauerkraut characterise German cooking. With around 1500 different varieties of sausage or wurst, it's no surprise that its use in German cooking is widespread.

Fondue is a well-known Swiss speciality which consists of melted cheese into which small pieces of bread are dipped. Smoked ham, sausages, pâtés, dried meat and fruit are also widely eaten.

Many of London's central European restaurants are heavily themed, so be prepared for cowbells, yodelling and waiters in lederhosen.

Cosmo   **1 G4**
4-6 Northways Pde, Finchley Rd NW3. 071-722 1398. The proprietor of this large, bright, continental restaurant is German-born, so the menu is dominated by solidly-cooked German dishes. Rheinischer sauerbraten, schnitzel and goulash. Apfelstrudel and cream to follow. Fast, attentive service. German beers or wine. *LD open to 23.00.* A.Ax.Dc.V. *££*

Kerzenstüberl   **6 D5**
9 St Christopher's Pl, off Wigmore Street W1. 071-486
3196. Authentic hearty Austrian food with dishes such as
leberknödel soup, bauernschmaus, goulash, Sacher Torte
and apfelstrudel. Lively accordion music, dancing, singing
and yodelling. *LD (Reserve D) open to 23.00. Closed L
Sat & LD Sun. Licensed to 01.00.* A.Ax.Dc.V. ££

Marché Mövenpick   **7 B6**
Swiss Centre, 1 Swiss Court W1. 071-734 1291. A free-
flow market restaurant where you pick fresh products
from market stalls and the food is then prepared in
front of you. Fondue, rösti, raclette. Muesli, quarktorte,
swiss ice-cream. Home-baked bread. *LD open to 24.00.*
A.Dc.V. ££

Prost   **9 D1**
35 Pembridge Rd W11. 071-727 9620. A modern
German restaurant which also offers specialities from
Hungary and Poland. Wild boar sausage, smoked
venison with Russian salad, spatzle (pasta dumplings)
and, for the vegetarian, vegetable strudel. Delicious
fried cheeses. Fruit-flavoured schnapps. Light lunches
on weekdays, Sunday brunches. *LD (Reserve) open to
23.00 Tue-Sun. Closed Mon.* A.Ax.Dc.V. ££

St Moritz   **6 F5**
161 Wardour St W1. 071-734 3324. Typical Swiss
decor, kitted out like a ski hut in the famous resort.
Cheese and beef fondues are the house speciality. Also
Berner Platte, which incorporates smoked ham, pork,
sauerkraut, beans, potato, boiled beef, sausage and
knoedels, and sliced veal in cream and mushroom sauce
served with rösti potatoes. Swiss chocolates accompany
the coffee. Nightclub downstairs. *LD (Reserve) open to
23.30. Closed L Sat & LD Sun.* A.Ax.Dc.V. ££

Tiroler Hut   **5 E5**
27 Westbourne Grove W2. 071-727 3981. This basement restaurant is decked out in chalet decor and is the
perfect place for a party – frothing steins of beer are
brought to your table by waiters in lederhosen, followed
by huge portions of pork, veal, sauerkraut and
dumplings. After your meal enjoy the festivities: cowbell
shows, yodelling, accordion playing, singing and dancing. *D open to 01.00, to 24.00 Sun.* A.Ax.Dc.V. ££

Twin Brothers   **9 E3**
51 Kensington Church St W8. 071-937 4152. Intimate,

old-style German restaurant where the ebullient proprietor (one of the twin brothers who started the restaurant up) will entertain you in his own inimitable style. Traditional dishes such as Bismarck herring, Schweizer onion soup and Wiener schnitzel. *D open to 23.30. Closed Sun.* No credit cards. ££

CHINESE

THERE are three main culinary regions of China – Canton, Beijing (Peking) and Szechuan – offering a huge variety of styles and ingredients. Most Chinese dishes are cooked simply and quickly in order to bring out the natural flavour of the food. Delicate tea accompanies food throughout China and is imbibed to clean the palate between mouthfuls. Try different dishes together – many restaurants serve banquets although it is usually necessary to book in advance. The heart of London's Chinatown is Gerrard Street in Soho.

Most of London's Chinese restaurants are Cantonese. The Cantonese come from the warm coastal south region and have highly savoury dishes. They also tend to blend meat and seafood such as beef with oyster sauce. Steamed *dim sum* are a feature of Cantonese cooking and are a great way to experiment with unfamiliar flavours; they are normally served *until 18.00*.

Food from Beijing (Peking) in the north is considered the highest form of Chinese cuisine. Drier and more highly seasoned than Cantonese, it shows Muslim and Mongolian influences. Typical dishes are Peking duck and Mongolian hotpot.

The cuisine of the isolated peasant communities of Szechuan and the west is characterised by strong flavours. Dishes are aromatic and spicy-hot, using chilli, onion, garlic, peanut, sesame and black beans. Double-cooked pork and tea-smoked duck are specialities.

Cheng Du   2 E5
9 Parkway NW1. 071-485 8058. This smart Camden
Town restaurant is tastefully decorated with fresh flowers and Chinese prints. Specialises in Cantonese and
Pekinese cuisine; the seafood dishes are excellent. Hot,
spicy dishes are marked on the menu. Set menus. *LD
open to 23.30.* A.Ax.V. £££

Chin's   13 C5
311-313 New King's Rd SW6. 071-736 8833. Plush
restaurant specialising in regional cuisine from Canton,
Szechuan and Beijing. Dine in one of the three elegant
feature areas – the Garden Room, Waterfall Room or
Dragon Room. Peking duck, served in the traditional
manner, is their speciality. *LD (Reserve Sat & Sun)
open to 23.45.* A.Ax.V. ££

Chuen Cheng Ku   6 F5
17 Wardour St W1. 071-437 1398. Vast Chinatown
restaurant serving authentic Cantonese food. Delicious
fish dishes such as whole bass in ginger, shrimp and
marinated prawns, and unusual dishes like ducks' feet
with fish lips. Excellent dim sum served from heated
trolleys in traditional Hong Kong style – can be very
busy with Cantonese families at *Sunday lunchtime. LD
(Reserve D) open to 23.45.* A.Ax.Dc.V. ££

Feng Shang   2 D5
Cumberland Basin, opposite 15 Prince Albert Rd NW1.
071-485 8137. Floating restaurant on the Regent's
Canal in the style of a Chinese boat. Light and airy
atmosphere in which to enjoy innovative dishes like
Mongolian lamb and Mou-shu pork served with pancakes. Exotic fruits for dessert. *LD open to 23.00, to
24.00 Sat & Sun.* A.Ax.Dc.V. £££

Fung Shing   6 G6
15 Lisle St WC2. 071-437 1539. Busy restaurant with a
well-deserved reputation for excellent innovative and
traditional dishes. Huge choice of seafood dishes. Slow-
cooked hotpots are their speciality. Try deep-fried squid
with prawn balls or chicken hotpot with clam sauce.
Excellent pre-booked banquets. *LD open to 23.30.*
A.Ax.Dc.V. ££

Gallery Rendezvous   6 F6
53 Beak St W1. 071-734 0445. You can dine in opulence in a banqueting suite at this restaurant which has
one of the best collections of original Chinese paintings
in London. Enjoy excellent Beijing cuisine; grilled

dumplings, Peking duck. Try their home-made egg noodles. *LD (Reserve) open to 22.45.* A.Ax.Dc.V. ££

Good Earth

233 Brompton Rd SW3. 071-584 3658.   **10 B5**
143-145 The Broadway NW7. 081-959 7011.
Predominantly Cantonese cuisine with a large selection of meat-free dishes such as faked yellow fish in hot piquant sauce. An ample menu for meat-eaters too which includes salmon steaks in Szechuan sauce, westlake pork fillet. *LD open to 23.00, to 22.30 Sun.* A.Ax.Dc.V. ££

Good Friends

139-141 Salmon Lane E14. 071-987 5498. Cantonese restaurant in London's original Chinatown at Limehouse, where the first wave of Chinese immigrants arrived as seamen in the late 18thC. Renowned for good, reliable cooking and East End hospitality. *LD (Reserve) open to 23.00, to 24.00 Sat & Sun.* A.Ax.Dc.V. ££

Green Cottage   **1 G4**

9 New College Pde, Finchley Rd NW3. 071-722 5305. Welcoming service attracts the local Chinese community to this Cantonese restaurant. Authentic barbecued roast meats and excellent vegetarian zhai cooking (where the tastes of meat and fish are created out of vegetarian ingredients). *LD open to 23.30.* A.Ax.V. ££

Hoizin   **10 E4**

72-73 Wilton Rd SW1. 071-630 5108. Hoizin means 'fresh taste of the sea' and the owner of this restaurant is a Gerrard Street fishmonger, so seafood dominates the menu. The seafood banquet comprises shark's fin, lobster and sea bass. Meat dishes are also available. Pavement tables *in summer. LD (Reserve) open to 23.30. Closed L Sun.* A.Ax.Dc.V. £££

Hunan   **10 D6**

51 Pimlico Rd SW1. 071-730 5712. Homely restaurant serving regional dishes from Hunan Province in central-southern China. Dishes are chilli-hot, but staff are happy to tailor your meal depending on how hot you like your food. Try Hunan duck (similar to Peking duck but basted in honey and soya) or lamb in a hot and spicy sauce. *LD open to 23.30, to 23.00 Sun.* A.Ax.V. ££

Ken Lo's Memories of China

67-69 Ebury St SW1. 071-730 7734.   **10 D5**
Harbour Yard, Chelsea Harbour, off Lots   **13 F4**
Rd SW10.
Ken Lo's cookery books and TV programmes have

popularised Chinese cuisine. Excellent regional dishes; Szechuan crispy beef, Cantonese sea bass and crispy king prawn kebab. Follow with delicious ginger and honey ice-cream with glazed Peking apple. Stunning views of the marina from the Chelsea Harbour branch. *LD open to 23.00, to 22.00 Sun.* A.Ax.Dc.V. **£££+**

Kew Rendezvous
110 Kew Rd, Richmond, Surrey. 081-948 4343. Stylish restaurant with an elegant three-floored glass façade. The eclectic menu covers the three main culinary regions of China; there are spicy Szechuan dishes, Cantonese seafood and Peking duck. *LD open to 23.30.* A.Ax.V. **££**

Ley-Ons   6 G5
56 Wardour St W1. 071-437 6465. Formerly a Lyons tea shop, this long-established Cantonese restaurant was the first place in Soho to serve dim sum. Try stuffed aubergine, crispy wun tun or steamed eel with black bean sauce. *LD open to 23.15, to 22.30.* A.Ax.Dc.V. **££**

Maxim Restaurant
155 Northfield Ave W13. 081-567 1719. A real find in Ealing is this family-run restaurant specialising in Beijing food. Try Peking duck, Szechuan chilli prawns, crispy lamb. Set meal for vegetarians. *LD open to 23.30. Closed L Sun.* A.Ax.Dc.V. **££**

Mayflower   6 G6
68-70 Shaftesbury Ave W1. 071-734 9207. Situated in the heart of theatreland and open into the early hours, this fashionable Cantonese restaurant is always busy. Specialities such as stir-fried crab, steamed scallops with garlic, yam-stuffed fried spiced duck. *D (Reserve) open to 04.00.* A.Ax.Dc.V. **££**

Mr Chow   10 D3
151 Knightsbridge SW1. 071-589 7347. Fashionable restaurant serving authentic Beijing cuisine in surroundings of old-style opulence. Peking duck, velvet chicken, Mr Chow's noodles. Banquets arranged for any number of people. *LD (Reserve) open to 23.45.* A.Ax.Dc.V. **£££**

Mr Kai of Mayfair   10 D1
65 South Audley St W1. 071-493 8988. Modern, stylish restaurant with simple decor and creative cuisine. Sizzling lamb, chilli prawns in fresh pineapple, steamed sea bass Peking-style. Efficient and friendly service. *LD (Reserve) open to 23.15.* A.Ax.Dc.V. **£££**

Now & Zen   **7 B6**
4a Upper St Martin's Lane WC2. 071-497 0376. You
walk over a glass gangplank to enter this stylishly-
designed restaurant, one of the Zen chain. Modern
Oriental menu; many cuisines of the Far East feature.
There is a snack menu in the bar *in the evenings*; eat as
many snacks as you like from a list of 50 which includes
minced chicken with Malaysian spices and Thai-style
pan-fried pomfret with chilli. Other branches. *LD
(Reserve at weekends) open to 23.30, to 23.00 Sun.*
A.Ax.Dc.V. £££+

Oriental   **10 D2**
Dorchester Hotel, 55 Park Lane W1. 071-629 8888.
Exquisite Cantonese cuisine in the sumptuous surroundings of this lavish hotel restaurant. Set menus or try one
of the chef's specials. Private rooms available. Correct
dress essential. *LD (Reserve) open to 23.00. Closed L
Sat & LD Sun.* A.Ax.Dc.V. £££+

Paper Tiger   **9 G4**
10-12 Exhibition Rd SW7. 071-584 3737. Select and
fashionable basement restaurant providing a high standard of Szechuan and Beijing cuisine. Spicy dumplings,
curried wun tun, steamed fish in rice wine sauce. Bang
bang chicken is one of the more exotic dishes. *LD
(Reserve) open to 24.00.* A.Ax.V. ££

Poons
4 Leicester St WC2. 071-437 1528.   **10 G1**
27 Lisle St WC2. 071-437 4549.   **10 G1**
50 Woburn Pl WC1. 071-580 1188.   **7 B3**
Whiteleys, Queensway W2. 071-792 2884.   **5 E5**
Unpretentious, usually crowded, family-run Cantonese
restaurants; the Lisle Street branch was the original.
Wind-dried meats such as duck and sausages are the
specialities but the extensive menus also include good
seafood and vegetable dishes. *LD (Reserve) open to
23.30.* No credit cards. £

Poons in the City   **8 B6**
2 Minster Court, Mincing Lane EC3. 071-626 0126.
The City branch of the Poons chain has a restaurant,
fast-food counter and private party rooms. Mainly
Cantonese food with an emphasis on seafood. *LD open
to 22.30. Closed Sat & Sun.* A.Ax.Dc.V. ££-£££

Poons of Covent Garden   **7 B6**
41 King St WC2. 071-240 1743. Up-market branch of

the Poons chain. The decor here is kept simple – a mural and a few pictures cover the brick walls. Built around the kitchen, the ceaseless activity of the chefs provides constant diversion. The menu includes many specialities, and, of course, Poons' wind-dried meats. Special Chinese New Year menu. Set menu changes frequently. *LD (Reserve D) open to 23.30. Closed Sun.* A.Ax.Dc.V. ££-£££

Qinggis   2 C3
30 England's Lane NW3. 071-586 8619. Specials from Beijing, Szechuan and Canton at this light, modern restaurant. Try steamed sea bass or fried squid with ginger and spring onion. Excellent service. *LD (Reserve) open to 23.00, to 23.30 Fri & Sat.* A.Ax.Dc.V. ££

Red Pepper   13 F2
7 Park Walk SW10. 071-352 3546. Sleek European-style restaurant decorated with modern prints and fresh flowers. Szechuan food; bang bang chicken salad, crispy pork fillet, sizzling lamb with spring onion. Three set menus. *LD open to 23.45.* A.Ax.Dc.V. £££

Royal China
13 Queensway W2. 071-221 2535.   5 E6
3 Chelverton Rd SW15. 081-788 0907.   16 A2
Both branches are smart and stylish with distinctive menus; Peking dumplings in chilli sauce, jellyfish with marinated pork, lobster with yellow-bean sauce. Always busy *at Sunday lunchtime.* Delightful service. *LD open to 23.00.* A.Ax.Dc.V. £££

Tai Pan
665 Commercial Rd E14. 071-791 0118. Large, bright and lively East End restaurant; the large round tables are ideal for group meals. Traditional-style Cantonese dishes with a few northern specials; try the delicious crispy Mongolian lamb. *LD (Reserve) open to 23.30, to 24.00 Fri & Sat.* A.Ax.Dc.V. ££

Tai Wing Wah   7 A6
7-9 Newport Pl WC2. 071-287 2702. A pleasant restaurant with friendly staff who are happy to explain the Chinese menu. One of the best places for dim sum in London; deep-fried squid cakes, grilled meat dumplings. *LD (Reserve) open to 23.30, to 24.00 Fri & Sat, to 22.30 Sun.* A.Ax.Dc.V. ££

Treasure of China
10 Nelson Rd SE10. 081-858 9884. Stylish restaurant

serving north Chinese food. All ingredients are bought fresh from Greenwich market each day. Sizzling dishes are very popular. Vegetarian set meals. *LD (Reserve) open to 23.30, to 24.00 Sat.* A.Ax.Dc.V. ££

Wong Kei   7 A6
41-43 Wardour St W1. 071-437 6833. Large, cheap and cheerful Cantonese caff on four floors. Expect to share a table and be prepared for the rudeness of the waiting staff. Excellent Singapore noodles and huge servings of wun tun soup. Free pots of Chinese tea. *LD open to 23.30.* No credit cards or cheques. £

Young's
154-155 Upper St N1. 071-226 8463.   3 E4
19 Canonbury Lane N1. 071-226 9791.   3 E4
An extensive choice of dishes from Beijing, Canton and Szechuan. Deep-fried prawns with chilli oil, bean curd with Chinese mushrooms, crispy duck Szechuan-style. The Upper Street branch is a large brasserie-style restaurant; Canonbury Lane is small and unobtrusive. *LD (Reserve D) open to 24.00.* A:Ax.Dc.V. ££

Young's Rendezvous
13 Bond St W5. 081-840 3060. This is an extremely smart, new-wave Chinese restaurant. Staff dress in traditional Chinese clothes, classical Chinese music plays in the background and an impressive collection of replica Ming and Qing dynasty gowns are on display. The wide-ranging menu offers Beijing and Cantonese dishes, plus some interesting specials. Dim sum *at lunchtime. LD (Reserve Fri & Sat) open to 23.45, to 24.00 Fri & Sat.* A.Ax.Dc.V. ££

Zen   10 B5
Chelsea Cloisters, Sloane Ave SW3. 071-589 1781. The unusual and luxurious surroundings of the original Zen restaurant include a rock-pool, waterfall and mirrored ceilings. The long and inventive menu covers all regional specialities; soft-shell crab, spicy ducks' tongues, Szechuan French beans. *LD (Reserve D) open to 23.30, to 23.00 Sun.* A.Ax.Dc.V. £££

Zen Central   10 E2
20 Queen St W1. 071-629 8103. More formal than the other Zen restaurants, the decor here is cool and stylish and the clientele in the expense account bracket. The menu offers hand-cut pork with dried shredded scallops, veal in black pepper sauce and some delicious

desserts; try the bean curd almond delight. *LD (Reserve) open to 23.00.* A.Ax.Dc.V. £££+

ZeNW3   1 F1
83 Hampstead High St NW3. 071-794 7863. Modern Chinese menu at the fashionable north London outpost of the Zen chain. Variations of Beijing and Szechuan dishes; Peking ravioli in a hot sauce, prawns steamed with fennel seeds, shredded jellyfish salad. *LD (Reserve) open to 23.30.* A.Ax.Dc.V. £££

EAST EUROPEAN

THIS section covers the cuisines of Hungary, Poland, Russia and the Czech Republic.

Paprika is used as a flavouring in many Hungarian dishes, usually accompanied by cream or a rich butter sauce. Favourite dishes include chicken *paprikash* or goulash, *porrlokt*, a national onion stew, and *letscho,* a mixture of peppers, tomatoes and onions.

Traditional Polish dishes are *blinis* (sweet or savoury pancakes filled with anything from herrings to cherries), *bigos* (stew with sauerkraut, sausages, bacon, mushrooms and red wine), and *zrazy* (beef roll filled with bacon, cucumber and mushrooms). Try accompanying your meal with flavoured vodkas, best downed in one go in the traditional manner!

If you're feeling rich, try the caviar and champagne menu to be found in the Russian establishments, or, at the other end of the price scale, a bowl of *borscht* (cold beetroot soup) or beef with dumplings.

Fish is common to each of these cuisines and comes served in a variety of ways. Dumplings and sausages are also common. Cabbage and sauerkraut are the traditional vegetables.

Borshtch 'n' Tears   **10 C4**
46 Beauchamp Pl SW3. 071-589 5003. Crowded, informal and lively Russian restaurant. Borscht, beef Stroganoff, chicken Dragomiroff and blinis. Portions are large and Russian vodkas flow. Very much a party restaurant. *LD open to 01.00.* Ax. ££

Czech Club   **1 E3**
Czechoslovak National House, 74 West End Lane NW6. 071-372 5251. London's only Czechoslovakian club, but you don't have to be a member to enjoy the excellent, authentic food. Try one of the meat soups or beef with dill sauce and dumplings. Czech beer. *LD (Reserve) open to 22.30. Closed L Mon-Fri & D Mon.* No credit cards. ££

Daquise   **10 A5**
20 Thurloe St SW7. 071-589 6117. Very popular with Polish émigrés and students, this restaurant serves simple, but very well-prepared dishes. Borscht, stuffed cabbage, sausages and shashlik. Also open for morning coffee and afternoon tea with some of the most delicious pastries in London. Flavoured Polish vodkas. *LD open to 23.30.* No credit cards. £

The Gay Hussar   **6 G5**
2 Greek St W1. 071-437 0973. Intimate, old-fashioned, much-loved Hungarian restaurant with a loyal following. Try the chilled wild cherry soup, pike with beetroot sauce, venison goulash or spiced Hungarian sausage. To follow, there are sweet cheese pancakes and poppyseed strudel. Hungarian wines. *LD (Reserve) open to 23.00. Closed Sun.* A.Ax.Dc.V. ££

Grove Gallery
69 The Grove W5. 081-567 0604. A delightful Polish café serving meals, snacks and delicious sweet pastries *all day*. Traditional dishes include bigos, sauerkraut, blinis and pancakes. Pavement tables *in summer*. Art gallery upstairs. *LD open to 23.00, to 22.30 Sun.* A.V. £

Kaspia   **6 E6**
18-18a Bruton Pl W1. 071-493 2612. In plush surroundings behind a caviar shop, this restaurant only serves fish and caviar. Choose from three set-price

menus, the Sanka, Troika and Trois Caviars, or sample specialities of smoked salmon, blinis and quails' eggs. Russian and Polish vodkas. *LD (Reserve) open to 23.30. Closed Sun.* A.Ax.Dc.V. ££-£££+

Lowiczanka

238-246 King St W6. 081-741 3225. Spacious first floor restaurant in the Polish Social and Cultural Centre. Changing menu always includes some East European dishes; try herring in cream sauce, pirozki or tripe soup. Home-made cakes. Polish bands *at weekends. LD open to 23.00, to 00.30 Sat.* A.Ax.Dc.V. £

Luba's Bistro   10 B4

6 Yeoman's Row SW3. 071-589 2950. Authentic Russian cooking in down-to-earth surroundings. Borscht, beef Stroganoff, kooliebaiaka (salmon pie), golubtsy, pojarsky. Seating at long tables. Unlicensed, but you can bring your own wine. *D open to 23.00. Closed Sun.* A.Ax.V. ££

Nikita's   13 E2

65 Ifield Rd SW10. 071-352 6326. An atmospheric cavernous restaurant, exquisitely decorated in red and gold, Nikita's introduced authentic Russian cuisine to London more than 20 years ago. Beef Stroganoff, scallops zubrovka, caviar. White Russian chocolate for dessert. Wide selection of vodkas. *D open to 23.30. Closed Sun.* A.Ax.V. £££

Ognisko Polskie   10 A3

55 Princes Gate, Exhibition Rd SW7. 071-589 4635. Quiet, elegant dining room in the Polish Hearth Club. Traditional cuisine; cold beetroot soup, meat dumplings, boiled beef. Breast of duck with blackcurrants is delicious. Hearty desserts; try the pancakes stuffed with cream cheese. Polish Pils. Flavoured vodkas. *LD (Reserve Fri & Sat) open to 23.00.* A.Ax.Dc.V. ££

Otchi   6 C4

43 Crawford St W1. 071-724 8228. Themed Russian restaurant where the waiters wear Georgian blouses and samovars adorn the walls. Otchi caviar, shashlik (kebabs), meat balls, chicken Kiev, beef Stroganoff. Set menu available. The wine list includes vodka and Russian wine. Live gypsy music *every night. LD open to 23.30. Closed L Sat & L Sun.* A.Ax.Dc.V. £££

Wodka   9 E4

12 St Alban's Grove W8. 071-937 6513. Built originally as a dairy in the 1880s, this is a stylish Polish restaurant

decorated in minimalist style. Imaginative menu includes wild boar sausages, herring fillet with dill cucumber, golonka (pork shank glazed with orange and honey), blinis with aubergine mousse. Delicious cream and chocolate-laden desserts. Home-made vodka, available in shots or half bottles. *LD (Reserve) open to 23.15. Closed L Sat.* A.Ax.Dc.V. ££

Zamoyski's   2 B2
85 Fleet Rd NW3. 071-794 4792. Above Zamoyski's wine bar this restaurant offers rich and robust Polish food; pierogi rozne (East European ravioli), blinis, marinated wild boar. Traditional puddings. Flavoured vodkas. *LD (Reserve Sat & Sun) open to 23.00.* A.V. ££

FRENCH

THE following restaurants provide a variety of styles of French cuisine. Some specialise in simple provincial cooking, others in sophisticated haute cuisine where dishes are delicate and artfully arranged. It should be noted that French food can be expensive as ingredients like foie gras, truffles and magret de canard are all imported.

The Ark   9 E2
122 Palace Gardens Ter W8. 071-229 4024. Good provincial French food in surroundings reminiscent of an Alpine chalet. Menu changes daily and may include champignons de campagne, moules marinières, wild rabbit (in season), fruits de mer, chicken pilaf. Crème brulée or chocolat au pot to follow. Branch at 35 Kensington High St W8 (**9 D4**) (071-937 4294) which serves modern French cuisine. *LD (Reserve) open to 23.15. Closed L Sun.* A.V. ££

L'Artiste Assoiffé   5 C6
122 Kensington Park Rd W11. 071-727 4714. Informal,
friendly restaurant in a large town house near Portobello
Road. Provincial French cuisine; snails with garlic, deep-
fried Camembert, filet Dijon, entrecôte au poivre. Small
garden for summer dining. Two resident parrots! *D open
to 23.00, L Sat only. Closed Sun.* A.Ax.Dc.V. £££

L'Artiste Musclé   10 E2
1 Shepherd Market, off White Horse St W1. 071-493
6150. Cheap and cheerful bistro on two floors with
pavement tables for outdoor eating *in summer*. Short
blackboard menu may include boeuf bourguignon, côte
du porc, smoked chicken. Fine cheese and wines. *LD
open to 23.30. Closed L Sun.* A.Ax.Dc.V. ££

Auberge de Provence   10 F3
St James's Court Hotel, 41 Buckingham Gate SW1.
071-821 1899. Rustic hotel dining room serving
Provençal-inspired cooking. Mediterranean herbs and
flavourings add zest to dishes like steamed sea bass with
tomato, basil and olive oil, noisettes of lamb with basil
and creamed aubergines. Provençal wines. Vegetarian
dishes. *LD (Reserve L) open to 23.00. Closed L Sat &
LD Sun.* A.Ax.Dc.V. £££+

L'Aventure   5 F1
3 Blenheim Ter NW8. 071-624 6232. Charming bistro
in a St John's Wood town house. You might find confit
of duck with lentils, carré of lamb, or chicken with
chanterelles on the fixed price menu which changes
daily. Delicious truffe au chocolate for dessert. Outside
tables *in summer. LD (Reserve) open to 23.00, to 22.00
Sun.* A.Ax.V. L ££ D £££

Boulestin   7 B6
1a Henrietta St WC2. 071-836 7061. Opened in the
1920s, Boulestin's heyday is over but it is still an outstanding restaurant in many ways. The interior is
sumptuous and spacious with a club-like atmosphere
and the menu has some interesting specialities. Dignified
service. Fine wines. *LD open to 23.15. Closed L Sat &
LD Sun.* A.Ax.Dc.V. £££+

Café des Amis du Vin   7 B5
11 Hanover Pl, off Long Acre WC2. 071-379 3444.
Very popular, lively spot with a wine bar in the basement and a café on the ground floor. The restaurant on
the first floor has an intimate atmosphere in which to

enjoy first-class regional French cuisine. Set pre-theatre menu. *LD (Reserve) open to 23.30. Closed L Sat & LD Sun.* A.Ax.V. £££

Le Café du Marché   7 E4
22 Charterhouse Sq EC1. 071-608 1609. Lively French restaurant in a converted warehouse near Smithfield Market. Set menu offers a large choice; salmon and leek terrine, bouillabaisse, pissaladière. Jazz *in the evenings. LD (Reserve) open to 22.00. Closed L Sat & LD Sun.* A.V. ££

Café Royal Grill Room   6 F6
68 Regent St W1. 071-439 6320. Superb food, wine and service in a wonderful setting; extravagant and unique rococo with mirrors, caryatids, gilding and painted ceiling. The menu is long and ambitious; classic French cooking and game (in season). Terrine de foie gras, tournedos Rossini, medallions of veal with foie gras. *LD (Reserve) open to 23.00. Closed L Sat & LD Sun.* A.Ax.Dc.V. £££+

The Capital   10 C3
The Capital Hotel, 22 Basil St SW3. 071-589 5171. This gracious hotel behind Harrods has one of the most outstanding French restaurants in London. Classic cuisine in an old-fashioned and charming atmosphere. Feather-light quenelles, tarte tatin, carré d'agneau, lobster bolognese. Set menus. *LD (Reserve) open to 23.00.* A.Ax.Dc.V. £££+

Chanterelle   9 F6
119 Old Brompton Rd SW7. 071-373 5522. Charming atmosphere at this ever-popular South Kensington bistro. Anglo-French dishes; bouillabaisse, Toulouse sausages, spinach roulade with walnuts and cream cheese. Set menus. Outdoor patio seating. *LD (Reserve) open to 23.30.* A.Ax.Dc.V. ££

Chez Gerard
8 Charlotte St W1. 071-636 4975.   6 F4
LD (Reserve) open to 23.00. Closed L Sat.
31 Dover St W1. 071-499 8171.   6 E6
LD open to 23.30. Closed Sun.
119 Chancery Lane WC2. 071-405 0290.   7 D5
L only Mon-Fri. Closed Sat & Sun.
Authentic and reliable French food in rustic surroundings. Charcuterie, soupe de poisson, escalope de veau, châteaubriand for two. Vast salads, tarts, mousses and cakes, cheeseboard. A.Ax.Dc.V. ££

Chez Moi 9 B2

1 Addison Ave W11. 071-603 8267. This charming restaurant has built a loyal following over the last 26 years. The menu is divided between traditional and eclectic dishes; lamb in Dijon mustard, roulade of smoked chicken, carré d'agneau. Chocolate pot or tarte au citron for dessert. *LD open to 23.00. Closed L Sat & LD Sun.* A.Ax.Dc.V. £££+

Chez Nico at Ninety Park Lane 10 D1

Grosvenor House Hotel, 90 Park Lane W1. 071-409 1290. The dining room of the Grosvenor House Hotel, this is a formal, yet relaxed restaurant. Nico Ladenis brings with him his classic dishes; rillette of smoked salmon with chopped herbs and tomato jelly, chicken and foie gras sausage with caramelized apples. For dessert, the poached pears with crispy almonds, chantilly and chocolate sauce is delicious. French cheeses and regional wines. New-style Gastronomic Menu has eight courses and is available at both lunch and dinner. *LD (Reserve) open to 23.00. Closed L Sat & LD Sun.* A.Ax.Dc.V. L £££ D £££+

Claridge's Restaurant 6 E6

Brook St W1. 071-629 8860. Distinguished French cooking in luxurious surroundings. The atmosphere is typical of the sedate '30s. Extensive menu includes lobster and crab fritters with soft quail eggs, seared sea bass, pot roasted guinea fowl with black pudding ballotine. Jasmin tea parfait with fresh melon, mille feuille aux deux chocolats to finish. Polished service. Large and notable wine list. Dinner dance *19.30-01.00 Fri & Sat. LD (Reserve) open to 23.15.* A.Ax.Dc.V. £££+

The Connaught 6 D6

The Connaught Hotel, Carlos Pl W1. 071-499 7070. Known as one of the grandest hotel dining rooms in the world. Old-fashioned panelling, mirrors and chandeliers are the setting for outstanding classical French and traditional English cuisine. The menu includes the famous Connaught terrine, oeufs de cailles Maintenon, filet de boeuf en croûte, langoustines, marvellous game. Superb wine list. Very formal with service by tail-coated waiters. Jacket and tie must be worn. *LD (Reserve) open to 22.15.* A.V. £££+

L'Epicure 6 G5

28 Frith St W1. 071-437 2829. With its distinctive flaming torches outside, this charming, old-fashioned

restaurant has been a Soho landmark for over 40 years.
Famous for its flambéed dishes; châteaubriand garni is
cooked over a flambé lamp and set alight. *LD (Reserve L)
open to 23.15. Closed L Sat & LD Sun.* A.Ax.Dc.V. £££

L'Escargot   6 G5
48 Greek St W1. 071-437 6828. Once very fashionable,
L'Escargot went into a decline and closed in 1992. It
underwent refurbishment and re-opened with a new-
look brasserie on the ground floor serving French bistro
food, and a more formal upstairs restaurant offering
traditional French dishes. Sole veronique, cassoulet, foie
gras topped with artichoke mousse. Excellent wine list.
LD open to 23.30. Restaurant closed L Sat & LD Sun.
A.Ax.V. Brasserie ££ Restaurant £££

L'Etoile   6 F4
30 Charlotte St W1. 071-636 7189. One of the oldest
French restaurants in London. Old-fashioned service
and atmosphere with a classic French menu; rognons,
ris de veau and tripes à la mode de Caen. Excellent wine
list. *LD (Reserve) open to 23.00. Closed L Sat & LD
Sun.* A.Ax.Dc.V. £££

Frederick's   3 E5
Camden Passage N1. 071-359 2888. A choice of
surroundings at this well-established restaurant – the
Conservatory, the airy Garden Room at the back, or
candlelit tables at the front. A la carte menu changes
monthly; fixed price menu changes weekly. Classic dishes; steamed asparagus with mint-scented hollandaise,
grilled tournedos of salmon and sole with fresh herbs,
grilled duck's breast with a light sauce scented with lime.
Innovative vegetarian dishes. Private rooms available *LD
(Reserve) open to 23.30. Closed Sun.* A.Ax.Dc.V. £££

Le Gavroche   6 D6
43 Upper Brook St W1. 071-408 0881. Run by Albert
Roux and his son Michel. Renowned for its luxurious
atmosphere and consistently faultless, imaginative haute
cuisine. The daily-changing set lunch menu is excellent
value. Magnificent wine list. *LD (Reserve) open to 23.00.
Closed Sat & Sun.* A.Ax.Dc.V. £££+ (set lunch menu £££)

Gavvers   10 D5
61-63 Lower Sloane St SW1. 071-730 5983. On the
original site of Le Gavroche, this is the less expensive
cousin of that acclaimed establishment. Food and service decidedly French; the all-inclusive menus are good

value. Classical cuisine; roast leg of rabbit, croustade of pheasant, sautéed scallops and tempura mussels. *LD (Reserve) open to 23.00. Closed L Sat & LD Sun.* A.Dc.V. £££

Le Gothique   17 A4
The Royal Victoria Patriotic Building, Fitzhugh Grove, Trinity Rd SW18. 081-870 6567. Housed in what was once an orphanage, a hospital and a home to the secret service, the walls of this restaurant are covered with historical photographs. Snails with garlic mushrooms, gigot d'agneau, and exquisite chocolate mousse to follow. *LD (Reserve) open to 22.30. Closed L Sat & LD Sun.* A.Ax.Dc.V. ££

Harvey's   17 B6
2 Bellevue Rd SW17. 081-672 0114. With the departure of Marco Pierre White to The Restaurant at the Hyde Park Hotel, Harvey's has been completely restyled and now has a lighter, fresher feel. The frequently changing menu has Mediterranean influences, but still maintains the high standards set by the former chef. *LD open to 23.00. Closed L Sat & D Sun.* A.Ax.V. £££+

Au Jardin des Gourmets   6 G5
5 Greek St W1. 071-437 1816. Owned by a wine merchant, this restaurant is famous for its climate-controlled cellar which harbours old and rare clarets. Elegant surroundings in which to enjoy modern and traditional French dishes. Snails, frogs' legs (seasonal), warm scallops on potato salad, sauté of fresh foie gras. Very good cheeseboard and home-made desserts. Set menus. *LD (Reserve) open to 23.15. Closed L Sat & LD Sun.* A.Ax.Dc.V. £££

Ma Cuisine   10 B5
113 Walton St SW3. 071-584 7585. This intimate family-run restaurant is comfortable and simply decorated. The menu is full of interest with dishes such as galettes de lotte et St Jacques au pistou, aiguillettes de boeuf Palois. Beautiful presentation, polite service. *LD (Reserve) open to 23.00. Closed L Sat & LD Sun.* A.Ax.Dc.V. £££

Magno's Brasserie   7 B5
65a Long Acre WC2. 071-836 6077. Gallic service at this slick establishment situated close to theatreland. Various dishes from the à la carte menu are included on the excellent pre-theatre menu; gigot d'agneau, truite aux

amandes. Tempting desserts. *LD open to 23.30. Closed L Sat & LD Sun.* A.Ax.Dc.V. £££ (pre-theatre set menu £)

Mange Tout
12 Royal Parade SE3. 081-852 2565. This small, pleasant restaurant overlooking Blackheath has a seasonal menu offering traditional French cooking with a twist. Starters include prawn bisque and baked blacked mushrooms. Follow with confit of duck in orange and lemon sauce, fillet of Scotch salmon and cod wrapped in puff pastry, or roast pigeon cooked in sherry. Friendly service. Occasional jazz. *LD open to 22.30. Closed D Sun & LD Mon.* A.Ax.Dc.V. £££

Mon Plaisir   7 B5
21 Monmouth St WC2. 071-836 7243. Typically French restaurant with a friendly atmosphere, helpful service and an unpretentious menu of classic provincial dishes. Coq au vin, cassoulet de canard, saumon grillé sauce bearnaise. Excellent plateau de fromages. Good wine list. Pre-theatre menu. *LD (Reserve) open to 23.15. Closed Sat & Sun.* A.Ax.Dc.V. ££-£££

Le Muscadet   6 D4
25 Paddington St W1. 071-935 2883. Small and intimate bistro with a loyal local clientele. Quality French cooking; fish soup, snails in puff-pastry, chicken liver terrine. *LD (Reserve) open to 22.45, to 22.00 Sat. Closed L Sat & LD Sun.* A.V. £££

Nico Central   6 F5
35 Great Portland St W1. 071-436 8846. What was formerly Chez Nico has become Nico Central with the departure of chef Nico Ladenis to Chez Nico at Ninety Park Lane (see above). Up-market brasserie with a menu of modern classics including Nico's boudin blanc (chicken and foie gras sausage). *LD (Reserve) open to 23.00. Closed Sat & Sun.* A.Ax.Dc.V. £££

Le Palais du Jardin   7 B6
136 Long Acre WC2. 071-379 5353. Lively and spacious, with the feel of a Parisian brasserie. Traditional French cuisine; steak haché, blanquette de veau, moules Parmentier. Oyster and shellfish bar at the front. *LD open to 24.00, to 23.00 Sun.* A.Ax.Dc.V. ££

Le P'tit Normand   16 D4
185 Merton Rd SW18. 081-871 0233. A deservedly popular local restaurant with a very friendly atmosphere. Hearty cooking; gambas au Calvados, côte de

veau normande, confit of duck. Magnificent French cheeseboard and vintage Calvados. *LD (Reserve D)* open to 22.30. *Closed L Sat.* A.Ax.V. ££

Pierre Victoire   16 B3
136 Upper Richmond Rd SW15. 081-789 7043. Informal, relaxed and friendly restaurant with a conservatory at the front and a roof garden. Roast monkfish tail with red wine, cinnamon and roasted garlic, Dover sole with lemon and black butter sauce. Delicious desserts. Pianist *Fri & Sat eve.* LD *(Reserve) open to* 23.00. *Closed D Sun.* A.V. L £ D ££

La Plume de ma Tante
381 King St W6. 081-748 8270. Warm and friendly Hammersmith bistro serving authentic French cuisine; deep-fried Brie, escargots, lambs' kidneys in port sauce, baby chicken stuffed with Provençal mincemeat. Small but select wine list. Pavement tables *in summer. LD* open to 23.00. *Closed L Sat & LD Sun.* A.V. ££

Le Poulbot   7 F5
45 Cheapside EC2. 071-236 4379. City partner of Le Gavroche, Le Poulbot has a busy brasserie-style operation on the ground floor and a plush restaurant in the basement. The restaurant offers a set menu of classic French food and has private booths which make an ideal setting for a business lunch. The brasserie serves standard bistro fare and is also open for breakfast. *L (Reserve) open to 14.30. Closed Sat & Sun.* A.Ax.Dc.V. Brasserie ££ Restaurant £££+

La Poule au Pot   10 D5
231 Ebury St SW1. 071-730 7763. A delightful, old-fashioned bistro with genuine French charm. Robust provincial food; ratatouille, mousse de poisson, poule au pot, garlic chicken in a lemon sauce, boeuf bourguignon, rabbit with mustard. Sorbets or crème brulée for dessert. *LD (Reserve) open to 23.15. Closed L Sat & LD Sun.* A.Ax.Dc.V. L ££ D £££+

Le Renoir   7 A6
79 Charing Cross Rd WC2. 071-734 2515. Friendly, efficient and right in the heart of theatreland. Good French cooking; grilled trout, steak frites, plus some simpler dishes such as croque-monsieur and omelettes. The menu is arranged in price brackets so all starters cost the same, as do main courses and desserts. *LD* open to 01.30. A.Ax.Dc.V. ££

La Rive Gauche   **11 D3**
61 The Cut SE1. 071-928 8645. South Bank restaurant
well situated for the National Theatre and the Old Vic.
A la carte or set pre-theatre menu which changes regularly and offers a good choice for each course. French
regional wines. *LD open to 23.00. Closed L Sat & LD
Sun.* A.Ax.Dc.V. Set menu ££ A la carte £££

R.S.J.   **11 D2**
13a Coin St SE1. 071-928 4554. Friendly and relaxing
French restaurant, handy for the South Bank arts complex. Imaginative Anglo-French food; hot scampi salad,
roast quail with raspberries and honey, supreme of
salmon with basil and white wine sauce. Set menus also
available. Fine selection of Loire Valley wines. Brasserie
downstairs serves lighter meals. *LD (Reserve) open to
23.00. Closed L Sat & LD Sun.* A.Ax.V. Set menu ££ A
la carte £££

Rue St Jacques   **6 F4**
5 Charlotte St W1. 071-637 0222. Formal restaurant
with a number of small, elegant dining rooms. Complex
combinations and unusual ingredients result in delights
such as roast monkfish with lentils, terrine of crab meat
in lobster sauce, light smoked haddock gâteau. Classic
French wines and excellent French cheeseboard. Set
price menus. *LD (Reserve) open to 23.15. Closed L Sat
& LD Sun.* A.Ax.Dc.V. L £££ D £££+

Les Saveurs   **10 E2**
37a Curzon St W1. 071-491 8919. Elegant basement
restaurant with a club-like atmosphere. Classic French
cooking with Mediterranean and Oriental flavours;
duck with fig compote and Thai spiced sauce, langous-
tine ravioli with pineapple and apple chutney, tomatoes
stuffed with sautéed frogs' legs and snails. Daily-changing set lunch menu. *LD (Reserve) open to 22.30. Closed
L Sat & LD Sun.* A.Ax.V. £££+

La Sémillante   **10 F1**
5 Mill St W1. 071-499 2121. From the bar and lounge
area on the ground floor you descend a wide staircase
leading to this stylish dining room. Contemporary furnishings and vivid colours are the backdrop for innovative dishes like tarte of sea scallops and caviar, mille-
feuille of quails' eggs and foie gras. Desserts are a speciality. French farmhouse cheeses. The restaurant is
non-smoking but you can smoke in the lounge. *LD
open to 23.15. Closed L Sat.* A.Dc.V. £££

1789
Fairfield Rd E3. 081-980 8233. A taste of France in the East End. Charming candlelit French bistro serving classic Gallic fare. Home-made pâté, fish soup, steak au poivre, coq au vin. *LD (Reserve) open to 22.30. Closed L Sat, LD Sun & LD Mon.* A.Ax.V. ££

Simply Nico   **10 F5**
48a Rochester Row SW1. 071-630 8061. Formerly Very Simply Nico, this busy branch of the Nico chain offers modern classics similar to Nico Central; Mediterranean fish soup, escalope of salmon with herb mayonnaise, veal braised with Madeira, and delicious quail pie. Traditional desserts. Set menu. *LD (Reserve) open to 23.15. Closed L Sat and LD Sun.* A.Ax.Dc.V. £££

La Tante Claire   **14 C2**
68 Royal Hospital Rd SW3. 071-352 6045. This is a highly-regarded and beautiful restaurant, serving innovative, perfectly-executed French cuisine. Chef Pierre Koffman has been awarded his third Michelin star. Traditional and modern dishes; mille-feuille d'escargots, quail stuffed with mushroom risotto, scallops with squid-ink sauce. Pig's trotters stuffed with sweetbreads are Pierre Koffman's speciality. Delicious desserts; the tarte tatin is legendary. Set lunch menu. Exceptional wine list. *LD (Reserve) open to 23.00. Closed Sat & Sun.* A.Ax.Dc.V. Set lunch menu £££ A la carte £££+

Thierry's   **14 A2**
342 King's Rd SW3. 071-352 3365. Romantic French bistro with a relaxed atmosphere. Authentic cooking; the set menus are excellent value, the à la carte menu offers classic bistro dishes; snails, plateau de fruits de mer, Toulouse cassoulet. French cheeses. Short French wine list. *LD open to 23.00, to 22.30 Sun.* A.Ax.Dc.V. Set menus ££ A la carte £££

Thomas de Quincey   **11 B1**
36 Tavistock St WC2. 071-240 3773. In the original house of the 19th-century opium-eating author, a warm and glittery room with a remarkable collection of paintings and Victorian chairs. Imaginative menu includes such dishes as terrine of foie gras, ballotine of salmon, sea bass with samphire. Desserts include white and dark chocolate bombe. *LD (Reserve) open to 23.00. Closed L Sat & LD Sun.* A.Ax.Dc.V. £££+

GREEK, TURKISH & CYPRIOT

GREEK, Turkish and Cypriot cooking uses fresh ingredients and interesting herbs and spices to produce sizzling meat dishes. Greek and Turkish food are very similar in style. Both use plenty of oil, herbs and spices such as oregano, coriander and cumin. Yoghurt is a common ingredient in Turkish cooking, and rice replaces whet in many dishes. A new style of cooking – *ocakbasi* – has become popular in London's Turkish restaurants. Similar to a barbecue, meat is grilled over charcoal in a narrow pit, in front of which you sit. Cypriot restaurants, which abound in London, combine the methods of both Greek and Turkish cooking.

Popular dishes include *shish kebab* – meat marinated with herbs and charcoal grilled on a skewer, *doner kebab* – lamb pressed down on a perpendicular spit and sliced off as it cooks, *moussaka* – layers of aubergine and minced lamb topped with béchamel sauce and baked, and *kleftiko* – a very tender lamb on the bone. A good way to sample dishes is to order *meze* – a selection of dishes from the menu, served like hors d'oeuvres. Desserts are very sticky and sugary. Two favourites are *baklava* and *hadeifij* – both filled with nuts and honey. To drink, try Turkish wine or Greek *retsina* – white wine stored in barrels to which resin has been added. *Ouzo* is a strong, aniseed aperitif rather like the French Pernod.

Anemos 6 F4
32 Charlotte St W1. 071-636 2289. A raucous atmosphere at this Greek party restaurant; plenty of plate-smashing and Greek dancing. Taramasalata, houmous, kebabs, stifado, moussaka. Drink retsina or Cypriot wines. Tables outside *in summer*. *LD (Reserve D) open to 23.30. Closed Sun.* A.Ax.Dc.V. ££

Apollo
134a Seven Sisters Rd N7. 071-263 4687. There are a few Cypriot restaurants in this area; this is one of the best. Large and lively with a very friendly atmosphere. Greek Cypriot food; charcoal grills predominate. Always packed at weekends when bouzouki bands, singers and dancers entertain. *LD (Reserve D Fri & Sat) open to 24.00. Closed L Sat & LD Sun.* A.Ax.Dc.V. ££

Beotys 7 B6
79 St Martin's Lane WC2. 071-836 8768. Old-fashioned atmosphere at this comfortable restaurant. Continental menu with Greek Cypriot specialities; stuffed vine leaves, kalamarakia (squid cooked in its own ink with wine), moussaka. Sweet pastries. European and Cypriot wines. Set menus. *LD open to 23.30. Closed Sun.* A.Ax.Dc.V. £££

Café Grec 6 F4
18 Charlotte St W1. 071-436 7411. Smart Greek restaurant offering authentic cuisine; the owner and chef are both from the Greek mainland. Unusual dishes include recipes from Ancient Greece which must be ordered two days in advance. Delicious desserts. Greek wine list. *LD (Reserve) open to 23.00. Closed L Sat & LD Sun.* A.Ax.Dc.V. ££

Costa's Grill 9 D2
14 Hillgate St W8. 071-229 3794. Old-fashioned and much loved for over 40 years, this friendly Greek restaurant near Notting Hill Gate offers robust Greek food; moussaka, stifado, kleftiko. Very friendly staff. Fish and chip shop next door serving huge portions of fresh, tasty fish. *LD open to 22.30. Closed Sun.* No credit cards. £

Efes Kebab House 6 F4
80 Great Titchfield St W1. 071-636 1953. Probably the best Turkish restaurant in London, this popular, lively place is generally packed with people from the nearby BBC. Food is in traditional style and consistently good;

hot and cold starters, lamb and chicken kebabs, char-grills. Finish with syrupy desserts and Turkish coffee. Turkish beer, wine and liqueurs. *LD (Reserve) open to 23.30. Closed Sun.* A.A.x.V. ££

Hodja Nasreddin   3 G2
53 Newington Green Rd N1. 071-226 7757. A small family-run Turkish restaurant with a homely atmosphere and exotic decor resembling a nomad tent. Sucuk (spicy sausage slices), boreks, feta cheese salad are all excellent. Always busy at weekends; open late *every night. LD (Reserve D Fri & Sat) open to 01.30, to 03.30 Fri & Sat.* A.A.x.V. £

Istanbul Iskembecisi   4 C1
9 Stoke Newington Rd N16. 071-254 7291. This popular Turkish restaurant serves food practically right through the night, as is customary in Turkish tripe houses. Unusual offal dishes are the speciality here; tripe soup, oven-roasted lamb's head, boiled brain. Also conventional Turkish fare for the less strong-stomached! *LD (Reserve D Thur-Sun) open to 05.00.* No credit cards. £

Lemonia   2 C5
89 Regent's Park Rd NW1. 071-586 7454. The new-look Lemonia (across the road from the original restaurant) has a brasserie feel to it; large and lively, it is as popular as ever. Extensive Cypriot menu; grills, stews, excellent choice of meze dishes. Good selection of vegetarian and fish dishes. *LD (Reserve D) open to 23.30. Closed L Sat & D Sun.* A.V. ££

Little Akropolis   6 F4
10 Charlotte St W1. 071-636 8198. Charming restaurant with intimate atmosphere and polite, attentive service. Greek favourites plus some European dishes. Specialities include avgolemono soup (chicken with egg and lemon), kleftiko and stifado. Rose petal jam pancakes for dessert. *LD (Reserve) open to 22.30. Closed L Sat & LD Sun.* A.A.x.Dc.V. ££

Mangal   4 C2
10 Arcola St E8. 071-249 0400. Popular restaurant run by one of the best Turkish chefs in London. Blue-tiled interior and waiters in embroidered waistcoats give this tiny establishment an authentic feel. Specialise in ocakbasi and lahmacun (Turkish pizza covered with spicy minced lamb). Unlicensed. *LD open to 24.00.* No credit cards. £

Mega Kalamaras   **9 E1**
76-78 Inverness Mews, off Inverness Pl W2. 071-727
9122. Also **Micro Kalamaras**, 66 Inverness Mews W2
(**9 E1**). 071-727 5082. Two relaxed and informal
restaurants sharing the same kitchen. **Micro** is smaller,
less expensive and unlicensed (no charge for corkage).
Mega is larger and has a more mellow atmosphere.
Both offer authentic Greek mainland food with superb
national dishes such as spanakotyropitas (paper thin
pastry with spinach and cheese) and tsirosalata (smoked
strips of salted fish). Delicious pastries and Greek
cheeses. *D (Reserve Fri & Sat) open to 24.00 (Micro to
23.00). Closed Sun.* A.Ax.Dc.V. **££**

Nontas   **2 E5**
14-16 Camden High St NW1. 071-387 4579. Bustling
Greek Cypriot taverna and ouzerie. Try fish kebabs,
moussaka or the Nontas Special – smoked sausage,
dolmas and kebabs on a bed of wheat. The meze is
excellent value. Yoghurt and honey for dessert. Ouzerie
serves snacks, teas and coffee. *LD (Reserve D) open to
23.30. Closed Sun.* A.Ax.Dc.V. **££**

Pasha   **3 E4**
301 Upper St N1. 071-226 1454. This modern, simply-
decorated Turkish restaurant serves a special Pasha
lunch and dinner – a selection of 12 different meze dishes includes Iman Bayildi (aubergines with a stuffing of
tomato, pepper, onion and garlic) and muskaborek
(fresh fried pastry with hot feta cheese and dill). Main
course dishes include the traditional Turkish dish of
Yogurtlu Iskender (minced lamb and chicken on pitta
bread, soaked in fresh tomato sauce with fresh herbs
and topped with yoghurt). *LD open to 23.30, to 24.00
Fri & Sat. Closed L Mon.* A.Ax.V. **££**

Psistaria   **10 F5**
82 Wilton Rd SW1. 071-821 7504. Psistaria means
grill, and grilled meat and fish are the specialities at this
Cypriot restaurant. Excellent food, good service and a
pleasant, calm atmosphere in light, airy surroundings.
LD (Reserve) open to 23.30, to 23.00 Sat. Closed Sun.
A.Dc.V. **££**

Sofra   **10 E2**
18 Shepherd St, off Hertford St W1. 071-493 3320.
This is one of the oldest Turkish restaurants in London.
Authentic food in light, pleasant, modern surroundings.
Extensive selection of meze, fish dishes, and a few inter-

national choices. Excellent dessert trolley. *LD (Reserve) open to 24.00.* A.Ax.Dc.V. £££

The Vineyard   15 G4
3-5 Camberwell Grove SE5. 071-708 5306. Attractive, simple restaurant in the street where John Ruskin once lived. The decor lives up to the name – grapes hang from trellises and lanterns provide soft lighting. Try the 'Vineyard Special' – all the menu's different kebabs on one plate, or the meze which has a selection of 18 house specialities. Greek wines. Pavement seating *in summer*. *LD open to 24.00.* A.Ax.Dc.V. £

White Tower   6 G4
1 Percy St W1. 071-636 8141. Old-fashioned and refined atmosphere at this Greek Cypriot restaurant established in 1938. The original menu, written in lyrical prose, is still used. Greek dishes with Middle Eastern and French influences. Chicken pilaff, stuffed courgettes, shashlik, duck with bulgur. *LD (Reserve) open to 22.30. Closed Sat & Sun.* A.Ax.Dc.V. £££

INDIAN

ALTHOUGH most of London's Indian restaurants are run by Bangladeshis, you will find various influences in the cooking. Hindu cooking uses fish and vegetables in rich liquid juices; Muslims use more meat and the food is drier. Moghul influences bring ingredients from the Middle East and also tandoori food (fish and meat marinated in yoghurt and spices and cooked in a clay oven). As a general rule, north Indian food comprises spicy curries eaten with rice and breads, while food from the south is predominantly vegetarian. Other regional features abound: in the west around Bombay, yoghurt is a common ingredient, whilst milk curd and vegetarian dishes such as *dhosas* and *idli* are a feature of Gujerati cooking. Goan food, from the south west coast, is particularly spicy, and fish is a speciality. Kashmiri cooking is the most elaborate, dishes often cooked in cream and almonds. Pakistani recipes rely heavily on meat, combined with vegetables, which is rare in India. In all Indian cooking classic spices and flavourings are used generously.

Typical dishes to be found on London menus are mild curries such as *korma* and *patia,* hot curries such as *madras* and *vindaloo, tikka* dishes – marinated with spices and fried, *nan* – doughy bread, *bhajis* – deep-fried snacks made with onion, *popadoms* – thin deep-fried wafers served with onions and chutney, *lassi* – yoghurt drink, and *kulfi* – cone-shaped, spiced ice-cream.

Many Indian restaurants in London specialise in vegetarian cuisine. More of these are listed under *Vegetarian & wholefood.* Particularly cheap Indian restaurants, of which there are many, are listed under *Inexpensive.*

Anarkali

305 King Street W6. 081-748 1760. Very popular Hammersmith haunt where the food is quite strongly spiced. Tandoori dishes, methi gosht, mughlai prawns, chicken dhansak; if you want something mild, try the prawn patia. *LD (Reserve D) open to 24.00.* A.Ax.Dc.V. ££

Bombay Bicycle Club   17 C5

95 Nightingale Lane SW12. 081-673 6217. This popular, fashionable restaurant serves unusual dishes with mild, subtle flavours. Try lamb with butter, onion and tomatoes, or fish in light, spicy batter. Good value buffet lunch on *Sunday. L(Sun only)D open to 23.30. Closed D Sun.* A.Ax.Dc.V. ££

Bombay Brasserie   9 F5

Courtfield Close, Courtfield Rd SW7. 071-370 4040. Fashionable new-wave Indian restaurant with sumptuous colonial decor – plants, fans, wicker chairs and an airy conservatory. First-class regional cuisine; representative dishes from all parts of the subcontinent include snacks from Bombay, tandoori dishes from the north west, spicy hot dishes from Goa. Excellent *lunchtime* buffet. *LD (Reserve D) open to 24.00* A.Ax.Dc.V. £££

Bombay Palace   6 B5

50 Connaught St W2. 071-723 8855. Modern, luxurious dining room serving north Indian dishes. Chicken kheema is a dish unique to the restaurant; minced

chicken breast with selected herbs and spices. *Lunchtime* buffet. *LD (Reserve D) open to 23.30, to 23.00 Sun.* A.Ax.Dc.V. ££

Café Lazeez 9 G5
93-95 Old Brompton Rd SW7. 071-581 9993. This trendy café bar/ restaurant adopts a European approach to Indian food. Pakistani specialities are developed into a western style; whole spring chicken stuffed with vegetables pilau, jumbo prawns marinated in freshly squeezed lime juice with ginger, spring onions, chillies, garlic and paprika. Café menu in the bar on the ground floor; intimate restaurant upstairs. *LD open to 01.00, to 22.30 Sun.* A.Ax.Dc.V. ££

Chutney Mary 13 F3
535 King's Rd SW10. 071-351 3113. London's first Anglo-Indian restaurant where chefs from different regions of India recreate the dishes which resulted from colonial days. Salmon kedgeree, Bangalore bangers and mash, masala roast lamb. Spicy 'Hill Station' version of bread and butter pudding to follow. Colonial decor, with wicker chairs, ceiling fans and palms. Conservatory and Verandah Bar where you can take tiffin. *Sunday* buffet. *LD (Reserve) open to 23.15, to 22.00 Sun (to 21.45 for buffet).* A.Ax.Dc.V. £££

Copper Chimney 6 F6
13 Heddon St W1. 071-439 2004. The London branch of a chain stretching to the Middle East and India. Plush and spacious, serving classic north Indian dishes which are beautifully presented. Delicately flavoured rice with lentils, dhal makhani, lassi to drink. Buffet lunch and set menus. *LD (Reserve D) open to 23.00, to 23.30 Fri & Sat, to 22.30 Sun.* A.Ax.Dc.V. ££

Covent Garden Rickshaw 7 B6
11 Henrietta St WC2. 071-379 5555. Very popular, bright, airy restaurant. The three founding partners are Muslim, Hindu and Sikh, which is reflected in the separate menus which cover all regions of India. From northern India try murgh tikka (chicken marinated in home-made spices and cooked in the tandoor over); from western India, salli murgh (chicken cooked with apricots and topped with a nest of potato straws); and from southern India, alu gosht (lamb cooked with onions and potatoes, with a blend of freshly ground spices). Kingfisher Indian beer to drink. *LD open to 23.15. Closed L Sat & LD Sun.* A.V. £

Diwan-E-Khas   6 F3
45 Grafton Way W1. 071-388 1321. Frequented by
local business people and Asians, this cavernous restaurant offers excellent tandoori dishes from north India.
Also Mogul chicken or lamb, and thalis (a selection of
small dishes including tandoori chicken, prawn bhuna
and Mogul mutton). *LD open to 23.45.* A.Ax.Dc.V. ££

Ealing Tandoori
9 The Green W5. 081-567 7606. Big and bustling, this
popular north Indian restaurant serves good food at
reasonable prices in a cheerful, busy atmosphere.
The kitchen is visible from the restaurant. Chicken tikka
masala, king prawn masala with peshwari or keema
nan; kulfi to follow. *LD (Reserve D) open to 23.30.*
A.Ax.Dc.V. £

Gopal's of Soho   6 G5
12 Bateman St, off Frith St W1. 071-434 1621. Up-
market restaurant in the middle of Soho. Popular for the
pleasant surroundings and high-quality cooking. King
prawns with spring onions, mutton xacutti (Goan dish
of lamb with coconut, vinegar and spices), south Indian
nariyal pilau rice. Excellent wine list. *LD (Reserve D)
open to 23.30, to 23.00 Sun.* A.Ax.Dc.V. ££

Great Nepalese   6 G2
48 Eversholt St NW1. 071-388 5935. Welcoming
restaurant near Euston Station. Simple decor with
Nepali hand-carved ornaments. Nepalese specialities
include masco bara (deep-fried black lentil pancakes),
Nepalese thali and an excellent tandoori mixed grill.
Rice pudding with raisins and cashew nuts to follow.
LD (Reserve Fri & Sat) open to 23.45. A.Ax.Dc.V. ££

Gurkha Brasserie
756 Finchley Rd NW11. 081-458 6163. Friendly
restaurant decorated with Gurkha artefacts. Wide
choice of Nepalese dishes; momo (steamed meat
dumplings), aloo ko achar (spiced potatoes with fresh
coriander), Nepalese thali. Also north Indian dishes. Set
menus. *LD (Reserve D Fri & Sat) open to 24.00, to
00.30 Fri & Sat, to 23.30 Sun.* A.Ax.V. £

India Club   7 C6
143 Strand WC2. 071-836 0650. This is one of the
oldest Indian restaurants in London and used to be
frequented by staff from the nearby Indian High
Commission. Surroundings are like a school canteen but

it is popular for its extensive choice of standard Indian fare at reasonable prices. Unlicensed. *LD open to 22.00, to 20.00 Sun.* No credit cards. £

Jashan
19 Turnpike Lane N8. 081-340 9880. Immensely popular with local Asians, this north London Indian produces excellent meat, fish and vegetable dishes. The three chefs were hired from Bombay and they supply Harrods food hall with foodstuffs. Freshly-prepared dishes include chicken Jashan served in a karahi (wok), tandoori fish, vegetable pakora. Good selection of breads. *LD (Reserve D Fri & Sat) open to 23.30.* A.Ax.Dc.V. ££

Karahi   1 E3
212 West End Lane NW6. 071-794 0228. Cool and light basement restaurant serving north Indian food with Kenyan-Asian specialities. Talapia (black bass from Lake Victoria), karahi chicken, khanvi (vegetarian pasta; available *weekends only*). Charming service. *D (Reserve weekends) open to 23.30.* A.Ax.Dc.V. ££

Khan's   5 E5
13-15 Westbourne Grove W2. 071-727 5420. The vast dining hall, with its oriental arches and palm tree pillars, was formerly a Lyons tea house. Cheap, cheerful, noisy and always busy. North Indian cuisine; specialities include kofti dilruba (spiced curried meatballs) and mattar panir (white cheese with peas and herbs). Service is hurried and erratic. No reservations, so expect to queue. *LD open to 24.00.* A.Ax.Dc.V. £

Kundan   11 A5
3 Horseferry Rd SW1. 071-834 3434. This lavishly-decorated basement restaurant is a popular haunt of MPs and government officials. Mogul-inspired Indian cooking; lamb jalfrezi, chicken makhani. Also succulent tandoori dishes. *LD (Reserve D) open to 23.30. Closed Sun.* A.Ax.Dc.V. ££

Lahore Kebab House   8 E5
2 Umberston St, off Hessel St E1. 071-488 2551. Unlicensed Pakistani 'caff' widely known for its authentic food and huge portions. Curried quails, sizzling chicken karahi, tandoori, tikka, kebabs. Freshly baked breads. Kheer (hot rice pudding) for dessert. *LD open to 24.00.* No credit cards. £

Lal Quila   6 F3
117 Tottenham Court Rd W1. 071-387 4570. This up-

market elegant restaurant was one of the first new-wave Indian establishments in London. North Indian cooking with subtly spiced dishes and unusual specialities; lamb brain masala, tandoori trout, fish curry. Cocktails. *LD (Reserve) open to 23.15.* A.Ax.Dc.V. **££**

Light of India 13 F2
276 Fulham Rd SW10. 071-352 5416. Romantic candlelit atmosphere. Special Moghlai dishes; murgh massalam, khurzi chicken and lamb (can be ordered in advance). Also good tandoori dishes. Staff are willing to show you the clay ovens. *LD (Reserve) open to 24.00.* A.Ax.Dc.V. **££**

Mumtaz 6 C3
4-10 Park Rd NW1. 071-723 0549. One of the most lavishly decorated Indian restaurants in London. Palms surround a goldfish pond on the patio. The maharaja set meal is very popular; an Indian mixed grill. Buffet lunches and dinners on *Sunday. LD open to 23.30.* A.Ax.V. **££**

Namaste 8 C5
30 Alie St E1. 071-488 9242. Situated on the fringe of the City, this simple restaurant offers some unusual dishes and Goan specialities. Lamb chops marinated in ginger, duck breast smoked in banana leaves, Bombay street snacks. Home-made kulfi and coconut sorbets. *LD (Reserve) open to 23.30.* A.Ax.Dc.V. **££**

Oval Tandoori 15 D3
46 Brixton Rd SW9. 071-735 7413. Cosy, intimate restaurant with alcoved tables. Chicken dupiaza, mutton badam pasanda and Kashmiri nan are among the delicacies on offer. *LD open to 00.30.* A.Ax.Dc.V. **££**

Ragam 6 F4
57 Cleveland St W1. 071-636 9098. Popular, friendly restaurant serving dishes from southern India. Specialities from the Kerala coast include kalan which is a dish made from buttermilk, coconut and sweet mangoes, and avial, a vegetable stew with a yoghurt and coconut sauce. Mango lassi to drink. *LD (Reserve) open to 23.30.* A.Ax.Dc.V. **£**

Rani
7 Long Lane N3. 081-349 4386. Formerly a tea shop, this family-run Gujarati restaurant is bright and friendly. Fresh, exotic vegetables and delicate spicing are used to create excellent vegetarian curries; stuffed aubergine

and potato, spiced mushroom and pea. Home-made chutneys. *LD (Reserve) open to 22.30. Closed L Mon, L Tue & L Sat.* A.V. ££

Ravi Shankar 6 F2
133 Drummond St NW1. 071-388 6458. Friendly, informal southern Indian restaurant serving authentic vegetarian dishes. Excellent Mysore masala dosai, thali and tasty snacks. It shares a kitchen with **Chutneys**, 124 Drummond St NW1 (**6 F2**). 071-388 0604. *LD (Reserve D) open to 22.30.* A.V. £

Red Fort 6 G5
77 Dean St W1. 071-437 2115. Attractive, luxurious surroundings in which to enjoy Bangladeshi food. Red Fort was a trend-setter in Bangladeshi fish dishes when it opened ten years ago. Unusual tandoori meals; duck, quail and trout. Elegant bar for pre-dinner drinks. *LD (Reserve) open to 23.15.* A.Ax.Dc.V. ££

Saheli Brasserie 7 B5
35 Great Queen St WC2. 071-405 2238. Country house decor, unusual for an Indian restaurant, is the attractive setting for well-prepared north Indian cuisine. Set lunch and pre-theatre menus. *LD open to 23.30. Closed Sun.* A.Ax.Dc.V. ££ (set menus £)

Salloos 10 D3
62-64 Kinnerton St SW1. 071-235 4444. Luxurious Pakistani restaurant tucked away in a mews in Knightsbridge. Dishes from the era of the Mogul emperors; haleem akbari, chicken jalfrezi, bataire masala (quail), authentic chicken karahi, lamb barra. Tandoori dishes are marinated for 24 hours and are always cooked to order. *LD open to 23.15. Closed Sun.* A.Ax.Dc.V. £££

Shampan 8 C4
79 Brick Lane E1. 071-375 0475. Bangladeshi cuisine at this smart restaurant which attracts a lot of custom from the nearby City. Innovative dishes; shatkora chicken is excellent. Wide selection of fish dishes. *LD (Reserve) open to 24.00.* A.Ax.Dc.V. ££

Shezan 10 B4
16-22 Cheval Pl SW7. 071-584 9316. Coolly decorated basement restaurant, acclaimed for the excellence of its Pakistani cooking. Try the tandoori favourite murgh tikka Lahori. Oriental milk puddings for dessert. *LD (Reserve D) open to 23.30.* A.Ax.Dc.V. £££

Sonar Gaon   3 E5
46 Upper St N1. 071-226 6499. Islamic tiling and prints
from Bangladesh decorate this bright Islington restaurant. Interesting dishes; prawns and crunchy fresh
herbs, duck masala and, for parties of 20, the chef will
prepare the kashi, a whole lamb marinated and stuffed
with rice and herbs. *LD open to 24.00.* A.Ax.Dc.V. ££

Star of India   13 F1
154 Old Brompton Rd SW5. 071-373 2901. One of
London's   longest-established   Indian   restaurants.
Unusual Renaissance setting in which to enjoy excellent
food and good service. Mogul dishes must be ordered a
day in advance. Prawn biryani, whole stuffed tandoori
chicken, kebabs. *LD open to 23.30, to 23.00 Sun.*
A.Ax.Dc.V. ££

Tandoori of Chelsea   10 B5
153 Fulham Rd SW3. 071-589 7617. Elegant furnishings and soft music at this fashionable Fulham Road
restaurant. High standard of regional cooking produces
traditional and innovative dishes. Tandoor clay ovens
are used; lamb and chicken are marinated with unusual
herbs and spices before cooking. *LD (Reserve) open to
24.00, to 23.30 Sun.* A.Ax.Dc.V. ££

Taste of India   11 C1
25 Catherine St WC2. 071-836 2538. Elegant and modern restaurant with a basement wine bar, the **Jewel in
the Crown,** popular with pre- and post-theatre crowds.
Regional menu includes meat and vegetable thalis,
freshly-cooked tandoori dishes and individually-spiced
lamb, chicken and seafood curries. Pre-theatre menu.
LD (Reserve) open to 24.00. A.Ax.Dc.V. ££

Veeraswamy   6 F6
99-101 Regent St (entrance in Swallow St) W1. 071-734
1401. Established in 1927, this is London's oldest
Indian restaurant. Turbaned doormen give it an up-
market, club-like feel. A good representation of regional
cooking; large choice of curries, kebabs, tandooris and
rice dishes. *Lunchtime* buffet. Delicate desserts. *LD
open to 23.15. Closed Sun.* A.Ax.Dc.V. ££

Viceroy of India   6 C3
3-5 Glentworth St NW1. 071-486 3401. Large and
elegant with fountains in the foyer and dining area. You
can watch appetising Indian dishes being prepared in
the open-view kitchen. Chicken pakora, fish masala,

well-executed tandoori specialities. *LD open to 23.00, to 22.30 Sun.* A.Ax.Dc.V. **££**

Zara's Kitchen   **15 G4**
51-53 Camberwell Church St SE5. 071-252 4587. East African Asian cooking at this friendly restaurant run by a mother and her son. Mombasa-style chapati is the house speciality. Unlicensed. *D open to 24.00, to 00.45 Sat, to 23.00 Sun.* No credit cards. **££**

INTERNATIONAL

T HESE restaurants fall into two categories. There are those which offer a wide selection of dishes from different countries, providing an array of authentic tastes from all corners of the globe. Others pick from the best dishes of the world, blending styles and flavours to create distinctive new ones.

Belgo   **2 E4**
72 Chalk Farm Rd NW1. 071-267 0718. Fashionable Belgian restaurant with an exceptionally modern design – you actually enter the restaurant through a tunnel. Waiters wearing monks' habits serve up moules et frites, wild boar sausages with stoemp and a huge variety of Belgian beer. *LD (Reservations taken from 11.00 on day) open to 23.00, to 01.00 Sat, to 23.30 Sun.* A.Ax.V. **££**

Blueprint Café   **12 C3**
Design Museum, Butler's Wharf SE1. 071-378 7031. Another Sir Terence Conran creation, this stylish restaurant on top of the Design Museum has spectacular views along the Thames. The international menu places emphasis on Mediterranean dishes; risotto milanese,

spinach and ricotta gnocchi, Portuguese fish stew. Outdoor tables on the terrace. *LD (Reserve L) open to 23.00. Closed D Sun.* A.Ax.V. ££

Deals

Deals Chelsea, Harbour Yard, Chelsea Harbour, **13 F4** off Lots Rd SW10. 071-376 3232. *LD open to 23.00.*
Deals West, 14-16 Foubert's Pl W1. 071-287 1001. **6 F5** *LD open to 23.00, to 02.00 Fri, to 03.00 Sat.* Live entertainment *Fri & Sat evening.*
Lively, New England-style diners decked out in bare wood and brickwork. The menu is American with Thai influences and is divided into 'Raw Deals' – salads, 'Big Deals' – ribs, steaks and burgers, and 'Hot Deals' – Thai curries. Huge portions of chocolate desserts. Deals Broadway, Hammersmith, is due to open in January 1994. A.Ax.Dc.V. ££

East of the Sun West of the Moon   11 D2

Gabriel's Wharf, Upper Ground SE1. 071-620 0596. Riverside location with fabulous views across the Thames to St Paul's. The interior is light and airy with windows looking out onto the river; there is also outside seating. Cuisine is a combination of east and west with a huge choice of dishes from China, South East Asia and eastern Europe; bangers and mash add a British touch. *LD open to 24.00, to 01.00 Fri & Sat.* A.Ax.Dc.V. ££

First Floor   5 C5

186 Portobello Rd W11. 071-243 0072. Above a Victorian pub, this restaurant has a classical interior and is crammed full of odds and ends. The modern international menu changes daily and may include Tuscan lamb stew, Thai fishcakes, chicken with ginger, honey and peppers. *LD (Reserve) open to 23.00.* A.Ax.V. £££

555   14 B5

555 Battersea Park Rd SW11. 071-228 7011. A warm welcome at this homely restaurant run by two Irish sisters. Small red dining room with outdoor seating in the backyard. Classic French main courses, plus seasonal choices of mixed ethnic origins. *D (Reserve) open to 23.30. Closed Sun & Mon.* No credit cards. ££

Mélange   7 B5

59 Endell St WC2. 071-240 8077. Stylish surroundings and an inventive menu make this a very popular spot.

Unusual dishes; Thai fishcakes, grilled polenta with Gorgonzola, warm lemon chicken salad with chilli. *LD (Reserve D) open to 23.30. Closed L Sat & LD Sun.* A.V. ££

Mulligans of Mayfair   6 F6
13-14 Cork St W1. 071-409 1370. Irish restaurant in the basement of a lively pub and oyster bar. The chef adds a modern touch to traditional Irish cooking with Mediterranean and modern British influences. Oyster, beef and Guinness casserole, pig's trotter fishcakes, Irish cheddar soufflé. *LD open to 23.15. Closed L Sat & LD Sun.* A.Ax.V. £££

Pera   2 D4
57-58 Chalk Farm Rd NW1. 071-916 0170. This modern restaurant has glass sliding panels at the front which open in good weather to provide pavement seating. Contemporary design with Eastern influences; Chinese screens on the walls. A huge variety of Eastern cuisines are on offer here; Indian, Chinese, Japanese, Thai, Russian and Turkish dishes feature on the menu. Large vegetarian menu. Indian and Japanese beers. Regular live music. *LD (Reserve) open to 23.30.* A.Ax.V. ££

Phood   6 F5
31 Foubert's Pl W1. 071-494 4192. An eclectic menu at this light and airy restaurant where tables spill out onto the street *in summer.* Popular dishes like Thai crispy duck with plum sauce and noisette of lamb with spinach are examples of the modern menu which shows influences from east and west. Snack menu offers steak sandwiches and salads from *17.30-19.30. LD (Reserve L) open to 24.00.* A.Ax.V. ££

Pomegranates   14 F2
94 Grosvenor Rd SW1. 071-828 6560. Highly original and adventurous restaurant with a truly cosmopolitan menu. Turkish, Malaysian and Chinese dishes happily rub shoulders with Welsh, Greek, Italian and French cuisine. All prepared from first-class ingredients. Multi-national wine list. *LD (Reserve D) open to 23.15. Closed L Sat & LD Sun.* A.Ax.Dc.V. L ££ D £££

Quaglino's   10 F2
16 Bury St SW1. 071-930 6767. Sir Terence Conran's large and glamorous brasserie seating 400. A sweeping staircase descends from the entrance foyer (where a shop sells foodstuffs offered on the menu) to a bar and

antipasti bar. From there a marble staircase descends to the main restaurant. Shellfish feature prominently on the menu; take your pick from the 'Crustacean Altar'. Also French, Italian and oriental dishes. Live music and dancing *to 03.00 Fri & Sat. LD (Reserve) open to 24.00, to 02.00 Fri & Sat, to 23.00 Sun. A.Ax.Dc.V.* **£££**

South of the Border   11 E2
8 Joan St SE1. 071-928 6374. Farmhouse decor in this spacious restaurant in a converted mattress factory. Outside terrace for summer dining. Indonesian food such as rijstafel, Japanese-style tempura prawns and some Australian dishes. Home-made desserts, ice cream or cheese. *LD open to 23.30. Closed L Sat & LD Sun.* A.Ax.Dc.V. **££**

The Wilds   13 F2
356 Fulham Rd SW10. 071-376 5553. An unusual mixture of African and European cuisine is reflected in the burnished walls and swagged wall-hangings. Memorable dishes include Gruyère and spinach crepes, spicy shrimp salad with chillis. *L(Sun only)D (Reserve) open to 23.00. Closed D Sun.* A.V. **£££**

ITALIAN

THERE are plenty of places to eat Italian food in London, from old-fashioned ristorantes and trattorias to the new style of restaurants where chefs draw on authentic ingredients and native herbs and spices to produce their own interpretations of traditional dishes. For pizza restaurants and pasta chains see the end of this section.

Al San Vincenzo   **6 B5**
30 Connaught St W2. 071-262 9623. Simple family-run
restaurant serving provincial Italian food. Fresh ingredients and an innovative approach to classic dishes; tagliolini with sun-dried tomatoes and basil, calf's kidneys
with pancetta and herbs. All-Italian wine list. Grappa.
LD open to 22.30. Closed L Sat & LD Sun. A.V. ££

Arts Theatre Café   **7 A6**
6 Great Newport St, off Charing Cross Rd WC2. 071-
497 8014. In the basement of the Arts Theatre, this tiny
café serves excellent Italian food. The daily-changing
menu always offers antipasti misti, spicy Italian
sausages and polenta, but may also include spinach,
salami and Parmesan cakes or baked halibut with mussel sauce. Regional Italian wines. *LD (Reserve) open to
22.00. Closed L Sat & LD Sun.* No credit cards. ££

Bertorelli's   **7 B6**
44a Floral St WC2. 071-836 3969. Stylish restaurant with
a simple menu offering new-wave Italian dishes; linguine
with sun-dried tomatoes, grilled tuna steak with tomato
and basil salsa. Also a selection of pasta dishes. Delicious
home-made breads and desserts. Wines from Italy and
California. Café/wine bar downstairs serves simpler meals.
Open to 23.30. Closed Sun. A.Ax.Dc.V. ££

Biagi's   **6 C5**
39 Upper Berkeley St W1. 071-723 0394. Small,
intimate trattoria. Large, varied menu; mozzarella
carrozza, villa alla biagi, scaloppine alla crema,
entrecote alla pizzaiola, tripe, saltimbocca. Tiramisu for
dessert. *LD (Reserve) open to 23.00.* A.Ax.Dc.V. ££

Billboard Café   **1 C4**
222 Kilburn High Rd NW6. 071-328 1374. Converted
warehouse offering Cal-Ital cuisine in a relaxed
atmosphere. Interesting ingredients are used to produce
delicious salads and fresh home-made pastas are served
with a variety of unusual sauces. Occasional live jazz.
LD open to 24.00. Closed L Mon-Wed & D Sun.
A.Dc.V. ££

Café Italien (des Amis du Vin)   **6 F4**
19-23 Charlotte St W1. 071-636 4174. A choice of
brasserie, wine bar or more formal dining room in which
to sample classic Italian dishes. Salads and pastas in the
wine bar; pasta, veal escalope, carpaccio in the brasserie;
and formal and elegant dining in the charming Bertorelli

Room. Tables on a raised platform outside *in summer*. *LD* wine bar *open to 22.30,* brasserie *open to 23.00,* restaurant *open to 23.00. Closed Sun.* A.Ax.Dc.V. Wine bar £ Brasserie ££ Restaurant £££

La Capannina   6 G6
24 Romilly St W1. 071-437 2473. Crowded Soho trattoria serving traditional Italian dishes. Good home-cooked pasta with a variety of sauces. Dishes of the day might include gnocchi, petto di pollo, vitello alla Gianni; good selection of desserts. Music *in the evening. LD open to 23.30. Closed L Sat & LD Sun.* A.Ax.Dc.V. ££

Cibo   9 B4
3 Russell Gdns W14. 071-371 6271. Decor is bright and modern at this fashionable restaurant. North Italian cuisine with an emphasis on seafood; sautéed langoustines, clams, mussels, squid and scallops, baked sea bass with herbs. Gnocchi in duck sauce is excellent. All-Italian wine list. *LD open to 23.00. Closed L Sat & D Sun.*A.Ax.Dc.V. £££

Como Lario   10 D5
22 Holbein Pl SW1. 071-730 2954. Lively and crowded trattoria run by an Italian family who have been here for years. The cooking is reliable and the service old-fashioned. Bresaola, wild mushroom trifolati, pollo sorpresa. *LD (Reserve D) open to 23.30. Closed Sun.* A.Ax.V. ££

Eleven Park Walk   13 F2
11 Park Walk SW10. 071-352 3449. Smart clientele in this stylish and lively restaurant. The menu is divided between modern Italian dishes and established favourites. Spaghetti with lobster, warm goose carpaccio, ravioli with tomato and basil, veal Milanese. *LD (Reserve) open to 24.00. Closed D Sun.* A.Ax.V. ££

La Famiglia   13 F2
5-7 Langton St SW10. 071-351 0761. This long-established trattoria is extremely popular and is always lively and noisy. Italian cooking with a Tuscan influence; wild boar sausages are the speciality. Huge outdoor seating area *in summer. LD (Reserve) open to 24.00.* A.Ax.Dc.V. £££

L'Incontro   10 D6
87 Pimlico Rd SW1. 071-730 6327. Modern, up-market restaurant where a wealthy clientele enjoy Venetian cooking. Pasta dishes and risottos are excellent. Try

tagliolini in fresh crab sauce or roast quail with polenta and wild mushrooms. Lunch menu. Excellent Italian wines. *LD (Reserve) open to 23.30, to 22.30 Sun. Closed L Sat & L Sun.* A.Ax.Dc.V. L ££ D £££+

Leoni's Quo Vadis 6 G5
26-29 Dean St W1. 071-437 4809. Relaxed elegance in one of Soho's oldest buildings – Karl Marx once lived here and started work on *Das Kapital* in a room upstairs; you can ask to see the room after your meal. Leoni's specialise in traditional Italian cooking using only the freshest ingredients. Excellent dessert trolley. Courteous service. *LD (Reserve) open to 23.15, to 22.30 Sun.* A.Ax.Dc.V. ££

Luigi's 7 B6
15 Tavistock St WC2. 071-240 1795. Something of an institution, Luigi's has old-world charm and elegance. Photographs of illustrious patrons from stage and screen adorn the walls. The food is classic Italian; cannelloni, mussels grilled with breadcrumbs and garlic, veal and chicken dishes. Extensive wine list. *LD (Reserve) open to 23.30. Closed Sun.* A.Dc.V. £££

Mimmo d'Ischia 10 D5
61 Elizabeth St SW1. 071-730 5406. Bright and lively restaurant decorated with autographed photos of famous stars posing with the ebullient owner, Mimmo. Competently-prepared pasta, fish and meat dishes. Rich desserts. *LD (Reserve) open to 23.15. Closed Sun.* A.Ax.Dc.V. £££

Neal Street Restaurant 7 B5
26 Neal St WC2. 071-836 8368. Sir Terence Conran's stylish design and Antonio Carluccio's wild mushrooms attract the glitterati and the very rich to this modern Italian restaurant. There is often a separate menu for the mushrooms; chanterelles, wild and cultivated horse mushrooms. Other dishes include rabbit casserole, tagliolini with truffle sauce, calf's liver Veneziana. *LD (Reserve) open to 23.00. Closed Sun.* A.Ax.Dc.V. £££

Opera Terrazza! 7 B6
45 East Terrace, The Piazza, Covent Garden WC2. 071-379 0666. Conservatory-style trattoria with large outdoor terrace overlooking Covent Garden piazza. Sunny, informal atmosphere in which to enjoy new-wave Italian cuisine; fresh pasta dishes, chargrilled chicken and fish. Lively bar with Happy Hour and live music.

Other branches in the same chain. *LD open to 23.30.*
A.Ax.Dc.V. ££

Orso   11 C1
27 Wellington St WC2. 071-240 5269. A fashionable
restaurant serving modern Italian food from the Tuscan
region. Frequently-changing menu may include grilled
scallops with roasted peppers, tagliatelle with spiced
sausage, tomato and herbs. There is always a selection
of pasta dishes plus excellent pizzas with various toppings. Always crowded. Two sittings at dinner. *LD
(Reserve) open to 24.00.* No credit cards. £££

Osteria Antica Bologna   17 C3
23 Northcote Rd SW11. 071-978 4771. Friendly and
relaxed restaurant with rustic surroundings. The cooking
is a blend of north and south Italian but is distinctive for
the 'assaggi' – the Italian version of meze – you can choose
a selection of small dishes at once. *LD (Reserve) open to
23.00, to 22.30 Sun. Closed L Mon.* A.Ax.V. ££

Palio   5 D5
175 Westbourne Grove W11. 071-221 6624. Stylish and
modern pasta restaurant serving fresh pasta dishes with
inventive sauces, plus a selection of chargrilled meat and
fish. Café/bar downstairs serves cappuccinos and snacks.
Very friendly atmosphere. *LD open to 23.00.* A.Ax.V. ££

Pasticceria Amalfi   6 G5
31 Old Compton St W1. 071-437 7284. Lively and
crowded Italian restaurant in Soho. Excellent veal,
chicken and home-made pasta dishes. Delicious pastries.
Cheeses imported from Italy. *LD open to 23.15, to
22.00 Sun.* A.Ax.Dc.V. ££

Portofino   3 E5
39 Camden Passage N1. 071-226 0884. Long-
established restaurant with many faithful regulars who
enjoy the intimate atmosphere and excellent cooking.
Fresh fish in season, calf's liver Veneziana, medaillon de
boeuf au beurre noir, steak tartare. *LD open to 23.30.
Closed Sun.* A.Ax.Dc.V. ££

La Preferita   17 D1
163 Lavender Hill SW11. 071-223 1046. Attractive
restaurant on two floors serving pasta, fish, meat and
chicken dishes. Speciality of the house is spaghetti al
cartoccio, which comes sealed in its own paper bag with
seafood and tomato sauce. All-Italian wine list. *LD
(Reserve D) open to 23.30.* A.Ax.V. ££

Riva

169 Church Rd SW13. 081-748 0434. This was one of the first new-wave Italian restaurants in London. Simple decor with mirrors, prints of classic architecture and high-tech lighting. The seasonal menu and imported ingredients result in dishes inspired by the cooking methods of northern Italy. Warm goose carpaccio, venison bresaola, black risotto with baby cuttlefish. Pavement seating *in summer. LD open to 22.30. A.V. ££*

River Café

Thames Wharf Studios, Rainville Rd W6. 071-381 8824. Riverside restaurant (without views unless you sit outside) serving excellent regional Italian dishes. Only the freshest ingredients are used and chargrilled dishes predominate; lamb with cannellini beans, squid with fresh chilli. Sorbets for dessert. *LD (Reserve) open to 21.30. Closed D Sun. A.V. £££*

San Frediano 10 B5

62 Fulham Rd SW3. 071-584 8375. Old-fashioned trattoria which has had a devoted following for years. Beautifully laid out cold table, clam salad, snails tagliatelle with cream and mushroom sauce. Good veal and liver dishes. Delicious zabaglione. *LD (Reserve) open to 23.15. Closed Sun. A.Ax.Dc.V. ££*

San Lorenzo 10 B4

22 Beauchamp Pl SW3. 071-584 1074. Charming, family-run establishment, which for a long time has been the favoured haunt of rich and famous celebrities. Dine in either the bright central raised area or at the more intimate surrounding tables. Daily-changing menu of familiar Italian dishes. Try the San Lorenzo pancake for dessert. *LD (Reserve) open to 23.00. Closed Sun.* No credit cards. £££+

Signor Zilli 6 G5

41 Dean St W1. 071-734 3924. Relaxed atmosphere at this Soho Italian which specialises in Venetian cooking. Hand-painted murals of Venice on the walls. Menu changes monthly; the risottos and fish dishes are excellent. Baked sea bass, fillet of beef in truffle and wild mushroom sauce, fresh clams. For dessert, try panacotta or tiramisu. Set lunch and pre-theatre menus. Children's entertainment *Sunday lunchtime. LD (Reserve) open to 23.30. A.Ax.Dc.V. ££*

Tiramisu 1 D2

327 West End Lane NW6. 071-433 1221. Smart and

unpretentious, decorated with prints evoking the sun-drenched Mediterranean. Home-made pasta, excellent seafood dishes, plus a 'natural cooking' menu which features such things as wholemeal tagliatelle with cabbage. *LD open to 23.30.* A.Ax.Dc.V. ££

Villa Bianca   1 F1
1 Perrins Court, off Hampstead High St NW3. 071-435 3131. This smart restaurant is situated in an appealing courtyard off Hampstead High Street where tables spill out onto the pavement *in summer.* Traditional Italian dishes; mixed fresh antipasti, grilled baby chicken with hot peppers. Excellent dessert trolley. *LD (Reserve D) open to 23.30.* A.Ax.Dc.V. £££

PIZZAS

THERE are basically two types of pizza – American-style deep-pan pizzas and Italian pizzas which have a thin, crispy base and are baked in clay ovens. Italian toppings tend to be simple and made up of easily mixed ingredients such as tomato, mozzarella and mushrooms, whereas American ones can be quite adventurous with unusual combinations such as chicken curry, spinach and bacon. You can normally create your own pizza from a list of toppings. The main pizza restaurant chains have branches all over London. They are **Pizza Hut, Perfect Pizza, Pizza Express, Deep Pan Pizza Co** and **Pizzaland.**

Calzone
2a Kensington Park Rd W11. 071-243 2003.   9 D1
66 Heath St NW3. 071-794 6775.
Stylish pizza restaurants offering a wide choice of toppings, including Inferno (tomato, mozzarella, onion and chilli) and Vegetali (mozzarella, artichokes, mushrooms, olives, capers, broccoli and courgettes). Italian starters and desserts. *LD open to 23.30.* No credit cards. £

Chicago Pizza Pie Factory   6 E5
17 Hanover Sq W1. 071-629 2669. The first to offer American deep-pan pizzas. Full of Chicago memorabilia; tapes of the local Chicago radio station and US football videos are flown in weekly. Also burgers, chilli and lasagne. Non-smoking section. *LD open to 23.45, to 22.30 Sun.* A.Ax.V. £

Condotti   10 F1
4 Mill St W1. 071-499 1308. Sophisticated and stylish restaurant serving authentic pizzas. Only the best ingre-

dients are used; try the Condotti which is topped with ricotta and Gorgonzola. Italian wines and Peroni beer. *LD open to 24.00. Closed Sun.* A.Ax.Dc.V. ££

La Delizia 10 B6
Chelsea Farmers Market, Sydney St SW3. 071-351 6701. One of London's most authentic Italian pizzerias, housed in two huts with lots of outside seating. Pizzas are made in the thin-and-crispy style with traditional toppings. *LD open to 23.00.* No credit cards. £

Gourmet Pizza Company
Gabriel's Wharf, Upper Ground SE1. 071-928 11 D2
3188.
42 New Oxford St W1. 071-580 9521. 7 B5
Mackenzie Walk, Canary Wharf E14. 071-712 9192.
Merton Abbey Mills, Watermill Way SW19. 081-545 0310.
Creative toppings using freshly-prepared ingredients. Try the Oriental Pork Calzone or the Chinese Duck Pizza. Pasta dishes and inventive salads. Continental ice-creams and sorbets. *LD open to 22.45.* A.Ax.V. £

LS Grunts' 7 B6
12 Maiden Lane WC2. 071-379 7722. Lively pizza hide-out in a converted electricity sub-station. Superior deep-pan pizzas. American salad bar. Polynesian cock-tails. *LD open to 23.30, to 21.00 Sun.* A.Ax.Dc.V. £

Kettners 6 G6
29 Romilly St W1. 071-437 6437. Great atmosphere in this turn-of-the-century Soho landmark, which is actually part of the Pizza Express chain. Sumptuous surroundings. Champagne bar. *LD open to 24.00.* A.Ax.Dc.V. ££

Mezzaluna 7 B5
Thomas Neal Centre, 22 Shorts Gdns WC2. 071-379 3336. Cheerful and colourful surroundings in this stylish new-wave Italian restaurant in the Thomas Neal Centre in Covent Garden. Innovative pasta dishes and salads, but the main attraction are the pizzas which are baked in a wood-fired stove. *LD open to 24.00, to 22.30 Sun.* A.Ax.Dc.V. ££

Pappagalli's Pizza Inc 6 F6
7-9 Swallow St, off Regent St W1. 071-734 5182. Large, lively restaurant serving wholemeal and white flour deep-pan and thin-crust pizzas. Also pasta dishes and salad bar. *LD open to 23.00. Closed Sun.* A.Ax.V. ££

Pizza on the Park   10 D3
11 Knightsbridge SW1. 071-235 5550. Stylish and fashionable restaurant. Innovative pizzas; leeks, parmesan and mozzarella, chilli *without* carne for vegetarians. Live jazz. *LD open to 24.00.* A.Ax.Dc.V. ££

Pizza Pomodoro   10 B4
51 Beauchamp Pl SW3. 071-589 1278. Tiny and extremely popular basement restaurant. Excellent pizzas. Live music *every night.* Lively and unconventional staff. *LD (no reservations) open to 01.00.* No credit cards. £

Pizza The Action   13 C5
678 Fulham Rd SW6. 071-736 2716. Fun and lively pizza place. Light and airy with bright decor. Traditional and more unusual pizzas, plus pasta dishes and burgers. *LD open to 24.00.* A.Ax.Dc.V. £

Soho Pizzeria   6 F6
16-18 Beak St W1. 071-434 2480. Large, modern dining room in the heart of Soho. A good selection of Italian-style pizzas plus calzone – a folded pizza. Live music *nightly. LD (Reserve) open to 24.00.* A.Ax.V. £

PASTA CHAINS

PASTA provides a cheap and healthy meal. The following are competitively-priced pasta restaurant chains with branches throughout London. They offer a variety of fresh pasta dishes in pleasant surroundings.

Bella Pasta   6 G6
22 Leicester Sq WC2. 071-321 0016. Authentic Italian pasta dishes in attractive, friendly surroundings. Menu offers meat, fish and vegetable pasta dishes, plus house specialities and traditional pizzas. *LD open to 24.00, to 03.00 Fri & Sat.* A.Ax.V. ££

Café Pasta   7 B5
184 Shaftesbury Ave WC2. 071-379 0198. Relaxed and friendly atmosphere. Wide choice of pasta dishes with some unusual choices; fusilli with Gorgonzola, penne with spicy Italian sausage. Vegetarian dishes. *LD open to 23.30, to 23.00 Sun.* No credit cards. £

Prima Pasta   7 B6
30 Henrietta St WC2. 071-836 8396. Choose from the huge selection of pasta dishes, or combine your own pasta choice with one of a variety of sauces. Also house

specialities, pizzas and salads. Italian wines and beers.
LD open to 23.45, to 23.00 Sun. A.Dc.V. £

Spaghetti House 6 F4
15-17 Goodge St W1. 071-636 6582. Oldest chain of
pasta joints in London. Traditional Italian dishes using
home-made pasta and fresh fruit and vegetables. Long
menu of pasta dishes which come with a bowl of salad.
*LD open to 23.00, to 23.30 Fri & Sat, to 22.00 Sun.
Closed L Sun.* A.Ax.Dc.V. ££

JAPANESE

JAPANESE cooking relies on using the freshest ingredients as a high proportion of the food is eaten raw.
Ingredients are cooked separately to preserve flavours
and are cut to emphasise the natural shape and texture
of the food. The Japanese eat all their dishes together as
the various tastes, colours and textures complement
each other. Typical Japanese dishes are *sukiyaki* – thinly
sliced beef and vegetables, boiled at the table and
dipped in raw egg, *tempura* – fish, shellfish and vegetables dipped in batter and deep-fried with soy sauce, and
yakitori – small pieces of skewered meat dipped into
sugary soy sauce and chargrilled. *Sushi* bars provide
snacks of finely sliced raw seafood on a small block of
rice, suffused with vinegar. In a *teppan-yaki* bar you sit
around the four sides of a large metal griddle while the
chef prepares food from the middle and deposits sizzling
slices of beef, fish and vegetables on your plate. *Kaiseki*
is a multi-course meal of Japanese haute cuisine which

is often served in *tatami* rooms. These are private rooms where you remove your shoes and sit on a heavy straw mat. Noodle bars are the latest trend in Japanese eating; huge bowls of noodles come served with various toppings. *Saké* (made by fermenting freshly steamed rice) is the traditional accompaniment to a Japanese meal. Green tea or whisky are also popular accompaniments. Etiquette plays a large part in Japanese restaurants, however staff are more than willing to explain the 'rules'.

Arisugawa   6 G4
27 Percy St W1. 071-636 8913. Smart modern restaurant decorated in Japanese style with exposed and polished natural wood. There is a teppan-yaki restaurant on the ground floor, and in the basement is a sushi bar and the main restaurant. Some unusual dishes; sea-urchin roe sashimi, sliced liver stir-fried with wild garlic. Set meals. *LD open to 23.00. Closed L Sat & LD Sun.* A.Ax.Dc.V. L ££ D £££

Asuka   6 C3
Berkeley Arcade, 209a Baker St NW1. 071-486 5026. Spacious, elegant restaurant with a main dining room, a sushi bar and private tatami rooms. Lengthy menu; unusual appetizers plus specialities of shabu shabu (beef and vegetables cooked over a flame in the middle of the table) and seafood genpei nabe, also cooked at the table. Set menus including a vegetarian set meal. *LD open to 22.30. Closed L Sat & LD Sun.* A.Ax.Dc.V. £££+

Aykoku-Kaku   7 G6
9 Walbrook EC4. 071-236 9020. Comfortable restaurant popular with Japanese businessmen. Most tastes and pockets catered for; there is a luxurious dining room where specialities such as salmon in saké, sashimi and tempura are expertly and delicately served. Also a sushi bar, teppan-yaki counters and private rooms. Kimono-clad waitresses. Set lunches. *LD (Reserve) open to 22.00. Closed Sat & Sun.* A.Ax.Dc.V. ££-£££+

Benihana   2 A4
100 Avenue Rd NW3. 071-586 7118. American-style Japanese restaurant which has branches all around the world. An elegant and enjoyable night out; diners are seated round a rectangular grill where teppan-yaki chefs prepare, with much twirling and flashing of blades, grilled vegetables, seafood, chicken and beef. 12-course

kaiseki meal available. *LD open to 24.00. Closed L Mon.* A.Ax.Dc.V. L ££ D £££

Ikeda 6 E6
30 Brook St W1. 071-629 2730. Bustling restaurant with both a sushi and a yakitori bar. Meals are beautifully presented and unusual simmered dishes include buta kakuni (pork simmered in a shoyu and saké broth) and sakani arani (fish on the bone with a soy sauce). *LD (Reserve) open to 22.30, to 22.00 Sat. Closed Sun.* A.Ax.Dc.V. £££+

Isohama 10 F5
312 Vauxhall Bridge Rd SW1. 071-834 2145. Small, simply-decorated restaurant close to Victoria Station. Excellent seafood menu plus sushi, sashimi, yakitori. Set meals. LD *(Reserve L) open to 22.30. Closed L Sat & LD Sun.* A.Ax.Dc.V. L £ D ££

Jin Kichi
73 Heath St NW3. 071-794 6158. This was one of the first yakitori bars in London. More than two dozen dishes on the menu from which you can try a set assortment. Sit round the bar to have your choices delivered sizzling onto your plate. Excellent sashimi set meal. Sushi bar upstairs. Kirin beer, whisky or saké to drink. *LD open to 23.30. Closed L Mon-Fri & D Tue.* A.Ax.Dc.V. £

Masako 6 D5
6-8 St Christopher's Pl, off Wigmore St W1. 071-935 1579. Authentic Japanese restaurant with private dining rooms attended by charming waitresses dressed in kimonos. A wide-ranging menu. Try the set sukiyaki, sashimi, sushi or kaiseki meals. Saké or Japanese beer. *LD open to 22.30. Closed Sun.* A.Ax.Dc.V. £££+

Matsuri 10 F2
15 Bury St SW1. 071-839 1101. Large, sumptuous restaurant where you can choose to eat at the sushi counter or round the teppan-yaki grill table. A la carte menu includes grated white radish with Japanese mushroom, salted crab meat, spring onion and seaweed with sweet vinegar. *LD (Reserve) open to 22.30. Closed Sun.* A.Ax.Dc.V. L £ D ££

Men's Bar Hamine 6 F6
84 Brewer St W1. 071-439 0785. 'Men' is Japanese for noodles, and large bowls of noodle soup are the mainstay at this new-wave Japanese diner. Also meat and

rice dishes, and excellent gyoza (grilled dumplings). *LD open to 24.00, to 02.00 Sat.* No credit cards. £

Miyama   10 E2
38 Clarges St W1. 071-499 2443. Stylish restaurant in the heart of Mayfair. Cool and elegant with modern decor – a reception, bar and main dining room on the ground floor and a teppan-yaki counter, sushi bar and tatami rooms downstairs. Teppan-yaki is a house speciality. Also excellent zensai starters. Set menus. Saké, Japanese beer and Suntory whisky. **City Miyama** at 17 Godliman St EC4 (7 F5), 071-489 1937, has a sushi bar and is very busy at lunchtime. *LD open to 22.30.* A.Ax.Dc.V. L ££ D £££+

Momo
14 Queens Parade W5. 081-997 0206. Small restaurant providing Ealing's Japanese community with authentic food, delicately prepared and served in traditional style. Good value one-dish lunches. Grilled eel and soft-shell crab on the main menu. *LD (Reserve D Fri & Sat) open to 22.00. Closed Mon.* A.Ax.Dc.V. L £ D £££

Nakano   10 B4
11 Beauchamp Pl SW3. 071-581 3837. Simply-decorated basement restaurant serving imaginative Japanese dishes. Cuttle fish marinated in saké, grilled salmon head. Specials menu changes monthly. Set menus. *LD (Reserve) open to 23.00. Closed L Sun & LD Mon.* A.Ax.Dc.V. L ££ D £££+

Neshiko   3 E4
265 Upper St N1. 071-359 9977. Named after a fishing village in the southern island of Japan, this bright, modern restaurant has a varied menu. Good selection of grilled, simmered and deep-fried dishes; simmered chicken and spring onion is delicious. Try the Japanese omelette. Sushi bar. *LD (Reserve D) open to 23.00. Closed Sun.* A.Ax.Dc.V. L ££ D £££+

Ninjin   6 E3
244 Great Portland St W1. 071-388 4657. Basement restaurant below its own supermarket. Comfortable and friendly, the perfect place to try Japanese food for the first time. Generous portions of sushi, tempura, kushiyaki. Chestnut and red bean ice-cream. Set menus. *LD (Reserve) open to 22.00. Closed Sun.* A.Ax.Dc.V. L ££ D £££

Sumos
169 King St W6. 081-741 7916. Simple restaurant

serving inexpensive Japanese meals. Sushi, sashimi, tempura, yakitori, teriyaki. Also yaki, a vegetarian dish of ground bean pancake with bean sprouts, carrot and onion. Set menus. *LD open to 23.00. Closed L Sat & LD Sun.* No credit cards. £

Suntory 10 F2
72 St James's St SW1. 071-409 0201. One of London's oldest Japanese restaurants, popular with ministers and officials from the Japanese Embassy. Elegant with traditional touches. Teppan-yaki room plus tatami rooms. Teppan-yaki dishes, lobster sashimi, sushi, tempura, shabu shabu. Set menus. *LD (Reserve) open to 22.00. Closed Sun.* A.Ax.Dc.V. £££+

Tatsuso 8 B4
32 Broadgate Circle EC2. 071-638 5863. One of London's top Japanese restaurants catering for a mainly business clientele. Serves *washoku* – authentic Japanese food, beautifully presented. Teppan-yaki bar. Tatami room (book well in advance). Waitresses in traditional dress. Set menus. *LD (Reserve L) open to 21.30. Closed Sat & Sun.* A.Ax.Dc.V. £££+

Tokyo Diner 6 G6
2 Newport Pl WC2. 071-287 8777. Bright and noisy Japanese diner. Service is Japanese-style; bowing waiters greet you on arrival. Standard fare; noodles, sushi, sashimi and bento boxes – complete meals served in a box. Japanese green tea. *LD open to 24.00.* No credit cards or cheques. £

Wagamama 7 B4
4 Streatham St, off Bloomsbury St WC1. 071-323 9223. Communal eating in a canteen atmosphere at this immensely popular Japanese noodle bar. Huge bowls of ramen noodle soup, fried rice or noodles with vegetable or seafood toppings, grilled dumplings, rice dishes and curries. All served by super-efficient waiters and waitresses wielding hand-held computer pads. No smoking. Expect to queue. *LD open to 23.00.* No credit cards. £

Yumi 6 C5
110 George St W1. 071-935 8320. Simple decor and traditional menu of grills, raw fish, steamed food and noodles. Sushi bar on street level; private rooms where you sit cross-legged at very low tables. Set meals available *at lunchtime. LD (Reserve) open to 22.30. Closed Sun.* A.Ax.V. £££+

JEWISH

ORTHODOX Jews are allowed to eat only fish with scales and cloven-hoofed animals which chew the cud, and may not mix dairy products with meat. Some Jewish restaurants in Britain are no longer 'kosher'. Menus usually show an East European and Middle Eastern influence and may include fried *latkes* (potato cakes), *gefilte fisch* (whitefish balls), salt beef or pickled herrings. American/Jewish cuisine, served in New York-style delis, is becoming more popular.

Bloom's
90 Whitechapel High St E1. 071-247 6001.   8 C5
LD open to 21.30. Closed D Fri & LD Sat.
130 Golders Green Rd NW11. 081-455 1338.
LD open to 23.00, to 04.00 Sat. Closed D Fri & L Sat.
Bloom's has been an institution for over 70 years since the original family premises were located in Brick Lane. Packed with Jewish families *on Sundays*. Good wholesome portions of salt beef, gefilte fisch, gedempte meatballs, bloomburgers. Lockshen pudding for dessert. A.Ax.Dc.V. **££**

Boobas   1 F3
4 New College Pde, Finchley Rd NW3. 071-483 0533. Basement restaurant with a café upstairs. Traditional East European dishes plus New York deli fare. Borscht, fried haddock with latkes, salads and sandwiches. *LD (Reserve D & L Sat) open to 24.00.* A.V. **£**

Grahame's Seafare   6 F5
38 Poland St W1. 071-437 3788. Simple, old-fashioned Kosher fish restaurant where you can have your fish deep-fried, grilled, steamed or cooked in milk and butter. Set lunch menu. *LD (Reserve L) open to 21.00, to 20.00 Fri & Sat. Closed Sun.* A.Ax.V. **££**

Harry Morgan's   **6 B1**
31 St John's Wood High St NW8. 071-722 1869.
All-Jewish menu, care of Mrs Morgan. Salt beef,
tongue, gefilte fisch, latkes, Hungarian goulash.
Takeaway deli. *LD open to 22.00. Closed D Fri.* No
credit cards. ££

Kosher Luncheon Club   **8 D4**
Morris Kasler Hall, 13 Greatorex St E1. 071-247 0039.
This is the last survivor of the East End Jewish eating
houses which were originally soup kitchens for Jewish
workers. Lunchtime restaurant serving home-cooked
East European food. Unlicensed. *L open to 15.00.
Closed Sat.* No credit cards. £

The Nosh Bar   **1 F3**
134 Finchley Rd NW3. 071-794 3434. Diner serving
New York deli fare; sandwiches, bagels, latkes, borscht.
Salad counter along one wall with a drinks bar. Seating
downstairs. *LD (Reserve L Sat & L Sun) open to 21.30,
to 15.30 Mon.* A.Ax.V. £

The Nosherie   **7 D4**
12-13 Greville St EC1. 071-242 1591. Authentic East
European Jewish food in this busy, friendly lunchtime
restaurant. Sandwich bar at the front and restaurant at
the back serving fish and meat dishes. *L open to 16.00.
Closed Sat & Sun.* No credit cards. £

Reuben's   **6 C4**
20a Baker St W1. 071-935 5945. Restaurant above a
simple kosher deli and takeaway in the oldest building
in Baker Street. Salt beef, chopped liver, gefilte fisch,
lockshen pudding. *LD (Reserve Sun) open to 22.00.
Closed D Fri & LD Sat.* A.V. ££

Uncle Ian's Deli Diner
8-10 Monkville Pde, Finchley Rd NW11. 081-458
3493. Lively atmosphere at this popular diner which is
always busy, so expect to queue. Deli-style sandwiches
plus traditional European dishes. Children are made
very welcome. Set menus. Unlicensed. *LD (no reservations) open to 23.30, to 16.00 Fri.* A.V. £

Widow Applebaum's   **6 E5**
46 South Molton St W1. 071-629 4649. New York deli
decorated with mirrors and photos of New York in the
jazz age. Matzo balls, salt beef sandwiches, hot pastrami,
apfelstrudel, ice-cream sodas. *LD open to 22.00.*
A.Ax.Dc.V. ££

BAGELS

Bagel King 11 F6
280 Walworth Rd SE17. 071-252 5057. Bagels with a huge choice of fillings. Also cakes and a small deli. *Open 24 hrs.* No credit cards.

Brick Lane Beigel Bake 8 C3
159 Brick Lane E1. 071-729 0616. Traditional Jewish bakery serving fresh bagels *all night*. Also pastries and doughnuts. *Open 24 hrs.* No credit cards.

Carmelli
128 Golders Green Rd NW11. 081-455 2074. Excellent bagels, bread and pastries. *Open to 24.00 Mon-Wed, Fri & Sun. Open 24 hrs Thur & Sat.* No credit cards.

Ridley Bagel Bakery 4 C2
13-15 Ridley Rd E8. 071-241 1047. Delicous fresh, hot bagels with wonderful fillings. Also a deli counter. *Open 24 hrs.* No credit cards.

KOREAN

KOREAN cuisine is a blend of Japanese, Thai and Chinese cooking and comprises odd mixtures of texture and taste. Common ingredients are sesame seeds, garlic, ginger and soy sauce. *Bulgogi* is the Korean speciality – meat marinated in a spicy sauce and barbecued at the table. Other traditional dishes include *yuk hwe* – shredded raw beef covered with strips of pear and egg yolk, *shinsonro* – meat soup with seaweed, seafood, eggs and vegetables, and *jeon gol* – strips of steak fried into pancakes with cabbage, mushroom, garlic, spices and onion. Seafood and fish also feature strongly. *Kim chee* is a preserved cabbage dish which accompanies everything. Desserts are simple, but fruit-cutting is a dazzling Korean art. Most restaurants offer set menus, and food is generally very well prepared and beautifully presented.

Arirang   6 F5
31-32 Poland St W1. 071-437 9662. London's oldest Korean restaurant where waitresses in national dress steer you through the large menu. Yuk kwe (beef strips with sugar, pears and spices), ojingo pokum (hot, sweet squid) and tangsaoyuk (sweet and sour meatballs) are some of the choices. For dessert, beautifully cut fruit. Saké, ginseng, Korean tea. *LD (Reserve D) open to 23.00. Closed Sun.* A.Ax.Dc.V. ££

Busan   3 D3
43 Holloway Rd N7. 071-607 8264. Friendly local restaurant with a great reputation. The extensive menu has specialities from Korea plus some Japanese classics. All dishes are beautifully presented; fruit and vegetables are artistically sculpted. Seafood is their speciality; try mixed seafood stir-fried in a chilli sauce. Saké, ginseng brandy. *LD (Reserve) open to 24.00. Closed L Sat & L Sun.* A.V. ££

The Garden
210 King Street W6. 081-748 5058. Relaxed atmos-phere in which to enjoy authentic Korean cuisine. Delicious traditional dishes are attractively presented and come in generous portions. Samgae tang (whole chicken stuffed with ginseng roots and rice) can be ordered 24 hours in advance. Korean rice cakes for dessert. Set meals. *LD (Reserve) open to 23.00. Closed Sun.* A.Ax.V. ££

Jin   6 G5
16 Bateman St, off Dean Street W1. 071-734 0908. Elegant Korean restaurant with smart white and gold frontage. All tables have a grill in the centre for barbecued specialities which are marinated and cooked at the table. Friendly, helpful service. Saké, Korean barley tea. *LD (Reserve) open to 23.00. Closed L Sun.* A.Ax.Dc.V. ££

Kaya Korean   6 G5
22-25 Dean St W1. 071-437 6630. Waitresses in

full national costume will talk you through the menu at this traditional Korean restaurant. The seafood special is worth tasting. So is the sliced, seasoned venison, which you won't find on many Korean menus. *LD (Reserve D) open to 23.00. Closed L Sun.* A.Ax.Dc.V. £££+

Seoul   8 C5
89a Aldgate High St EC3. 071-480 5770. Informal restaurant popular with Japanese and Korean business-men at lunchtime. Extensive menu of authentic Korean dishes; bulgogi, kim chee, squid in spicy sauce, fish fried in egg and batter. *LD (Reserve L) open to 21.00. Closed Sat & Sun.* A.V. ££

Shilla   6 F5
58-59 Great Malborough St W1. 071-267 1147. Charming service guides you through this restaurant's speciality – barbecue dishes – with the barbecue at your table and you as the chef. Delicious sauces accompany the beef, chicken or seafood chosen. Popular with businessmen. Set menus available. *LD open to 23.00. Closed L Sun.* A.Ax.Dc.V. ££

You Me House
33 Pratt St NW1. 071-267 1147.   2 F5
510a Hornsey Rd N19. 071-272 6208.
Family-run restaurants. Try bintatok (Korean pizza topped with minced beef, spring onions, crab meat, garlic and mixed vegetables). Artistically cut fresh fruit for dessert. Set menus. Good service. N19 branch unlicensed. *LD (Reserve) open to 24.00. Closed L Sun.* A.V. (No credit cards at N19 branch.) ££

Young Bin Kwan   7 F4
3 St Alphage High Walk, London Wall EC2. 071-638 9151. A strange setting for this restaurant, high on the Barbican walkway. Popular with businessmen at lunchtime and theatre-goers in the evening. The bi bim bap set lunch is good value; raw beef and egg, vegetables and rice, with miso soup and kim chee. Japanese beer to accompany your meal. *LD (Reserve L) open to 23.00. Closed Sat & Sun.* A.Ax.Dc.V. ££

MALAYSIAN, INDONESIAN & SINGAPOREAN

SOUTH East Asian cuisine, from Malaysia, Indonesia and Singapore, has been influenced by Chinese and Indian cooking, although dishes tend to be lighter and fresher, and coconut and peanut replace soy and garlic as the prominent flavours. Seafood, chicken and beef are often stir-fried after marinating. Those of delicate palate should beware *sambals* – fiery pickles served as sauces or accompaniments.

Malaysian specialities include *satay* – strips of meat marinated in coconut milk, grilled on a skewer and served with a spicy peanut dip, *gado gado* – salad with satay sauce made from ground peanuts, chilli, onions and sugar, and *nasi goreng* – special fried noodles.

Indonesia is famous for its *rijstafel* (literally 'rice table') – a banquet of small dishes served with rice.

Mild and creamy curries are the pride of Singapore, as is *laksa* – a noodle soup with prawns, chicken, bean sprouts, fish cakes and chillis on a base of coconut.

Bali   **6 B5**
101 Edgware Rd W2. 071-723 3303. Attractive restaurant on two floors. Decorated with bamboo furnishings, palms and pastel colours. Authentic South East Asian food; excellent rijstafel, laksa, gado gado. *LD (Reserve) open to 23.15.* A.Ax.Dc.V. ££

Bintang 2 E4
93 Kentish Town Rd NW1. 071-284 1640. Tiny,
family-run restaurant bringing the delights of sunny
Malaysia to north London. Bamboo and palm matting,
tropical fish tanks and Malaysian artefacts. A mixture
of Malaysian, Indonesian and Singaporean fare.
Seafood is their speciality. Singaporean Tiger beer
to drink and Malaysian pop music to listen to.
LD (Reserve) open to 23.30, to 01.30 Fri & Sat. A.V.
££

Circle East 12 C3
The Circle, Queen Elizabeth St SE1. 071-403 9996. Just
behind Butler's Wharf in the Circle development, this
designer restaurant is visually stunning. The bar area
contains two huge aquariums with coral reef displays
and tropical fish. Malaysian, Indonesian and
Singaporean dishes predominate, but there are also
choices from China and Thailand. Pianist *nightly. LD
open to 23.00, to 23.30 Fri & Sat, to 22.30 Sun.*
A.Ax.Dc.V. L ££ D £££

Indorasa 18 B6
53a Streatham Hill SW2. 081-671 5919. Indonesian
restaurant run by two sisters who are half Javanese and
half Sumatran. Rijstafel is the speciality; choose from a
variety of set meals incorporating dishes from all the
main Indonesian islands. Balinese-style beef, Javanese
chicken. Coconut banana pancake for dessert. *LD
(Reserve Fri & Sat) open to 23.30. Closed L Sat.*
A.Ax.Dc.V. ££

Melati 10 G1
21 Great Windmill St W1. 071-437 2745. Lively and
popular restaurant serving authentic Malaysian,
Indonesian and Singaporean cuisine. Excellent laksa
soup, satay dishes, Malaysian chicken curry. Exotic
fresh fruit. Indonesian Bintang beer, Singaporean Tiger
beer. *LD (Reserve) open to 23.30, to 00.30 Fri & Sat.*
A.Ax.Dc.V. ££

Minang 6 G5
11 Greek St W1. 071-287 1408. This smart restaurant
is an offspring of **Melati** and is somewhat less frenetic
than its parent restaurant with a pleasant and relaxed
atmosphere. The Indonesian buffet lunch is good value;
soto Minang soup, followed by a main course incorporating six dishes. *LD (Reserve D Fri & D Sat) open to
23.30.* A.Ax.Dc.V. ££

Nusa Dua   6 G5
11-12 Dean St W1. 071-437 3559. Cheerfully-decorated
Indonesian restaurant on two floors. The extensive
menu includes excellent chicken, beef, prawn and beancurd satays, fish grilled in banana leaf and some good
vegetarian choices. Indonesian Bintang beer. *LD
(Reserve D Fri & D Sat) open to 23.30. Closed L Sat &
LD Sun.* A.Ax.Dc.V. ££

Penang Satay House
9 Turnpike Lane N8. 081-340 8707. Bright restaurant
decorated with bamboo and batik. Menu of spicy dishes
from Penang and Singapore. Sambal udang is the house
speciality; king prawns in shrimp sauce. Excellent satay
dishes; try satay halibut. *D (Reserve Fri & Sat) open to
22.45, to 24.00 Fri & Sat. Closed Sun.* No credit cards.
££

Rasa Sayang
10 Frith St W1. 071-734 8720.   6 G5
38 Queensway W2. 071-229 8417.   5 E6
Simple restaurants serving authentic Malaysian and
Indonesian food. Dishes worth trying are orange chick-
en and rendang (cutlets of beef in coconut gravy). *LD
(Reserve) open to 22.30, to 24.00 Fri & Sat. Closed L
Sat.* A.Ax.Dc.V. ££

Rasa Sayang West
146 The Broadway W13. 081-567 6821. Ealing branch
of the Rasa Sayang chain. The emphasis at this restaurant is on Indonesian dishes. Try dendeng asam pdas
(beef steak in hot and sour sauce) or grilled prawns with
butter and orange sauce. *L(Sun only)D (Reserve D Fri
& Sat) open to 23.00, to 24.00 Fri & Sat. Closed L
Mon-Sat & D Mon.* A.Ax.V. ££

Singapore Garden   1 F4
83 Fairfax Rd NW6. 071-328 5314. Homely restaurant,
very popular with Singaporean and Chinese families at
weekend   lunchtimes.   Excellent   Malaysian   and
Singaporean cuisine; sizzling dishes, Malaysian chicken
and beef curries, chilli lobster, Singapore noodles. *LD
(Reserve L Sat & Sun and D Mon-Sun) open to 22.30,
to 22.45 Fri & Sat.* A.Ax.Dc.V. ££

Singapura   13 B5
839 Fulham Rd SW6. 071-736 9310. A stylish restau-
rant serving dishes from all over South East Asia.
Vietnamese   spring   rolls,   Indonesian   gado   gado,

Singapore noodle soup. Deep-fried banana for dessert. All dishes are beautifully prepared and presented. Occasional live music. *D (Reserve) open to 23.00. Closed Sun.* A.Ax.Dc.V. ££

Straits   10 E2
5 White Horse St W1. 071-493 3986. Bright Malaysian/Indonesian restaurant decorated with bamboo and lots of plants. Cuisine is from the Straits of Malacca and is influenced by Chinese and Indian cooking. Also some Singaporean dishes. *LD (Reserve) open to 23.45. Closed L Sat & LD Sun.* A.Ax.Dc.V. £££

Tiger Under The Table
643 Finchley Rd NW11. 081-458 9273. A bright and cheerful Singaporean restaurant serving innovative dishes. Try soft-shelled crab or ro teocheow fishball soup. *Sunday lunchtime* buffet offers a choice of ten main dishes and four desserts. *LD (Reserve D Thur-Sun) open to 23.15.* A.Ax.Dc.V. ££

MEXICAN

Mexican food is basically a peasant cuisine, and typical dishes are largely variations on the theme of *tortillas* – thin corn or flour pancakes, minced or shredded meats, *frijoles* – refried beans, and chilli. *Tacos* – crisp tortillas folded and filled with shredded meat, salad and spicy sauce, *burritos* – soft tortillas wrapped around meat and beans, and *enchiladas* – burritos baked in chilli sauce, are all typical. More ambitious dishes include *ceviche* – raw fish marinated in lime juice, chicken *mole* – in a spicy chilli and bitter chocolate sauce, and *tamales* – suety pancakes of meat slow-baked in corn husks. Rice is a common accompaniment, often cooked in tomato sauce. Avocados, tomatoes, lettuce and beans are often included to balance the spicy heat of dishes.

Arizona   **2 E5**
2a Jamestown Rd NW1. 071-284 4730. Loud, lively
and bustling Tex-Mex restaurant and bar just off
Camden High Street. Nachos, tacos, enchiladas and
vegetarian quesada. Wash down with Sol or Corona
beers, margueritas and tequila slammers. Outside tables
on the roof terrace. *LD open to 24.00.* A.Ax.V. ££

Break for the Border
8 Argyll St W1. 071-734 5776.   ⌝ **6 F5**
LD (Reserve) open to 23.45.
5 Goslett Yard, off Charing Cross Rd WC2.   ⌐ **6 G5**
071-437 8595. *D open to 23.30 Sun-Tue, to 02.00*
Wed-Sat.
Saloon-style bar and restaurant, evoking memories of
the gold-rush. Always packed with party crowds
attracted to the loud music, cocktails and Tex-Mex
food. Nachos, enchiladas, burritos, chimichangas, fajitas.
Cocktails and Mexican beers. A.Ax.V. ££

Café Mexicano   **15 G4**
53 Camberwell Church St SE5. 071-252 5477. The
bright decor, lively atmosphere, live music and late opening hours make this a popular spot. Huge portions of
nachos, tacos, chimichangas and burritos. Mexican beers.
LD open to 01.00, to 23.30 Sun. Closed L Sun. A.V. ££

Café Pacifico   ⌐ **7 B5**
5 Langley St WC2. 071-379 7728. Crowded cantina in
a converted warehouse where a young crowd enjoys the
loud and lively atmosphere. No booking at night, but
you can have a cocktail at the long bar while you wait.
Guacamole, nachos, tacos, enchiladas, quesadillas,
tostadas, chilaquiles. Fresh pineapple or helados to
follow. A dozen different tequilas, Mexican cocktails
and beers. Occasional Mexican music. *LD (Reserve L)*
open to 23.45, to 22.45 Sun. A.Ax.V. ££

Chiquito   ⌐ **7 A6**
20-21 Leicester Sq WC2. 071-839 6925. Large and bright
restaurant decorated with artefacts and colourful wall-
hangings. Fresh ingredients and mild spices are used to
prepare traditional north Mexican cuisine. Pollo Mon-
terrey, enchiladas, tacos, guacamole, chimichangas,
Mexican pizzas. Mexican fried ice-cream for dessert.
Pitchers of sangria and margueritas. Mexican beers. *LD (no*
reservations) open to 23.45, to 22.45 Sun. A.Ax.Dc.V ££

La Cucaracha   ⌐ **6 G5**
12-13 Greek St W1. 071-734 2253. London's first

Mexican restaurant, in the cellars of a converted monastery. Decorated in hacienda style with alcoves and a sunny covered terrace. Try the Mexican national dish, mole poblano de guajolote (roasted turkey in a cocoa nut sauce) or avocado Mexicano (baked and stuffed with crab meat). Finish with copa vallarta (sorbet with fresh melon and mango). Mexican guitarist *in the evening. LD open to 23.30. A.Ax.Dc.V. ££*

Down Mexico Way   16 F6
25 Swallow St, off Regent St W1. 071-437 9895. Originally a Spanish restaurant owned by the Martínez family, the dining room floors and walls are covered in hand-painted tiles given to the family by King Juan Carlos. An interesting menu includes Mexican soup, jalapeno muffins, mesquite smoked dishes, sizzling fajitas. Plenty of choice for vegetarians. Mexican hot chocolate, tequila slammers and Chilean wine. Late night bar *open to 03.00 Mon-Sat (with entertainment Thur-Sat). LD (Reserve) open to 23.45, to 22.15 Sun.* A.Ax.Dc.V. ££

El Gran Taco   17 B2
43 St John's Hill SW11. 071-585 3050. A popular restaurant, brightly-decorated with Mexican wall-hangings. Authentic Mexican food; alitas de pollo (chicken wings in barbecue sauce), pez espada (swordfish steak). Also a 'menu variado' which offers a selection of dishes from the menu. Occasional live music. *D (Reserve Fri & Sat) open to 23.30, to 22.30 Sun.* A.Ax.V. ££

Jeepers   16 E3
350 Old York Rd SW18. 081-870 5491. Lively Mexican restaurant with an attractive central conservatory full of plant life. Always busy with diners enjoying chicken, beef and vegetarian chilli, Mexican pizza, tangy spare ribs. Unusual desserts; Mexicali cake, apple chimichanga. Margueritas and Sol beer. *LD open to 23.30, to 22.30 Sun.* A.Ax.Dc.V. ££

Los Locos
24 Russell St WC2. 071-379 0220.   11 B1
14 Soho St, off Oxford St W1. 071-287 0005.   6 G5
Lively Mexican bar and restaurant with lots of Tex-Mex specials. Mexican beer and cocktails. Disco *from 23.30 every night. D (Reserve Fri & Sat) open to 21.30. Bar food until 03.00.* A.Ax.Dc.V. ££

Richmond Cantina
32 The Quadrant, Richmond, Surrey. 081-332 6262.

Authentic Mexican restaurant decorated in terracotta and blue. The menu goes beyond standard Tex-Mex fare; calamari, tinga poblana (diced pork with chillis, chorizo, tomatoes and potatoes). Delicious lime cheesecake for dessert. Frozen margueritas. *LD open to 23.00, to 22.00 Sun.* A.Ax.V. **£**

Roxy Café Cantina   3 E5
297 Upper St N1. 071-226 5746. A relaxed atmosphere at this brightly-lit modern diner. Good selection of dishes; as well as burritos, tacos and nachos, you can have southern-fried chicken and chargrilled burgers. Vegetarian choices include mushroom chimichanga and enchiladas with cheese and onion filling. *LD (Reserve D Fri & Sat) open to 23.30, to 22.45 Sun.* A.V. **££**

Texas Lone Star West
154 Gloucester Rd SW7. 071-370 5625.   9 F5
117a Queensway W2. 071-727 2980.   5 E5
50-54 Turnham Green Ter W4. 081-747 0001.
Lively frontier-style restaurants with rough wood, heaps of straw and Tex-Mex dishes. Guacamole, tacos and burritos, plus burgers, ribs and steaks. Cocktails. Live music *Mon-Sat. LD open to 23.30 Sun-Wed, to 00.15 Thur-Sat.* No credit cards. **££**

MIDDLE EASTERN

THIS section covers Afghani, Arabic, Iranian, Lebanese, Moroccan and Tunisian cuisines. Charcoal grilling is a popular method of cooking throughout these areas, and dishes are often spicy. Yoghurt is a common ingredient, as are ginger, almonds, nutmeg, coriander and cinnamon. It is a good idea to order two or three dishes per person. They are usually accompanied by salad, olives and unleavened bread. Typical dishes are *kibbeh* – deep-fried mince and cracked wheat balls, *tabouleh* – finely chopped parsley, tomatoes, onions, cracked wheat, olive oil and lemon juice, *borek* – small flat pastries which are baked or fried and filled with cheese or spinach, and kebabs in a variety of forms – *doner, kofta* or *shish*.

Adam's Café
77 Askew Rd W12. 081-743 0572. During the day this is a humble café but in the evenings it becomes a Tunisian restaurant. The friendly and helpful staff will steer you through the menu. Couscous is the speciality, but you can also choose from traditional dishes such as chorba (Tunisian lamb soup) and gargoulette (Tunisian spicy lamb casserole). Tunisian pastries for dessert. Unlicensed, but you can bring your own wine. *D (Reserve) open to 22.30. Closed Sun.* No credit cards. ££

Al Alysse　　　　3 E5
134 Upper St N1. 071-226 0122. North London Lebanese restaurant with an excellent lunchtime buffet. Atmosphere is more intimate in the evenings. A good selection of meze, and interesting dishes such as basturma (spiced beef) and shish taouk (chicken in garlic). *LD open to 24.00. Closed L Mon & LD Sun.* A.V. ££ (set buffet lunch £)

Al Basha　　　　9 D4
222 Kensington High St W8. 071-937 1030. Smart restaurant near Holland Park which has outside tables on the terrace *in summer.* Excellent Lebanese food; kofta antabiyeh (minced kebab with spicy tomato sauce), shawarma (slices of lamb marinated in vinegar and spices, and grilled on an upright spit). Lebanese wine. Live music *nightly. LD (Reserve D Fri & D Sat) open to 24.00.* A.Ax.Dc.V. ££

Al Bustan　　　　10 D4
27 Motcomb St SW1. 071-235 8277. Al Bustan means 'the garden' and the light, airy decor at this Lebanese restaurant conveys this theme. A good selection of Lebanese and Middle Eastern dishes; meze, main course grills including firreh (grilled quail), raw lamb dishes. Cardamom-flavoured Turkish coffee. *LD (Reserve D) open to 23.30.* A.Ax.Dc.V. £££

Al Hamra　　　　10 E2
31-33 Shepherd Market, off White Horse St W1. 071-493 1954. Long-established Lebanese restaurant. The spacious dining room has three sides which look out onto the market; the other is covered in mirrors. Huge range of hot and cold meze dishes followed by a variety of charcoal-grilled meats and sweet, sugary desserts.

Outside tables *in summer*. Lebanese wine or arak to drink. *LD open to 23.30.* A.Ax.Dc.V. £££

Caravan Serai 6 D4
50 Paddington St W1. 071-935 1208. One of only two restaurants in London serving Afghani food. The other is **Buzkash**, 4 Chelverton Rd SW15 (**16 A2**). 081-788 0599. Caravan Serai is small, decorated with artefacts. Authentic Afghani dishes include ashak (pasta filled with minced meat, yoghurt and spices), bonjon (aubergine, tomatoes, garlic and capsicum), samorook (mushrooms with tomatoes and fresh coriander). Home-made ice-cream for dessert. *LD (Reserve) open to 23.00, to 22.30 Sun.* A.Ax.Dc.V. ££

Fakhreldine 10 E2
85 Piccadilly W1. 071-493 3424. Huge and elaborately-decorated Lebanese restaurant overlooking Green Park. Extensive list of meze dishes, charcoal grills, falafel, kibbeh. Excellent pastry trolley. Lebanese wine. Live music *nightly*. *LD (Reserve D) open to 01.00, to 24.00 Sun.* A.Ax.Dc.V. £££

Hafez 5 D5
5 Hereford Rd W2. 071-221 3167. This is one of the few Iranian restaurants in London. Delicious, authentic food; chelo kebabs are the speciality. Traditional flat breads are baked in the huge mosaic oven at the front and are served hot with herbs, feta cheese, yoghurt and shallots. **Hafez II** is at 559 Finchley Rd NW3 (**1 E2**). 071-431 4546. *LD open to 24.00.* No credit cards. £

The Lebanese Restaurant 6 B5
60 Edgware Rd W2. 071-262 9585. Sample authentic Lebanese dishes in an oriental atmosphere. Mirrors, arches, dim wall lights and carved chairs inlaid with brass. Montabar (baked aubergine with sesame sauce, lemon, olive oil and garlic) is worth trying. For dessert, usmalieh (pieces of shredded wheat in cream and syrup). Finish off with proper mint tea made with mint leaves. *LD open to 24.00.* A.Ax.Dc.V. ££

Maroush I 6 C5
21 Edgware Rd W2. 071-723 0773.
Maroush II 10 B4
38 Beauchamp Pl SW3. 071-581 5434.
Maroush III 6 C5
62 Seymour St W1. 071-724 5024.
Ever-popular chain of authentic Lebanese restaurants.

Large selection of mezes and charcoal grills. Fresh bread baked on the premises. Music *nightly* at Maroush I. *LD open to 24.00.* A.Ax.Dc.V. No cheques. ££

The Olive Tree   6 G6
11 Wardour St W1. 071-734 0808. Simple restaurant serving Middle Eastern food with Arabic and Greek specialities. A separate vegetarian menu features several Lebanese dishes. *LD open to 23.00, to 21.00 Sun.* A.V. £

Phoenicia   9 D4
11-13a Abingdon Rd W8. 071-937 0120. Attractive family-run Lebanese restaurant with a spotlit internal garden. Specialities are mezes and charcoal grills. Katayaf with honey, nuts and cream cheese for dessert. *LD open to 23.45.* A.Ax.Dc.V. £££

La Reash Cous-Cous House   6 G5
23-24 Greek St W1. 071-439 1063. Not all couscous, despite the name; a variety of other Lebanese and Moroccan dishes. Try chicken tageen which is served piping hot in a traditional Moroccan cooking pot. Vegetarian meze. *LD (Reserve D Fri & D Sat) open to 24.00.* A.V. ££

Soraya   9 F4
36 Gloucester Rd SW7. 071-589 5745. Popular with ex-patriate Iranians, this restaurant serves traditional Persian cuisine; Persian stews, khorosh fesenjan (meat-balls in sweet and sour sauce), khosh badenjan (lamb in tomato, lime and aubergine). Nightclub in the base-ment. *LD (Reserve D Fri & D Sat) open to 01.00, to 02.00 Thur-Sat.* A.V. ££

Tageen   7 B6
12 Upper St Martin's Lane WC2. 071-836 7272. Moroccan restaurant decorated in traditional style; tiles, lanterns, cushions, Moroccan tablecloths and tableware. Food arrives at your table in tageens, traditional Moroccan cooking pots. Start with harira, a thick and spicy soup. Try the Moroccan national dish, bastela, a sweet pie with chicken, saffron, almonds and cinnamon. Main dishes are all wonderfully marinated, tangy or pleasantly spiced. *LD open to 23.30. Closed L Sat & LD Sun.* A.Ax.Dc.V. ££

MODERN EUROPEAN

MODERN European cuisine is based on the techniques of French and English cooking but also incorporates ideas and ingredients from around the world. Individuality is the trademark, with interesting and daring adaptations of classic French and other European dishes as well as some equally bold new ideas. Regularly changing menus ensure that the freshest ingredients are used and presentation is an important factor. Modern European restaurants can be quite expensive, but are normally attractive and pleasant places to eat.

Alastair Little   6 G5
49 Frith St W1. 071-734 5183. Celebrity chef Alastair Little uses the freshest ingredients to produce his very distinctive style of cooking. Very fashionable restaurant with minimalist decor and a wide-ranging menu which changes frequently. Dishes are all beautifully presented. Chinese-style glazed Bresse pigeon, sautéed squid with ink sauce, chicken wrapped in cabbage and pancetta. Set lunch menu. *LD (Reserve) open to 23.30. Closed L Sat & LD Sun.* A.Ax.V. £££+ (set lunch menu ££)

Beauchamp Place   10 B4
15 Beauchamp Pl SW3. 071-589 4252. Spacious restaurant on three floors. Modern decor; glass roof, bright colours, modern designs and lighting. The ground floor bar has a menu of light dishes. The restaurant menu offers tagliatelle with lobster, crab, escalope of salmon. Apricot and almond brulée for dessert. *LD (Reserve) open to 24.00. Closed Sun.* A.Ax.Dc.V. L ££ D £££

The Belvedere   9 C3
Holland Park, off Abbotsbury Rd W8. 071-602 1238.
Housed in what was the original summer ballroom
of Holland House, this bright restaurant overlooks
Holland Park. The interior has been stylishly revamped
and is a pleasant contrast to the classic exterior. The
cuisine is carefully prepared and beautifully presented.
Specialities are caramelised onion tart, roasted sea
bream, risotto with sun-dried tomatoes. Outdoor tables
on a small balcony *in summer. LD (Reserve L Sat & L
Sun) open to 22.30. Closed D Sun.* A.Ax.Dc.V. £££

Bibendum   10 B5
Michelin House, 81 Fulham Rd SW3. 071-581 5817.
Lofty dining room on the first floor of the unusual 1910
Michelin building bought and redeveloped by Sir
Terence Conran, Paul Hamlyn and Simon Hopkinson.
Traditional and contemporary French, English and
Mediterranean dishes created by respected chef Simon
Hopkinson. Baltic herrings à la crème, rabbit in a pep-
pered sauce, ox tongue with spinach dumplings. Coffee
is served with chocolate truffles. Extensive wine list. Set
lunch menu. Oyster bar downstairs. *LD (Reserve) open
to 23.30, to 22.30 Sun.* A.V. £££+ (set lunch menu £££)

Bistrot 190   9 F4
190 Queen's Gate SW7. 071-581 5666. Antony Worrall-
Thompson's fashionable bistro serving Mediterranean
cuisine. Always crowded, and there are no bookings, but
you can have a drink in the bar while you wait for a table.
Imaginative dishes include chargrilled squid, chicken with
peperonata and pesto potatoes, duck livers with rösti. A
popular choice is the AWT chargrilled pizza. Seafood
bistro downstairs. *LD (no reservations) open to 23.30.
Closed Sun.* A.Ax.Dc.V. £££

The Brackenbury
129 Brackenbury Rd W6. 081-748 0107. This double-
fronted restaurant has a faithful local following but also
lures diners from further afield who are attracted by the
daily-changing menu of simple, modern dishes. Duck
confit on braised cabbage, lamb shank with haricots
and spinach, roast hake with pesto mash. Prune and
Armagnac mousse for dessert. Cheeses are served with
home-made biscuits. *LD (Reserve) open to 23.00.
Closed LD Mon, L Sat & D Sun.* A.Ax.V. ££

The Canteen   13 F4
Harbour Yard, Chelsea Harbour, off Lots Rd SW10.

071-351 7330. Owned by Michael Caine and Marco Pierre White, this light and airy restaurant has magnificent views of the marina. Varied menu includes sea bass, lobster, rump of lamb. Bisquit glacé or lemon tart for dessert. *LD (Reserve) open to 23.45, to 22.45 Sun.* A.V. £££

Cantina del Ponte   12 C2
36C Shad Thames, Butler's Wharf SE1. 071-403 5403. The younger sister of Le Pont de la Tour (see below). Excellent views of the Thames, Tower Bridge and the City from riverside tables. Inside, a mural covering the entire back wall depicts life on the river. Relaxed atmosphere in which to enjoy Mediterranean cuisine and high quality pizzas. *LD (Reserve) open to 23.00. Closed D Sun.* A.Ax.Dc.V. £££

Le Caprice   10 F2
Arlington House, Arlington St SW1. 071-629 2239. Tucked behind the Ritz, this fashionable restaurant is stylishly decorated with David Bailey prints and lots of fresh flowers. Modern brasserie fare; tomato and basil galette, baked salmon with treviso, grilled rabbit with rosemary. Also traditional favourites; Lancashire hotpot, eggs Benedict. *LD open to 24.00.* A.Ax.Dc.V. £££

Clarke's   9 D2
124 Kensington Church St W8. 071-221 9225. Relaxed and friendly restaurant offering set lunch and dinner menus with little choice at lunch and no choice at dinner. However, dishes are always satisfying, constantly changing and imaginative; inspiration comes from California, the Mediterranean and the Far East. Main course meat and fish dishes are often chargrilled. Delicious desserts. Cheeses are served with home-made oatmeal biscuits. Sally Clarke's bakery/delicatessen is next door. *LD (Reserve) open to 22.00. Closed Sat & Sun.* A.V. L £££ D £££+

Daphne's   10 B5
110-112 Draycott Ave SW3. 071-589 4257. Fashionable restaurant, popular with shoppers at lunchtime and Chelsea locals in the evening. Italian cuisine with Mediterranean influences; lobster ravioli, sauté of wild mushrooms with grilled polenta. Set menus. *LD (Reserve Mon-Fri) open to 23.30. Closed L Sat & LD Sun.* A.Ax.Dc.V. L ££ D £££

dell 'Ugo   **6 G5**
56 Frith St W1. 071-734 8300. This fashionable Soho restaurant is another Antony Worrall-Thompson venture. On street level is a café serving salads made with fresh Mediterranean produce. The first floor restaurant is dominated by one wall of abstract painting, and the top floor restaurant is the most formal. The long restaurant menu includes chargrilled squid, pan-grilled steak tartare and a choice of one-pot dishes. Delicious desserts. *LD (Reserve, no reservations for café and first floor restaurant) open to 23.00 (café to 00.30). Closed Sun.* A.Ax.V. ££

The Eagle   **7 D3**
159 Farringdon Rd EC1. 071-837 1353. This is actually a pub, transformed into a lively restaurant serving modern Mediterranean cuisine. Portuguese soup, Italian spicy sausages, grilled vegetables on focaccia. Always crowded, and no bookings, so expect to fight for a table. *LD open to 22.30. Closed Sat & Sun.* No credit cards. ££

Granita   **3 E4**
127 Upper St N1. 071-226 3222. Minimalist decor and designer furniture at this fashionable Islington restaurant. Only the freshest ingredients are used and everything is home-made including bread and ice-cream. The menu changes weekly; chargrills predominate but you may also find interesting dishes such as wilted spinach salad and Tuscan potato bake. Follow with bittersweet chocolate cake, coffee crème anglaise, maple spice cake with raisin ice-cream. *LD (Reserve) open to 22.30, to 22.00 Sun. Closed LD Mon & L Tue.* A.V. ££

The Ivy   **7 A5**
1 West St, off Shaftesbury Ave WC2. 071-836 4751. Sister restaurant to Le Caprice (see above) this glamorous, old-fashioned dining room has been a favourite with stars of the stage and screen since the 1930s. It has an up-market brasserie menu where modern Mediterranean dishes sit alongside traditional favourites. Dover sole, grilled squid and bacon, tagliatelle of lobster and scallops, salmon fishcakes with sorrel sauce. *LD (Reserve) open to 24.00.* A.Ax.Dc.V. £££

Julie's   **9 B1**
135 Portland Rd W11. 071-727 4585. A much-loved local restaurant with a relaxed atmosphere. Modern European cuisine is served in a maze of rooms; the Gothic Room, the Original Forge, the Conservatory, the

Garden Room and the Banqueting Room. Avocado and smoked chicken terrine with basil sauce, roast quail with fresh pear and blackcurrants, calf's liver with red onions and polenta. Wine bar upstairs. *LD (Reserve) open to 23.15, to 22.15 Sun.* A.Ax.Dc.V. £££+

Kensington Place 9 D2
201-207 Kensington Church St W8. 071-727 3184. This huge restaurant has an all-glass frontage and a stark, modern interior. Bright and lively, the style of cooking is modern. Start with foie gras served on a sweetcorn pancake, follow with hake and potate torte or partridge with spiced cabbage. Delicious desserts; poached pears with red wine, cinnamon ice-cream. *LD (Reserve) open to 23.45, to 22.15 Sun.* A.V. £££

Langan's Bistro 6 D4
26 Devonshire St W1. 071-935 4531. This was Peter Langan's first restaurant. It has an intimate, relaxed atmosphere and is decorated with original Hockneys and Proctors and inverted parasols. Dishes include vegetarian couscous with Provençal vegetables, lamb steak with mustard sauce, pan-fried monkfish with prawns and mushrooms. *LD (Reserve) open to 23.30. Closed L Sat & LD Sun.* A.Ax.Dc.V. £££

Langan's Brasserie 10 E2
Stratton St W1. 071-493 6437. The original fashionable brasserie, still popular with a glamorous clientele. Long menu of brasserie dishes, traditional English dishes and some more eclectic choices. Quail's egg tart, grilled Dover sole, smoked goose breast, bangers and mash with white onion sauce. Live music *from 22.00 nightly* in the bar. *LD (Reserve) open to 23.45, to 24.00 Sat. Closed L Sat & LD Sun.* A.Ax.Dc.V. £££

The Lexington 6 F6
45 Lexington St W1. 071-434 3401. This is a smart, simple restaurant lined with high, dark green leather banquettes. The menu changes daily and offers such delights as warm pigeon and parsnip soup, wild mushroom risotto with shaved parmesan and roast haunch of hare with savoy cabbage. *LD (Reserve) open to 23.00. Closed L Sat & LD Sun.* A.Ax.Dc.V. £££

Mijanou 10 E5
143 Ebury St SW1. 071-730 4099. Intimate and friendly restaurant with a small patio at the rear for outdoor eating *in summer*. The cooking is French with

Mediterranean influences. Try ravioli filled with vegetable purée or carré d'agneau cooked in saffron and yoghurt. Excellent wine list; the menu is marked with wine recommendations for each dish. Set menus. *LD (Reserve) open to 23.00. Closed Sat & Sun.* A.Ax.V. L ££ D £££+

Museum Street Café   7 B4
47 Museum Street WC1. 071-405 3211. An informal atmosphere and simple decor at this unpretentious restaurant. Innovative Mediterranean cuisine; salmon and fennel soup, penne with broccoli, tomato and Parmesan. Breads and desserts are excellent, and the cheeses come from Neal's Yard. Unlicensed, but you can bring your own wine. No smoking. Set menus. *LD (Reserve) open to 23.00. Closed Sat & Sun.* No credit cards. ££

Odette's   2 C5
130 Regent's Park Rd NW1. 071-586 5486. Pretty restaurant in Primrose Hill with tables spilling out onto the street *in summer*. Inside, dark green walls are covered with gilt-framed mirrors. Inventive cooking; rock oysters with spicy Thai-style sausages, smoked eel niçoise, calf's kidney with shallot purée. *LD open to 23.00. Closed L Sat & LD Sun.* A.Ax.Dc.V. £££

Odin's   6 D4
27 Devonshire St W1. 071-935 7296. Stylish, luxurious restaurant. The walls are lined with Peter Langan's art collection. Frequently changing menu may include dishes like red mullet pâté, stewed eels and mash, steamed monkfish with saffron sauce. Also seasonal specialities such as game, lobster and mussels. Home-made ice-cream and lemon curd tart to follow. Extensive wine list. *LD (Reserve) open to 23.30. Closed L Sat & LD Sun.* A.Ax.Dc.V. £££

192   5 C6
192 Kensington Park Rd W11. 071-229 0482. This underground, post-modernist restaurant is spacious, cool and relaxed. The menu changes twice daily and offers the type of modern food developed by Alastair Little when he was chef here. Duck platter, sun-dried tomato risotto, roast chicken with couscous. Deep-fried ice-cream for dessert. Excellent wine list. Wine bar at street level. *LD (Reserve) open to 23.30, to 23.00 Sun.* A.Ax.V. ££

Le Pont de la Tour   12 C2
36D Shad Thames, Butler's Wharf SE1. 071-403 8403.

Sir Terence Conran's complex in a converted Thames-side wharf comprises a restaurant, bar and grill, bakery, foodstore and wine merchant. The restaurant is big and buzzing with spectacular views of Tower Bridge and the Thames. *In summer*, tables on the terrace provide superb open-air dining. Modern cuisine with British, Irish, French and Italian influences; marinated mozzarella, roast pepper and aubergine salad, Arbroath smokies with tomato and Gruyère, saffron risotto. Much use is made of the open charcoal grill and seafood is very fresh. Extensive wine list. The **Butler's Wharf Chop House**, Conran's latest venture, is due to open in the complex in late 1993, offering a primarily English menu. *LD (Reserve) open to 24.00, to 23.00 Sun. Closed L Sat.* A.Ax.Dc.V. L £££ D £££+

Snows on the Green
166 Shepherd's Bush Rd W6. 071-603 2142. Attractive bistro; warm yellow and terracotta decor with prints of Mediterranean scenes give a Provençal feel. Modern menu; pumpkin risotto, bollito misto, salmon with pancetta, bruschetta and chargrilled vegetables. Delicious desserts; clementine tarte tatin, caramelised rice pudding. Set lunch menu. *LD (Reserve D) open to 23.00. Closed L Sat & D Sun.* A.V. ££

Stephen Bull   6 C5
5-7 Blandford St W1. 071-486 9696. Large, bright and airy modern restaurant. The menu is changed frequently but always includes interesting and inventive dishes. Fish plays a prominent part; skate with chillis, salmon with lentils and sherry vinegar, fillet of brill with oyster mushrooms and rosemary. Extensive wine list. *LD (Reserve) open to 22.45. Closed Sat & Sun.* A.V. £££

Stephen Bull's Bistro & Bar   7 E2
71 St John St EC1. 071-490 1750. Stephen Bull has moved from his West End establishment to this stylish restaurant and bar in the City. The short daily menu includes original dishes like terrine of duck confit and cabbage and stir-fry of beef with sesame, ginger and coriander. For dessert try the delicious lemon and lime curd pots with crumbled biscuits. *LD (Reserve L) open to 23.00. Closed L Sat & LD Sun.* A.V. ££

Wilson's   9 A4
236 Blythe Rd W14. 071-603 7267. Ceiling fans, hanging plants and white table cloths contribute to the light, homely atmosphere in this restaurant. Set menu with

dishes such as avocado pear with strawberry French dressing, escalope of salmon with asparagus sauce, chocolate marquise with coffee bean sauce. Vegetarian dish. Sunday lunch recommended. *LD (Reserve) open to 22.00. Closed LD Mon, L Sat & D Sun.* A.Ax.V. ££

Zoe   6 D5

3-5 Barrett St, St Christopher's Pl W1. 071-224 1122. This restaurant, café and bar is another Antony Worrall-Thompson's venture. Post-modernist decor and a vast restaurant menu of eclectic Mediterranean cuisine. Dishes are divided into Country and City; the Country menu puts the emphasis on meat dishes, the City menu on pasta and fish. Desserts are delicious; ice-cream sandwich and pan-roasted pear cake. The café and bar have their own menus. *LD open to 23.30. Closed L Sat & LD Sun.* A.Ax.Dc.V. ££

SCANDINAVIAN

SCANDINAVIAN food is healthy, with the emphasis on fresh, natural raw materials. It includes plenty of fish, salads, vegetables, fruit, cheese and wholegrain bread. The traditional smörgåsbord is a good way to sample lots of dishes at once and consists of bread and butter with cheese, smoked salmon, herring, beef or pork and piquant salads. Seafood features prominently on many menus; much of it is smoked, marinated, pickled or served with sour cream. Try hams, sausages and regional cheeses, too.

Anna's Place   4 A2

90 Mildmay Park N1. 071-249 9379. Charming restaurant with a homely atmosphere and a pretty garden at the rear. Hospitable service from either Anna or her daughter; they are more than happy to steer you through the menu of Swedish dishes. Try gravlax, duck breast with Swedish cabbage, home-cured herring.

Delicious desserts; Swedish apple cake or chocolate truffle cake. *LD (Reserve) open to 22.45. Closed Sun & Mon.* No credit cards. ££

The Causerie 6 E6
Claridge's Hotel, Brook St W1. 071-629 8860. Smörgåsbord lunches in the bright and summery restaurant of one of London's most prestigious hotels. Smoked and cured delicacies include gravlax, smoked eel, herring dishes. Excellent choice from the dessert trolley. *L (Reserve) open to 15.00. Closed Sat & Sun.* A.Ax.Dc.V. L £££

Copenhagen Pâtisserie 2 C3
196 Haverstock Hill NW3. 071-435 7711. A bright café serving snacks and coffee. Excellent open sandwiches, which are typical in Denmark; toppings include tuna fish and sliced egg with herring. Also cakes and Danish pastries. Pavement tables *in summer. Open 07.30-21.00, to 19.30 in winter.* No credit cards. £

Gamla Eken 10 E5
Scandic Crown Hotel, 2 Bridge Pl SW1. 071-834 8123. 'The Old Oak Tree' restaurant serves Swedish, French and continental cuisine in an informal, relaxed atmosphere. The decor is Swedish in design with warm coloured walls and an open fire *in winter.* Smörgåsbord at *lunchtime,* and also for group bookings *in the evening.* Typical dishes from the main menu include the popular Swedish starter toast Skagen (pan-fried bread topped with prawns, mayonnaise, dill and diced red onion), main course beef and pork fillet strips stir-fried with oriental vegetable and oyster sauce, baked rainbow trout stuffed with prawns and capers. Fraise romanoff for dessert. *LD open to 22.45.* A.Ax.Dc.V. ££

Garbo's 6 C4
42 Crawford St W1. 071-262 6582. Intimate restaurant serving Scandinavian home cooking. Try the herring salad Baltic, smoked eel, cabbage stuffed with minced pork, beef and rice. *Lunchtime* smörgåsbord. Imported Swedish beer and Schnapps. *LD (Reserve) open to 23.30. Closed L Sat & L Sun.* A.Ax.V. ££

Three Crowns Restaurant 12 G2
Scandic Crown Hotel, 265 Rotherhithe St, Nelson Dock SE16. 071-231 1001. This simple, spacious restaurant has a waterside location with views stretching over Canary Wharf. Smörgåsbord menu *every day* for lunch and dinner. *LD (Reserve) open to 22.30.* A.Ax.Dc.V. ££

SPANISH, PORTUGUESE & SOUTH AMERICAN

ALTHOUGH Spanish cuisine varies from region to region, fish and seafood are the mainstays, often cooked in garlic and olive oil. A typical Spanish meal might include *gazpacho* – chilled soup of tomatoes, garlic, breadcrumbs, green pepper, cucumber, oil and vinegar, followed by *paella* – a famous national dish of saffron-flavoured rice to which chicken, prawns, clams and squid are added. *Zarzuela* is a traditional fish stew and *chorizo* is a delicious peppery red sausage often stewed with red beans. Tapas bars, serving simple snacks which can be eaten as a snack with a drink or as a main meal, are still popular in London.

Stews, soups and simple fish dishes form the basis of Portuguese cooking. *Bacalhau* is a typical and popular dish – cod served either *a transmontana* – with garlic, onion and tomatoes, or *a gomes de sa* – with potatoes in place of tomatoes. Pork is also widely used, often marinated in wine and garlic. Cinnamon and *piri piri* – a very hot pepper from Angola, are the most commonly-used spices.

The Brazilian national dish is *feijoada* – a casserole of black beans, pork and sausages served with rice. Typical dishes throughout South America include rich broths and meat-based stews, which are normally served with rice or potatoes and sweet corn.

Albero & Grana   10 B5
Chelsea Cloisters, 89 Sloane Ave SW3. 071-225 1048.
Stylish Spanish bar and restaurant decorated in striking
ochre and red. Traditional and modern food; escabeche
of duck liver, lasagne of black pudding. Sugary desserts.
Good selection of Riojas and beers. Tapas bar. *D open
to 23.30, to 22.30 Sun.* A.Ax.Dc.V. £££

Amazonas   5 E5
75 Westbourne Grove W11. 071-243 0090. Pleasant
Brazilian restaurant; a tropical mural, exotic palms and
colourful tablecloths add to the bright atmosphere.
Authentic Brazilian food; the house speciality is camarao
no molho de goiaba (sautéed prawns with lime juice,
coriander, parsley and mint served with a creamy guava
sauce). There is also a vegetarian menu and a balanced
light menu with a calorific breakdown of each dish. Live
Brazilian music on *Friday and Saturday evenings. LD
open to 23.30. Closed Sun & Mon.* A.Ax.V. ££

Bar Escoba   9 F6
102 Old Brompton Rd SW7. 071-373 2403. Lively
tapas bar with a quieter restaurant at the back. Sit outside on the patio *in summer.* Typical dishes include fried
calamares and steamed mussels with garlic. Spanish and
Mexican beers. Live Latin music *several nights a week.
LD open to 23.00, to 22.30 Sun.* A.V. ££

Bar Gansa   2 E5
2 Inverness St NW1. 071-267 8909. One of the liveliest
and most popular tapas bars in London, always packed
in the evenings. A long, narrow room decorated with
Spanish ceramics. Well-prepared tapas with vegetarian
choices; liadillos Sevillanos (cabbage rolls), tartaletas de
puerros (leek and nutmeg tartlet). To follow, crema
Catalana, manchego cheese and celery. Good choice of
Spanish wines. Spanish singer on *Mon evenings. LD
open to 23.30, to 22.30 Sun.* A.V. £

Café Portugal   15 B2
6a Victoria House, South Lambeth Rd SW8. 071-587
1962. In the basement of a pastelaria serving coffee and
delicious cakes you will find this tiny restaurant. Sample
caldo verde (cabbage soup) followed by huge portions of
Portuguese meat stews. Very hospitable, Portuguese staff.
LD open to 22.00. Closed Wed. No credit cards. ££

Caravela   10 B4
39 Beauchamp Pl SW3. 071-581 2366. Small, intimate

basement restaurant with white walls and a ceramic mosaic floor. The menu offers an extensive range of seafood and fish; freshly-grilled sardines, king prawns piri piri or regional specialities like arroz a Nazare (a rice and seafood combination). Delicious torta de laranga, an orange roll dessert. Portuguese wines. Fado singer *Friday or Saturday evenings. LD (Reserve) open to 01.00, to 24.00 Sun. Closed L Sun.* A.Ax.Dc.V. £££

Casa Santana 5 B4

14 Golborne Rd W10. 081-968 8764. This informal Portuguese restaurant is a focal point for the Portuguese community, with its lively, jolly atmosphere and rustic feel. Hearty servings of traditional Portuguese soups, stews and fish dishes. Live music *at weekends. LD open to 23.30.* A.Ax.Dc.V. ££

Churrasqueira 15 B3

168a Old South Lambeth Rd SW8. 071-793 0744. Churrasqueira means 'grill house' and the majority of fish and meat dishes here are chargrilled on the barbecue. Huge portions of squid, trout, salted cod, pork chops. Live guitar music on *Friday and Saturday evenings. LD (Reserve) open to 24.00, to 22.30 Sun.* A.Ax.V. ££

Costa Dorada 6 G5

47-55 Hanway St W1. 071-636 7139. Lively atmosphere at this Spanish flamenco restaurant. Tapas bar and restaurant; authentic dishes include fried calamares, pulpo a la Galicia (spicy octopus), mixed fish and seafood grill. Two flamenco shows *nightly. D open to 02.00, to 24.00 Sun.* A.Ax.Dc.V. £££

Don Pepe 5 G3

99 Frampton St NW8. 071-262 3834. London's oldest tapas bar, immensely popular with the local Spanish community. The restaurant at the back serves fish and seafood dishes, plus Galician specialities such as caldo Gallego (traditional stew) and zorza (strips of pork cooked with red peppers). Guitarist plays *most evenings. LD (Reserve) open to 00.15. Closed D Sun.* A.Ax.Dc.V. ££

O Fado 10 B4

50 Beauchamp Pl SW3. 071-589 3002. One of the oldest Portuguese restaurants in London, established in 1969. Decorated in continental style. House speciality is rosa de marisco, a type of Portuguese paella. Home-

made desserts. Traditional Portuguese music (O Fado) played on 12-string guitars with singers *from 20.30 Wed-Sun. LD open to 01.00, to 23.30 Sun.* A.Ax.V. ££

Galicia 5 C5
323 Portobello Rd W10. 081-969 3539. Traditional tapas bar with a restaurant at the back. Very popular with the local Spanish community. The Spanish chef prepares authentic dishes; avocado prawns and fried squid to start. Main courses are mainly fish dishes; hake Galician style, grilled Dover sole, paella. Good selection of Galician wines. *LD (Reserve D Fri & Sat) open to 23.30. Closed Mon.* A.Ax.V. ££

El Gaucho 10 B6
Chelsea Farmers Market, Sydney St SW3. 071-376 8514. Lively atmosphere at this Argentinian restaurant housed in a brightly painted shack in the Farmers Market. Plenty of seating outside. Try Argentinian beef, meat-filled pasties, sausages, with salads, baked potatoes and corn on the cob. Unlicensed, but you can buy drinks from the bar next door. *LD open to 23.00.* No credit cards. ££

La Mancha 16 B2
32 Putney High St SW15. 081-780 1022. Bright and lively tapas bar with an intimate balcony restaurant upstairs. Extensive choice of tapas with some unusual dishes; jerezanos (mushrooms with chorizo, ham and peppers), tortitas de gambas (prawn and cod pancakes). The restaurant upstairs is more relaxed and offers authentic Spanish food plus some international dishes. Live music *every evening.* Good Spanish wine list. *LD (Reserve D Fri & D Sat) open to 23.00.* A.V. ££

Paulo's 13 A2
30 Greyhound Rd W6. 071-385 9264. A lively party atmosphere at this Brazilian restaurant which offers a set buffet dinner. Choose from over 20 dishes; pork, chicken, beef and prawns in various stews and sauces, accompanied by beans and rice. Brazilian cocktails. Portuguese and Brazilian wines. *D open to 22.30. Closed Sun.* No credit cards. ££

La Piragua 3 E4
176 Upper St N1. 071-354 2843. Small Latin American restaurant with a barbecue at the back. Try different national dishes; from Patagonia, pastel de choclo (beef stew with olives and raisins); from Mexico, sanconcho

(chicken in rich broth with plantains and potato). Served with tropical vegetables. Wines, beers and spirits are all South American. Regular live music. *LD open to 23.00, to 01.00 Fri & Sat.* No credit cards. ££

El Prado 13 C4

766 Fulham Rd SW6. 071-731 7179. A small local restaurant and tapas bar. Classic tapas, main dishes such as paella and Castilian roast lamb, plus regional specialities from Andalucia and the Basque country. South American music and occasional flamenco. *LD (Reserve D) open to 24.00.* A.V. ££

Rebato's 15 B3

169 South Lambeth Rd SW8. 071-735 6388. Pleasant atmosphere at this friendly tapas bar and restaurant. Authentic tapas in the front bar, and a mixture of Spanish and international dishes in the elegant restaurant. Menu is predominantly seafood; monkfish, prawns served with tasty sauces, paella. Live music *every evening.* Set menu. *LD (Reserve) open to 23.00. Closed L Sat & LD Sun.* A.Ax.Dc.V. ££

Los Remos 6 B5

38a Southwick St W2. 071-723 5056. A selection of over 40 tapas in the basement tapas bar and an authentic Spanish menu in the restaurant. Choose from paella, zarzuela of fish, parrillida of meat. Typical home-made desserts include traditional Spanish cake. *LD (Reserve D) open to 24.00. Closed Sun.* A.Ax.Dc.V. ££

El Rincón Latino 17 G1

148 Clapham Manor St SW4. Very popular restaurant run by two half-Spanish, half-Colombian sisters. Authentic Spanish and Latin American food with a first-class wine list. Spanish breakfast of chocolate con churros is served *11.00-14.00 Sat. LD (Reserve) open to 24.00. Closed Sun.* A.Ax.V. ££

The Rock 13 C4

619 Fulham Rd SW6. 071-385 8179. A simple and traditional bar and restaurant run by a Gibraltarian. Flamenco fans and posters of bull-fighters adorn the walls. Authentic Spanish food; a choice of 30 tapas dishes awaits you at the bar, with more substantial dishes in the restaurant. Specialities plus favourites like tortilla española, fresh sardines and piping hot chorizo. *LD (Reserve D Fri & D Sat) open to 01.00, to 23.30 Sun.* A.V. ££

La Rueda   17 G2
68 Clapham High St SW4. 071-627 2173. Lively and friendly place divided into a tapas bar and restaurant. Wagon wheels (la rueda) form a central part of the decor – on the walls and outside the restaurant. Good traditional food such as paella, patatas bravas, prawns in garlic. A stockpile of wines stacked into the enormous false ceiling runs into hundreds of bottles with over 72 Spanish varieties. *LD (Reserve) open to 23.00.* A.V. £

Salvador's El Bodegon & Tapas Bar   13 F2
9 Park Walk SW10. 071-352 1330. This is one of London's longest-established Spanish restaurants. A small dark tapas bar in the basement and a restaurant on the ground floor. The food is well presented and the waiters are charming. Authentic cuisine; gambas al pil-pil (prawns in a hot garlic sauce), zarzuela, paella. *Year-round* patio seating. *LD open to 24.00.* A.Ax.Dc.V. ££

Triñanes   2 E3
298 Kentish Town Rd NW5. 071-482 3616. Very popular tapas bar, serving the same food upstairs and down. Tapas are divided into vegetable, meat and seafood varieties. Small selection of more substantial dishes. Traditional Spanish entertainment in the form of live music and flamenco dancing on *Friday and Saturday evenings. LD open to 02.00, to 01.00 Sun. Closed L Sat.* No credit cards. ££

Valencia   13 D2
1 Empress Approach, Lillie Rd SW6. 071-385 0039. Tucked behind Earl's Court, this is London's oldest Spanish restaurant. Large menu of regional dishes and a lengthy wine list strong in Rioja and Catalan wines. Spanish guitarist *every night*, flamenco show on *Sun. D open to 00.15.* A.V. ££

Viva Brazil   6 F5
4 Winsley St W1. 071-637 3969. Relaxed atmosphere at this Brazilian-style café and tapas bar done out in green and beige, the colours of the national flag. Try petiscos (Brazilian tapas), feijoada, arroz brasileiro especiale (Brazilian rice). Good range of cocktails. **Bar Madrid**, which has a disco and Latin American music *nightly,* is downstairs. *D open to 01.30 Mon-Sat.* A.Ax.V. £

THAI

THAI cuisine encompasses many different flavours and styles of cooking, and offers diversity of taste, texture and colour accentuated by use of exotic herbs and spices. Distinctive ingredients are coriander, chilli, lemon grass, coconut and *nam pla* (a fish essence). Garlic, ginger, lime leaves and sweet basil are also much used. Dishes are often interesting mixtures of meat, seafood and vegetables and can be hot and spicy, or mild and delicately flavoured. Popular desserts are coconut ice-cream and banana cooked in coconut milk. Dishes are always beautifully presented.

Bahn Thai   6 G5

21a Frith St W1. 071-437 8504. Stylish decor and high-quality cooking have contributed to the popularity of this restaurant, which was one of the first to offer authentic Thai cuisine in London. Some ingredients are imported from the Far East, and spicing is subtle and complex. Dishes are even chilli-rated for spiciness! Specialities are crispy frogs' legs and Thai blue swimming crab. The soups, chargrilled meats and green curries are also excellent. Private dining room. *LD (Reserve) open to 23.15.* A.Ax.V. ££

Bangkok   10 A5

9 Bute St SW7. 071-584 8529. Long-established Thai restaurant which has been run by the same family since it opened over 25 years ago. Short menu; beef and pork satay, Thai noodles, chicken fried in garlic or prepared with ginger. Exotic fruit for dessert. *LD (Reserve) open to 23.15. Closed Sun.* A.V. ££

Bedlington Café

24 Fauconberg Rd W4. 081-994 1965. One of the new breed of Thai-run cafés which serve traditional fry-ups at

lunchtime and eastern stir-fries and curries in the evening. Relaxed atmosphere and charming service. High-quality spicy dishes; jungle curry and spicy pork minced meat are two examples. Sweet Thai desserts. Unlicensed, but you can bring your own wine or beer. *LD (Reserve) open to 22.00.* No credit cards or cheques. **££**

Blue Elephant   13 D3
4-6 Fulham Broadway SW6. 071-385 6595. This lavish restaurant has an exotic setting resembling a tropical jungle. The food is excellent, beautifully presented and served by unobtrusive waiters and waitresses in Thai costume. The menu features unusual dishes; jungle salad, laab phed (marinated duck breast stir-fried with herbs and spices) and the magnificent 17-dish Royal Thai banquet. Vegetarian menu. *LD open to 00.30, to 22.30 Sun. Closed L Sat.* A.Ax.Dc.V. **£££+**

Blue Jade   10 E5
44 Hugh St SW1. 071-828 0321. Intimate restaurant with a relaxed, candlelit wine bar downstairs. Waiting staff in elegant Thai costume serve authentic dishes which are prepared to order from the freshest ingredients. Try kaeng ped (beef curry), stir-fried seafood, yam yai (spiced mixed salad), all beautifully presented. Thai desserts include delicious coconut ice-cream. You can have a drink, a snack or a full meal in the wine bar. *LD open to 24.00. Closed Sun.* A.Ax.Dc.V. **£££**

Busabong Too   13 F2
1a Langton St SW10. 071-352 7414. A pleasant restaurant with a loyal following. Low tables and cushions provide relaxed but elegant surroundings, and the service is charming. Menu features a lot of spicy specialities, and also includes fisherman's soup, satay beef, pork with minced water chestnuts. Thai egg custard or coconut bananas for dessert. *D (Reserve) open to 23.00.* A.Ax.Dc.V. **££**

Busabong Tree   14 A3
112 Cheyne Walk SW10. 071-352 7534. Sister of Busabong Too, this light and airy restaurant has a welcoming, friendly atmosphere. Three domed sky lights have stained glass motifs of a lotus, the English word for busabong. Classical Thai dishes; spicy soft shell crab, oriental crispy duck with almonds and peppercorns, king prawns with garlic and coriander. Outdoor tables on the garden terrace. Extensive wine list. *LD (Reserve) open to 23.15.* A.Ax.Dc.V. **££**

Chaopraya   **6 D5**
22 St Christopher's Pl, off Wigmore St W1. 071-486
0777. Classy minimalist basement restaurant with a few
tables upstairs. Authentic Thai dishes include tom yum
soup, Penang curry, flaming chicken in red wine sauce.
For dessert, kanom sai sai (coconut cream in coconut
leaves). *LD (Reserve) open to 23.00. Closed L Sat &
LD Sun.* A.Ax.Dc.V. ££

Chiang Mai   **6 G5**
48 Frith St W1. 071-437 7444. Modelled on a
traditional Thai stilt house, the restaurant occupies two
floors and has an air of calm and serenity. Try chicken
with chilli and peanuts, pad Thai noodles, som tam
(chilli-hot grated papaya salad). Specialises in food from
northern Thailand. Vegetarian dishes. Thai whisky or
beer. *LD (Reserve) open to 23.00.* A.V. ££

Khun Akorn   **10 B4**
136 Brompton Rd SW3. 071-225 2688. Smart
Knightsbridge restaurant decorated in traditional Thai
style. The head chef was the Thai Royal Family's chef
for over 20 years. The tongsai platter for two persons
consists of a selection of appetizers, and is highly
recommended. Other dishes from the menu include
drunken duck, king prawns with lemon grass sauce,
nua thip (sliced fillet of beef with thai salad dressing).
LD (Reserve) open to 23.00, to 22.30 Sun. A.Ax.Dc.V.
£££

Oriental Brasserie   **10 D4**
Grouse & Claret pub, Wilton Mews SW1. 071-245
6734. A Belgravia mews pub is an unlikely location for
a Thai restaurant, but this smart wood-panelled dining
room above the Grouse & Claret serves excellent Thai
cuisine. The Thai manageress will guide you through a
menu of unusual dishes such as deep-fried soft shell
crab with ginger or chicken Penang. *LD open to 24.00,
to 23.00 Sun. Closed L Sun.* A.Ax.Dc.V. ££

S & P Patara   **10 B4**
9 Beauchamp Pl SW3. 071-581 8820. Beautiful restaurant with Thai silk furnishings, wooden floors, and
single lotus flowers on each table. Dishes include sweet
and tangy crispy noodles with prawns, chargrilled
prawns in lemon grass and lime dressing, coconut beef
curry with sweet basil. Set lunch menus. Branch at 181
Fulham Rd SW3 (**13 G1**). 071-352 5692. *LD open to
22.30. Closed L Sun.* A.Ax.Dc.V. £££

Sri Siam   6 G5
14 Old Compton St W1. 071-434 3544. Popular Thai
restaurant which attracts a fashionable crowd with its
stylish interior and authentic Thai food. Extensive
menu; king prawn satay, roast duck curry with pineapple and grapes, chicken curry with lime leaves. Good
choice of vegetarian dishes. Singha Thai beer. There is a
sister restaurant in the City; **Sri Siam City**, 85 London
Wall EC2 (**7 G4**). 071-628 5772. *LD (Reserve D) open
to 23.15, to 22.30 Sun.* A.Ax.Dc.V. ££

Tamnag Thai
50-52 Westow Hill SE19. 081-761 5959. A charming,
subtly-lit restaurant with a wrought iron spiral staircase
just inside the entrance. Authentic Thai cuisine; deep
fried fish cakes, mee krob (crispy rice noodles with
prawns and pork), pud ped pla muk (fried squid with
chilli). Wide choice for vegetarians. Charming, attentive
service. *D (Reserve Sat & Sun) open to 23.00.*
A.Ax.Dc.V. ££

Thai   9 D4
209 Kensington High St W8. 071-937 2260. Simple
basement restaurant serving daily specialities such as
tom yum soup with squid, red Thai chicken curry,
steamed fish with soya beans and ginger. Various fried
noodle dishes. Try thont yip (egg yolk in syrup) for
dessert. *LD (Reserve) open to 22.30.* A.Ax.Dc.V. ££

Thai Pavilion   6 G6
42 Rupert St W1. 071-287 6333. Authentic Thai food
in a relaxed atmosphere. Eat in the Swasdee Room –
'highest heaven' – where you sit shoeless on low
cushions in a room decorated in typical Thai-style with
natural bamboo cladding and Thai figures. Try the
Royal Thai; a mixture of prawns, asparagus and black
mushrooms. Vegetarian menu. *LD (Reserve) open to
23.15, to 22.30 Sun.* A.Ax.Dc.V. ££

Thailand
15 Lewisham Way SE14. 081-691 4040. Small, friendly
restaurant in Lewisham run by an ethnic Laotian and
her Scottish husband. Specialities from north-east
Thailand and Laos. Try the unusual Laotian dishes;
chicken with black pepper and garlic, hot-and-sour
papaya, lime, garlic, chilli and mudfish, steak chargrilled with lime juice, toasted rice and chillis. Huge
selection of malt whiskies. *D (Reserve) open to 23.00.
Closed Sun & Mon.* A.Ax.V. ££

VIETNAMESE

VIETNAMESE cuisine is often described as a combination of Chinese and French cooking as a result of the French colonisation of Vietnam. There is always a balance of tastes between sweet, sour, salty, bitter and hot in cooking. Root ginger, coriander, coconut milk, chilli and lemon grass are common ingredients, and *nuoc nam* is a fish sauce that is added to many dishes. Seafood, prawns and squid are common. Presentation is important; fruit and vegetables are often carved into elaborate designs.

Bonjour Vietnam   13 C4
593-599 Fulham Rd SW6. 071-385 7603. One of the Zen chain of restaurants. A huge 30ft fish tank is part of the relaxed, welcoming atmosphere. Sample traditional and new-wave Vietnamese dishes such as Saigon spicy chicken with chilli or steamed scallops. *LD open to 23.30, to 23.00 Sun.* A.Ax.Dc.V. ££

Lemongrass Restaurant   2 F4
243 Royal College St NW1. 071-284 1116. Pleasant restaurant with an eclectic menu; dishes from Vietnam, Thailand, Cambodia and China. Try the vegetarian spring rolls or the samosas to start with, followed by the hot and spicy chicken Saigon or the highly-recommended French steak cooked with crispy fried shallots, ginger and of course, lemon grass. *LD (Reserve) open to 23.00, to 22.45 Sun. Closed L Sat & L Sun.* A.V. ££

Mekong   10 F5
46 Churton St SW1. 071-630 9568. Bistro-like atmosphere in which to try a blend of Vietnamese and

Chinese cuisine. Worth trying are their excellent spring
rolls, crispy fried fish, aromatic duck with steamed
pancakes and plum sauce. Mango pudding for dessert.
Vegetarian dishes and set price menus. *LD (Reserve)
open to 23.30.* A.V. ££

Nam Long at Le Shaker   13 E1
159 Old Brompton Rd SW5. 071-373 1926. Behind the
bustling cocktail bar lies a stylish restaurant serving
excellent Vietnamese cuisine. Aromatic duck, prawns in
garlic sauce, beef and lemon grass. *LD (Reserve D)
open to 23.30. Closed L Sat & LD Sun.* A.Ax.V. ££

Pho   6 G6
2 Lisle St WC2. 071-437 8265. A very popular, thriving
café serving large portions of Vietnamese food at reasonable prices. The decor is very basic and you just sit
where you can find space at one of the round tables. Try
the Vietnamese soup (pho) which contains noodles and
slices of raw beef and comes with a plate of coriander,
mint and onions. *LD open to 23.30.* No credit cards. £

Saigon   6 G5
45 Frith St W1. 071-437 7109. A smart, comfortable
Vietnamese restaurant with a vast, imaginative menu.
Exotic starters such as papaya salad followed by
seafood specialities. Try dae huong cua (spiced crab
with garlic, lemon grass and herbs). All dishes are
beautifully presented. *LD (Reserve) open to 23.30.
Closed Sun.* A.Ax.Dc.V. ££

Saigon House   14 G4
252 Wandsworth Rd SW8. 071-498 0337. A welcoming atmosphere and delicious Vietnamese home cooking
have ensured this restaurant a strong local following.
Crispy shredded seaweed with dried scallop, chicken
Saigon (sauted with ginger and onions), prawns
wrapped in rice paper with barbecue sauce. *D open to
23.00, to 24.00 Fri & Sat.* A.Ax.Dc.V. ££

Van Long   6 G5
40 Frith St W1. 071-434 3772. An attractive, modern
Vietnamese restaurant. The menu is long and the set
menus can be a helpful alternative for the uninitiated.
Lemon grass features strongly in the cooking. The soups
are excellent, almost a meal in themselves. Superior
seafood dishes; hot and sour seafood soup, fried
seaweed with scallops. *LD open to 24.00.* A.Ax.Dc.V.
££

FISH

Some of London's best restaurants specialise in fish. They can be expensive, but we also list some establishments at the lower end of the price scale. Exotic types of fish can be found in London's markets so menus are interesting and varied. Try angel fish, snapper, parrot fish, swordfish, shark, pomfret and mahi mahi. We have not listed the good old British fish and chip shops as they are too many to mention and can be found on most high streets.

Bentley's   **6 F6**
11-15 Swallow St, off Regent St W1. 071-734 4756. Traditional fish and seafood restaurant established in 1916. Classical seafood dishes in club-like surroundings. Choose between the upstairs dining-room, the ground floor oyster bar and the basement bar. Oysters are a speciality, but the main fish dishes are also excellent. *LD (Reserve) open to 22.30. Closed Sun.* A.Ax.Dc.V. £££

Bibendum Oyster Bar   **10 B5**
Michelin House, 81 Fulham Rd SW3. 071-589 1480. Elegant oyster bar which is always packed. Native and rock oysters, clams, crab, langoustines and lobster. Excellent plateau of seafood. Also brasserie fare and some dishes from the **Bibendum** menu upstairs. *LD open to 23.00, to 22.30 Sun.* A.V. ££

Bill Bentley's
Swedeland Court, 202 Bishopsgate EC2. 071-283   **8 B5**
1763.
31 Beauchamp Pl SW3. 071-589 5080.   **10 B4**
5 Minories EC3. 071-481 1779.   **8 C6**

18 Old Broad St EC2. 071-588 2655.   **8 A5**
St George's Lane, off Pudding Lane EC3.   **8 A6**
071-929 2244.
Willies Wine Bar, 107 Fenchurch St EC3.   **8 B6**
071-480 7289.
Old-style establishments serving superbly-prepared fish
and shellfish, supplemented by roasts and grills. Tiger
prawns, oysters, smoked salmon, Dover sole, steamed
John Dory. *L open to 15.00. Closed Sat & Sun.*
Beauchamp Place branch *open for lunch Sat (to 14.30)
and for dinner Mon-Sat (to 22.30). Closed Sun.* A.V. £££

Café Fish   **10 G1**
39 Panton St, off Haymarket SW1. 071-930 3999. Bright
and spacious with maritime prints and paintings on the
walls. All-fish menu includes oysters, moules marinières,
bouillabaisse, plateau de fruits de mer, seafood casserole.
The downstairs wine bar has a shorter menu of snacks
and light meals. *LD (Reserve) open to 23.30. Closed Sun.*
Wine bar *open to 23.00.* A.Ax.Dc.V. ££

Chez Liline
101 Stroud Green Rd N4. 071-263 6550. A Mauritian
fish restaurant with a menu that changes daily according to what is best at the market. Mauritian food has
Indian, African, Chinese and French influences.
Everything is cooked to order; king prawns chow chow
(prawns with tropical fruit), plateau de fruits de mer,
grilled fish, Mauritian bouillabaisse. *LD (Reserve) open
to 23.00.* A.Ax.V. ££

La Croisette   **13 E2**
168 Ifield Rd SW10. 071-373 3694. A spiral staircase
leads down to this excellent fish restaurant. Fish is
supplied fresh from the Channel ports. Famed for its
plateau de fruits de mer; crab, oysters, mussels, clams,
langoustines and winkles. *LD open to 23.30. Closed
LD Mon & L Tue.* A.Ax.Dc.V. £££

Downstairs at 190   **9 F4**
190 Queen's Gate SW7. 071-581 5666. In the basement
of Bistrot 190 is this seafood brasserie. Stylish wood-
panelled Edwardian room decorated with paintings and
lots of plants. Modern fish dishes; chargrilled turbot
steak, crumbly crab and corn fish cakes, grilled squid
with rocket, saffron and mussel risotto. *D (no reservations) open to 24.00. Closed Sun.* A.Ax.V. £££

Flounders   **7 B6**
19-21 Tavistock St WC2. 071-836 3925. Informal

bistro with rustic decor. Try lobster bisque, marinated salmon or traditional cod and chips. Home-made desserts. Pre-theatre set dinner. *LD open to 23.30, to 24.00 Sat. Closed Sun.* A.Ax.Dc.V. ££

La Gaulette 6 F4
53 Cleveland St W1. 071-580 7608. Delightful Mauritian fish restaurant specialising in exotic tropical fish. Red snapper, capitain, vacqua, parrot fish, all prepared using subtle Mauritian and Eastern spicing. Bistro downstairs has a very reasonable set menu. *LD open to 23.30. Closed L Sat & LD Sun.* A.Ax.Dc.V. ££

Geale's 9 D2
2-4 Farmer St, off Uxbridge St W8. 071-727 7969. One of London's oldest and best-loved fish restaurants. Simple and informal with cheerful service. Traditional fish and chips with the batter made of beef dripping. Other dishes include deep-fried clams and parrot fish. Bar upstairs. *LD open to 23.00. Closed Sun & Mon.* A.V. £

Green's Restaurant & Oyster Bar 11 A4
Marsham Court, off Marsham St SW1. 071-834 9552. Traditional restaurant with a club-like atmosphere, a favourite with politicians from the nearby Houses of Parliament. Mahogany panelling and leather banquettes with old prints on the walls. Try smoked eel with horse-radish, smoked salmon with blinis, dressed crab. Also at 36 Duke St SW1 (**10 F2**). 071-930 4566. *LD (Reserve) open to 23.00. Closed Sat & Sun.* A.Ax.Dc.V. £££

Lobster Pot 11 E5
3 Kennington Lane SE11. 071-582 5556. French restaurant, done out like a ship's cabin, full of nautical knick-knacks. The menu focuses on fish and changes regularly. Bouillabaisse Bretonne, skate with raspberry vinegar, seafood platter. Also bistro dishes such as coq au vin and filet de boeuf. *LD open to 23.30. Closed Sun & Mon.* A.Ax.Dc.V. £££

Lou Pescadou 13 F1
241 Old Brompton Rd SW5. 071-370 1057. Authentically Gallic restaurant with a nautical feel to the decor. Informal and friendly atmosphere. Delicious dishes; they get daily supplies of fresh fish from Brittany. Oysters, noodles with baby clams, assiette de pêcheur (a soup of mussels, fish and potato). *LD open to 24.00.* A.Ax.Dc.V. ££

Lucullus 10 C3
48 Knightsbridge SW1. 071-245 6622. An elegant

restaurant with a superb array of fresh fish displayed on banks of ice, above a tank of live lobsters, crabs and langoustines. Your choice of fish can be charcoal grilled or cooked in a sauce – specialities include lobster flamed in whisky, salmon stuffed with a broccoli mousse wrapped in filo pastry and served with a champagne sauce. They also have beef and poultry dishes on the menu. *LD open to 23.00.* A.Ax.Dc.V. £££

Manzi's   6 G6
1-2 Leicester St WC2. 071-734 0224. London's oldest seafood restaurant. Downstairs is bustling and lively; the Cabin Room upstairs is grander, more sedate, with a fuller menu. Wide range of fish and shellfish with simple dishes such as salmon or turbot, grilled or poached. Italian wines. Also at Turnberry Quay, Pepper St E14. 071-538 9615. *LD (Reserve) open to 23.30. Closed L Sun. Upstairs closed Sun.* A.Ax.Dc.V. £££

Overton's
5 St James's St SW1. 071-839 3774.   10 F2
LD open to 22.45. Closed Sat & Sun. A.Ax.Dc.V. £££
4-6 Victoria Bldgs, Terminus Pl SW1. 071-834   10 E4
3774.
LD open to 22.45. Closed Sun. A.Ax.Dc.V. ££
Traditional restaurants in which to enjoy familiar fish dishes prepared from first-class ingredients. Notable oysters and lobsters. Extremely polite service. Fine wine list.

Poissonnerie de l'Avenue   10 B5
82 Sloane Ave SW3. 071-589 2457. Old-fashioned restaurant and oyster bar, tastefully decorated with marine artefacts. Dependable cooking, using a variety of high-quality fresh fish; they have their own fishmonger's shop next door. Sole, turbot, halibut, mackerel, Dublin Bay prawns, oysters, mussels and scallops in season. *LD (Reserve) open to 23.30. Closed Sun.* A.Ax.Dc.V. £££

Le Quai St Pierre   9 D4
7 Stratford Rd W8. 071-937 6388. Bright French restaurant decorated with striped umbrellas and pictures of the south of France. Impressive range of French seafood, including mussels, oysters, langoustines, sea urchins and scallops. The main speciality is the plateau de fruits de mer. Some meat dishes too. *LD open to 24.00. Closed LD Sun & L Mon.* A.Ax.Dc.V. £££

Rock & Sole Plaice   7 B5
47 Endell St WC2. 071-836 3785. Cheerful chippie in the heart of Covent Garden. Impressive glass frontage,

simple inside with fresh flowers, quick and friendly service and generous portions of fresh fish. Follow up with ice-cream, banana fritters or apple pie. Pavement seating *in summer*. Unlicensed, but you can bring your own wine. *LD open to 22.30. Closed Sun.* No credit cards. £

Rudland & Stubbs 7 E4

35-37 Greenhill Rents, Cowcross St EC1. 071-253 0148. Up-market fish and chip shop serving a wide selection of high quality fish and seafood. Oysters (in season), jellied eels, rollmops, mussels with cream and white wine, trout, salmon, lobster, turbot, bass and exotic fish such as baby shark and barracuda. Vegetarian dishes available. Lager and draught Guinness as well as an extensive wine list. *LD (Reserve) open to 22.45. Closed L Sat & LD Sun.* A.V. ££

Scott's 10 D1

20 Mount St W1. 071-629 5248. Restaurant, oyster bar and caviar bar serving splendid oysters and fresh, skilfully-cooked fish. The Cornish crab claw, soft herring roe and smoked eel are memorable. Impeccable service and good wine list. *LD (Reserve) open to 22.45 Mon-Fri. Closed L Sat & LD Sun.* A.Ax.Dc.V. £££+

Seashell 6 A3

49-51 Lisson Grove NW1. 071-723 8703. Reputed to be one of the best fish and chip shops in London, this clean, modern chippie offers 14 varieties of fish. Hot crisp haddock and halibut are particularly good. *LD open to 22.30. Closed Sun.* A.Ax.Dc.V. ££

Sheekeys 7 B6

28-32 St Martin's Court, off St Martin's Lane WC2. 071-240 2565. Old-style fish restaurant established in 1898. Situated in the heart of theatreland, the pre-theatre menu is good value, and they stay open late for post-theatre orders. Specialities continue to be oysters, lobsters and turbot; other dishes include salmon in dill sauce, lemon sole fillets and seafood platter. *LD open to 23.15. Closed L Sat & LD Sun.* A.Ax.Dc.V. £££

Le Suquet 10 B5

104 Draycott Ave SW3. 071-581 1785. Casual and cheerful French seafood restaurant. The plateau de fruits de mer is the main feature on a menu of fresh fish and shellfish. Other dishes include turbot with champagne sauce, bouillabaisse, scallops with saffron sauce. Efficient service with true Gallic charm. Good wine list. *LD (Reserve) open to 23.30.* A.Ax.Dc.V. £££+

Sweetings   **11 E1**
39 Queen Victoria St EC4. 071-248 3062. Tiny 150-year-old City lunchtime restaurant. Splendid oysters, salmon, fish pie, herrings with mustard. Good cheeses and traditional puddings served by staff with old-fashioned courtesy. Very popular; expect to queue as they don't take bookings. *L open to 15.00. Closed Sat & Sun.* No credit cards. ££

Upper Street Fish Shop   **3 E5**
324 Upper St N1. 071-359 1401. Cheerful bistro atmosphere at this Islington fish and chip shop. Wide range of fish from rock to Dover sole, plus fish soup and fish lasagne. Delicious home-made desserts. Unlicensed, but you can bring your own wine. *LD open to 22.00. Closed LD Sun & L Mon.* No credit cards. ££

Walsh's Seafood & Shellfish Restaurant   **6 F4**
5 Charlotte St W1. 071-637 0222. Run by the grand-daughter of the man who started Wheeler's (see below), this traditional British fish restaurant comprises an oyster bar and several small dining rooms. The menu is divided into species of fish, and features classic and modern dishes; you can choose between Dover sole Veronique and lobster ravioli. Fresh oysters are served raw, grilled or au gratin. Traditional desserts. Carefully-chosen wine list. *LD open to 23.00. Closed L Sat & LD Sun.* A.Ax.Dc.V. £££+

Wheeler's
A well-known chain dating back over 100 years to the fish shop in Old Compton Street which today is one of the many London branches. Although each restaurant has its own character, there are certain similarities; green painted exteriors, leaded windows, panelling and plush surroundings. Many have an oyster bar and all offer a range of fresh fish and shellfish, cooked simply and well. Specialities include lobster and sole. Service is cheerful and the restaurants have a loyal following. Several branches are listed below. A.Ax.Dc.V. £££

Alcove   **9 D4**
17 Kensington High St W8. 071-937 1443.
LD open to 22.30. Closed L Sat & L Sun.

Vendôme   **6 E6**
20 Dover St W1. 071 629 5417
LD open to 22.30. Closed L Sat & L Sun.

Wheeler's Old Compton Street   **6 G5**
19 Old Compton St W1. 071-437 2706.
LD open to 23.15, to 22.30 Sun.

VEGETARIAN & WHOLEFOOD

INTEREST in vegetarian food has increased in recent years and as a result there are now many more restaurants and cafés offering meat-free dishes. The most innovative of these restaurants tend to be run by committed individuals who use organic produce and imaginative ingredients to produce creative vegetarian dishes. However, these establishments are few and far between, and most of the places listed in this section are basic vegetarian cafés offering wholesome cuisine and healthy snacks in pleasant, if somewhat spartan, surroundings. For an alternative, see under *Indian;* the cuisine of southern India is predominantly vegetarian.

For further information contact the Vegetarian Society. They publish the *International Vegetarian Travel Guide* which has a directory of vegetarian restaurants, shops, guest houses and hotels throughout the UK and the world. They can be contacted at Parkdale, Dunham Rd, Altrincham, Cheshire WA14 4QG. 061-928 0793.

Blah Blah Blah
78 Goldhawk Rd W12. 081-746 1337. Simple restaurant/café serving imaginative and mouth-watering dishes. Try fennel and apple korma, sesame crêpes filled with spinach, courgettes and ricotta. The menu includes dishes from India and the Middle East. Unlicensed. No smoking. *LD open to 23.00. Closed Sun.* No credit cards. ££

Café Santé 7 B6
17 Garrick St WC2. 071-240 7811. New-style vegetarian café with sleek black tables and chairs. Interesting salads, hot dishes which change daily, plus a few non-vegetarian meals. Unlicensed. *LD open to 23.30, to 18.00 Sun.* No credit cards. £

The Cherry Orchard 8 F2
241-245 Globe Rd E2. 081-980 6678. Brightly decorated café run by a group of Buddhist women. Imaginative vegetarian and vegan cuisine; cauliflower and cashew filo pie, watercress crumble. Delicious desserts. Unlicensed. No smoking. *Open 11.00-16.00 Mon-Fri, to 19.00 Tue & Wed.* A.V. £

Country Life 6 F6
1 Heddon St W1. 071-434 2922. Large basement restaurant with a health food shop upstairs. Vegetarian and vegan menu; everything is home-made and no dairy produce is used. The set lunch is good value and consists of soup, a hot dish with salad or vegetables and a pudding. The menu changes daily. Unlicensed. No smoking. *L open to 15.00, to 14.00 Fri. Closed Sat & Sun.* No credit cards. £

Cranks 6 F5
8 Marshall St W1. 071-437 9431. This branch was the first of London's original healthfood restaurants. Having been bought out of receivership, the chain has been re-launched and is once again serving innovative vegetarian dishes. Try the vegan tofu-topped lentil quiche or the nut burger with couscous, beans and almonds. Other branches. *LD (Reserve D) open to 20.00. Closed Sun.* A.V. ££

Food for Thought 7 B5
31 Neal St WC2. 071-836 0239. Simple, whitewashed Covent Garden restaurant. The daily-changing menu always features a soup, a salad, stir-fried vegetables and a few hot dishes. Good choice of puddings too. Unlicensed, but you can bring your own wine. *LD open to 20.00, to 16.00 Sun.* No credit cards. £

Fungus Mungus 14 B5
264 Battersea Park Rd SW11. 071-924 5578. Not the most attractive name for this laid-back 1960s-style cluttered bar. International vegetarian dishes are well prepared and beautifully presented. Exotic beers. Occasional live music. *D (Reserve Fri & Sat) open to 24.00, to 23.00 Sun.* No credit cards. ££

The Gate
51 Queen Caroline St W6. 081-748 6932. Tucked behind the Hammersmith Apollo above a Christian Community Centre, this is an airy, spacious restaurant serving vegetarian food inspired by European, Middle Eastern and Oriental dishes. Vegetable roulade with cream cheese and crunchy vegetables, wild mushroom cannelloni, spinach lasagne. Organic wines and beers. Live music. No smoking. *LD open to 22.45. Closed Sun.* A.Ax.Dc.V. ££

Govinda's   6 G5
9 Soho St, off Oxford St W1. 071-437 3662. Pleasing surroundings in this vegetarian restaurant run by members of the Hare Krishna movement. Good range of Indian dishes plus pizza, ratatouille, vegeburgers and salads. Vegetarian cheese and no eggs are used in the cooking. Herbal teas. Unlicensed. No smoking. *LD open to 19.00. Closed Sun.* No credit cards. £

The Greenhouse   6 G4
Drill Hall, 16 Chenies St WC1. 071-637 8038. A charming, simple restaurant serving excellent vegetarian and vegan dishes. Pumpkin soup, aubergine pâté, walnut balls with tomato and basil sauce, leek and mushroom croustade. Mouthwatering display of desserts and pâtisseries; carob nut flan, date and banana lattice, plum and sour cream flan. Unlicensed. Non-smoking. *LD open to 20.15, to 19.00 Mon. Closed Sun. (D Mon women only.)* No credit cards. £

de Las Casas   17 G2
153 Clapham High St SW4. 0710738 8760. A trendy restaurant/café decorated in bright colours. Very relaxed atmosphere; newspapers, chess and backgammon boards can be borrowed on request. Soups are delicious; try blue cheese and celery, followed by tofu and fennel goulash with rice or apple. Occasional jazz and flamenco. *LD open to 23.00, to 18.00 Sun & Mon.* No credit cards. £

Leith's   5 C6
92 Kensington Park Rd W11. 071-229 4481. Up-market restaurant with an excellent vegetarian menu in addition to their modern British dishes. Hot and cold starters such as artichoke pie and asparagus mousse. Beautifully-presented main courses and home-made desserts. Vegans also catered for; it is advisable to give notice. *D (Reserve) open to 23.30.* A.Ax.Dc.V. £££

Mamta 13 C5
692 Fulham Rd SW6. 071-736 5914. A smart Indian restaurant offering imaginative home-cooked vegetarian meals. Flavoursome dishes like sev puri (pastry filled with potatoes and topped with yoghurt, tamarind sauce and noodles) and aubergine with ginger and garlic are worth trying. Vegan thali. *LD open to 23.00, to 24.00 Thur-Sun.* A.Ax.Dc.V. ££

Mandeer 6 G5
21 Hanway Pl, off Hanway St W1. 071-323 0660. This atmospheric basement restaurant was the first in London to offer completely vegetarian Indian cooking. Specialities include aubergine bhajis, thali Mandeer or puffed lotus savoury. The lunchtime self-service buffet is good value. Wholemeal Indian breads, organic wine. Special diets are catered for. *LD open to 21.45. Closed Sun.* A.Ax.Dc.V. £

Manna 2 C4
4 Erskine Rd NW3. 071-722 8028. Good, reliable food and a welcoming atmosphere at this well-established vegetarian restaurant. Cool stone floors and massive pine tables help to create a farmhouse kitchen atmosphere. All the food is made on the premises, including bread. Nut loaf, curries, quiche, vegetable casserole, celery and apple salad with curd cheese. A choice of wine, beers and juices. *D open to 23.00.* No credit cards. ££

Mildred's 6 G5
58 Greek St W1. 071-494 1634. Glass-fronted café serving excellent vegetarian and vegan dishes. Also fish and seafood dishes on the daily-changing menu. They use no preservatives or additives and use organic produce where possible. The vegetable stir-fry in satay sauce with noodles is popular. To follow, iced lemon poppyseed cake or home-made brown bread ice-cream. *LD open to 23.00. Closed Sun.* No credit cards. £

Millward's
97 Stoke Newington Church St N16. 071-254 1025. A pretty restaurant with a bistro atmosphere. Dishes are imaginative and well presented. Vegetable terrine, broccoli and Brie pancakes, cauliflower and chickpeas in an apricot sauce. There is always a vegan dish. Helpful and friendly service. *D open to 22.30 Mon-Sun. L open to 17.00 Sun.* A.V. ££

Neal's Yard Dining Rooms 7 B5
14 Neal's Yard WC2. 071-379 0298. A light, airy vege-

tarian restaurant where you can either sit at the bar or at large shared tables. International dishes include Egyptian pitta, Indian thali, Turkish meze and Indonesian sambal. Unlicensed, but you can bring your own wine. No smoking. *LD open to 20.00 Tue-Fri, to 18.00 Sat, to 17.00 Mon. Closed Sun.* No credit cards. £

The Nuthouse   6 F6
26 Kingly St W1. 071-437 9471. Self-service restaurant on two floors with a take-away service. Produce is all organically grown and freshly cooked. Macrobiotic dishes are also available. Nut rissoles, nut roast and several salads every day. To follow, fruit crumble and yoghurt. Drink wine, fresh fruit juice or herbal teas. *L open to 19.00. Closed Sun.* No credit cards. £

The Place Below   7 F5
St Mary-le-Bow, Cheapside EC2. 071-329 0789. Situated in the crypt of St Mary-le-Bow, this is an excellent self-service café offering a short menu of lunch dishes and a gourmet vegetarian menu on *Thursday and Friday evenings.* Imaginative dishes include Roquefort terrine and aubergine and fennel casserole. Home-made olive and garlic bread. Fresh exotic fruit. Set menu. Unlicensed, but you can bring your own wine *in the evenings. L open to 15.00. D (Reserve) open to 22.30 Thur & Fri only. Closed Sat & Sun.* No credit cards. L £ D ££

Raw Deal   6 C4
65 York St W1. 071-262 4841. Small, friendly vegetarian café serving soups, salads and hot daily specials. Risotto, savoury pancake, stuffed vegetables, a splendid variety of salads and quiches. To follow, fruit salads, pies and cakes, which are made on the premises from wholemeal flour. Unlicensed, but you can bring your own wine. *LD open to 21.30. Closed Sun.* No credit cards. £

Richmond Harvest
5 Dome Buildings, The Quadrant, Richmond, Surrey. 081-940 1138. Stylish restaurant catering for vegans as well as vegetarians. Try spicy lentil pâté, courgette and tomato lasagne, celery and mushroom croustade. For dessert there's banoffi pie, carrot cake, hot fruit crumble. Extensive wine list. *LD (Reserve D) open to 23.00, to 22.00 Sun.* No credit cards. ££

Seasons   6 B4
22 Harcourt St W1. 071-402 5925. Smart, stylish interior

with an open kitchen. Daily-changing menu which may include lasagne, stir-fried vegetables, leek, mushroom and barley pie, butter bean and broccoli bake. Also salads, baked potatoes and a choice of soups. Country wines offered include strawberry leaf and nettle. *LD open to 21.30. Closed Sun.* A.Ax.V. £

Vegetarian Cottage   2 C3
91 Haverstock Hill NW3. 071-586 1257. Small and simple restaurant offering a varied menu of Chinese vegetarian food. The chef comes from the oldest vegetarian restaurant in Hong Kong and prepares imaginative dishes such as deep-fried buns with vegetable stuffing, fried beancurd with mushrooms and stir-fried mange tout. Also some seafood dishes. *L(Sun only)D open to 23.15.* A.V. £

Vijay   1 C5
49 Willesden Lane NW6. 071-328 1087. Simple, modern decor at this south Indian vegetarian restaurant. Try vegetables cooked in yoghurt and coconut or masala dosai. Coconut and lemon rice are specialities. To follow, genuine Indian desserts and kulfi. They also serve meat curries for non-vegetarians. *LD (Reserve D) open to 22.45, to 23.45 Fri & Sat.* A.Ax.Dc.V. £

Wholemeal Café
1 Shrubbery Rd SW16. 081-769 2423. Busy Streatham café with a country cottage atmosphere. Meals are served all day. Choose from a wide selection of salads and jacket potatoes or try the daily special. Good choice of desserts. No smoking. *LD open to 22.00.* A.V. £

Wilkins   11 A4
61 Marsham St SW1. 071-222 4038. Vegetarian, vegan and macrobiotic café with pavement tables *in summer*. Menu changes daily; lots of soups, curries, flans, pies, pastas – all made on the premises. They also bake their own bread. Get there by about *12.00* for a full range as they tend to run out. Unlicensed. No smoking. *L open to 17.30. Closed Sat & Sun.* No credit cards. £

Windmill Wholefoods   13 E3
486 Fulham Rd SW6. 071-385 1570. Cheery restaurant with a big open window at the front and a fire in winter. Large portions of salads, quiches and hot savoury dishes – all home-made. A vegan dish is always available. Crumble, banana cream or cake to follow. Large range of organic wines; also additive-free beers and ciders. Herbal teas. *LD open to 23.00.* A.V. £

DINNER AND ENTERTAINMENT

A night out for dinner can mean more than just a meal in a pleasant restaurant. London offers all sorts of dinner and entertainment combinations, whether it be live music, a dinner dance or a full cabaret show. Alternatively there are theme restaurants where you can take part in an Elizabethan banquet or be entertained by jugglers and jesters.

Some of the restaurants listed below are in night-clubs for which you will have to pay an entrance fee. (**M**) means membership is necessary but most clubs have guest membership arrangements.

Annabel's   **6 E6**
44 Berkeley Sq W1. 071-629 3558. Famous fashionable nightclub; like the members, the food is of a distinguished quality. Raspberries in December, asparagus in January. Very exclusive; all visitors should ask a member to arrange entry in advance. *D open to 03.00. Closed Sun.* (**M**). Ax.Dc.V. **£££+**

Barbarella 1   **13 E3**
428 Fulham Rd SW6. 071-385 9434. Stylish and sophisticated Anglo-Italian restaurant where you can dance until the early hours. Dance floor visible from wherever you sit. A Barbarella Special consists of whipped cream, strawberry and liqueur with crushed macaroons clustered on top. Private rooms available. **Barbarella 2** is at 43 Thurloe St SW7 (**10 A5**). 071-584 2000. *D (Reserve) open to 01.00, to 02.00 Sat. Dancing to 03.00. Closed Sun.* A.Ax.Dc.V. **£££**

Bass Clef   **8 B2**
35 Coronet St N1. 071-729 2440. Primarily a venue for live jazz, Latin, African, rare groove and soul music, there is also a small restaurant offering imaginative, well-prepared food, including some vegetarian choices. Entrance charge for the club depends on who is playing. *D open to 01.00.* A.Ax.Dc.V. **££**

Bizarro   **5 G5**
18-22 Craven Rd W2. 071-723 6029. Wine, dine and dance in a lively Mediterranean atmosphere. Comprehensive Italian menu. Eating upstairs amidst alcoves and arches, dancing downstairs to a resident

band to *02.00 (Mon-Sat)*. *D (Reserve weekends) open to 01.00*. A.Ax.Dc.V. ££

Brick Lane Music Hall   8 C4
152 Brick Lane E1. 071-377 8787. Music hall entertainment for the 1990s in the Old Bull & Bush style. Traditional three-course English dinner which is served at long tables. Then follows the show with singalongs and slapstick. *Meal served 19.30 Wed-Sat; show starts 21.00*. A.Dc.V. £££

Canal Café Theatre   5 E4
Bridge House Pub, 2 Delamere Ter W2. 071-289 6054. Small and inexpensive theatre restaurant overlooking the Regent's Canal at Little Venice. Flexible cabaret programme; Newsrevue, which is topical comedy, runs from *Thur-Sun*. *Phone for details*. Simple, homely food can be ordered throughout the show. Menu changes daily; vegetarian dishes available. *D open to 22.30. Closed Mon.* A.V. ££

Concordia Notte   5 G5
29-31 Craven Rd W2. 071-723 3725. Sophisticated, baroque dining room patronised by stars and sometimes royalty. Haute cuisine Italian menu prepared by more than ten chefs. Caviar, oysters, lobster. Special dishes like El Marinaro, shellfish mixed with veal, ham and beef, in white wine, garlic and tomatoes. Excellent sweet trolley. Latin American cabaret and dancing to a resident band. *D (Reserve) open to 01.00. Closed Sun.* A.Ax.Dc.V. £££+

Costa Dorada   6 G5
47-55 Hanway St W1. 071-631 7139. Lively atmosphere at this Spanish flamenco restaurant which features singers and musicians in addition to the dancers. Tapas bar and restaurant serving authentic dishes. Two flamenco shows *nightly. D open to 02.00, to 24.00 Sun.* A.Ax.Dc.V. £££

Elysée   6 G4
13 Percy St W1. 071-636 4804. Lively, ethnic restaurant serving Greek food with some English and French dishes. Dancing to the resident four-piece band; bouzouki music. Taverna atmosphere, plate-smashing is encouraged. Roof garden open *in summer. D (Reserve) open to 03.00. Closed Sun. Cabaret 23.00, 01.00 & 02.30.* A.Ax.Dc.V. ££

Entrecôte   7 B4
124a Southampton Row WC1. 071-405 1466.

Romantic, candlelit restaurant with resident dance band *21.00-01.00 Fri & Sat.* Formal but relaxed atmosphere. International cuisine with a French influence. *D (Reserve) open to 23.45, to 22.45 Sun.* A.Ax.Dc.V. *££*

Flanagan's
100 Baker St W1. 071-935 0287.   6 D4
14 Rupert St W1. 071-434 9201.   6 G6
A warm and friendly atmosphere at these unique, turn-of-the-century theme restaurants. Edwardian dining rooms with sawdust for spitting on and plenty of cockney songs – a truly colourful extravaganza. Elegantly-costumed waiters and serving girls dish up tripe, jellied eels, game pie, steak 'n' kidney pudding, enormous plates of fish and chips. *D open to 23.00.* A.Ax.Dc.V. *££*

L'Hirondelle   6 F6
99-101 Regent St W1 (entrance in Swallow St). 071-734 1511. Comfortable and pleasant restaurant which has live music and two floor shows *nightly.* Well staged and flamboyant. Dancing to live music *from 21.30.* International menu in grand style; suprême de volaille Princesse, escalope de veau Hirondelle. A really spectacular evening out. *D (Reserve) open to 02.00. Closed Sun. Floor shows 23.00 & 01.00.* A.Ax.Dc.V. *£££*

London Entertains
All reservations 081-568 1616. This organisation runs special evenings at three different venues, each with its own distinctive character. All three are operated on advance bookings and are open according to demand. The price is the same for all, and includes a four- to five-course meal, unlimited drink and a show. There is a surcharge on *Sat. D (Reserve). Phone for times.* A.Ax.Dc.V. *£££+* The three venues are:

Beefeater by the Tower of London   12 C2
Ivory House, St Katharine's Dock E1. In the historic vaults of the Ivory House you will be treated to an evening of British pageantry. A traditional medieval banquet with Henry VIII and his court providing the entertainment. Traditional English cider on arrival, followed by a five-course banquet.

The Cockney   6 G4
161 Tottenham Court Rd W1. Music Hall entertainment; cockney sing-along routines, spoof magic shows,

can-can dancing and other cabaret acts. Honky-tonk piano greets you. Traditional English dinner.

The Talk of London   7 B5
Drury Lane WC2. Elegant surroundings at one of London's most luxurious cabaret restaurants. Features dancers and top international cabaret stars. Dancing to a resident band. Begin with cocktails, followed by dinner.

My Fair Lady   2 E4
250 Camden High St NW1. 071-485 4433/6210. Live entertainment on board an attractive canal wideboat which travels down the Regent's Canal. Modern British cuisine. Melon with raspberry coulis, smoked salmon and cream cheese roulade, lamb noisettes, guinea fowl. Singer/guitarist entertains. *D (Reserve) open to 23.00. Closed Sun & Mon.* A.V. £££

The Old Palace
Hatfield Park, Hatfield, Herts. (0707) 262055. Spend an evening with 'Good Queen Bess' in the palace where the original held her first Council of State. Five-course meal, unlimited wine and 'Elizabethan' entertainment. *Strictly by advance booking only.* Coach picks up from and returns to London. Evening begins *19.30. D (Reserve). Closed Mon & Wed.* A.V. £££

Palookaville   7 B6
13a James St, off Covent Garden Piazza WC2. 071-240 5857. This basement restaurant and wine bar is situated in a converted banana warehouse. Jazz bands play to a lively audience. Small dance floor. Admission charge after *21.30 Fri & Sat. D (Reserve) open to 00.15. Bar open to 01.00.* A.Ax.Dc.V. ££

Rio   5 D5
103 Westbourne Grove W2. 071-792 0312. Brazilian carnival shows, lambada floor shows, dancers and musicians provide the entertainment at this supper club. Menu is a strange mixture of South American, Greek and international dishes. *D open to 00.30. Closed Sun. Show 22.30 Fri & Sat.* A.Ax.Dc.V. ££

Ronnie Scott's   6 G5
47 Frith St W1. 071-439 0747. World-class jazz acts at London's legendary jazz venue. Always packed, so it is advisable to book in advance. British and continental cuisine. *D open to 02.00. Closed Sun. First set 21.30.* (**M**) available, but not essential to gain entry. A.Ax.Dc.V. ££

The Roof Gardens   9 D4
99-121 Kensington High St W8. 071-937 7994.
Nightclub and restaurant in a spectacular setting –
beautiful gardens with trees, streams, fountains and
flamingoes six floors above the Kensington streets.
Private club two nights a week; dinner and disco *Thur*
and *Sat*. Owned by Virgin's Richard Branson, it has a
smart clientele. (**M**). *D (Reserve) open to 23.30.*
Dancing to 03.00. Closed D Mon, Tue, Wed, Fri, Sun.
A.Ax.Dc.V. £££

Royal Roof Restaurant   9 E3
Royal Garden Hotel, 2-24 Kensington High St W8.
071-937 8000. An Anglo-French restaurant with excellent views over Kensington Gardens, Kensington Palace
and Hyde Park. Dinner dances on *Sat evenings*. Good
menu and wine list. *D (Reserve) open to 22.30, to*
23.00 Sat. Closed Sun. Dancing to 24.00. A.Ax.Dc.V.
£££+

The Savoy Restaurant   7 C6
The Savoy Hotel, Strand WC2. 071-836 4343. Elegant
and formal restaurant where the resident quartet and
dancing contribute to the grand hotel manner. World-
famous, well-deserved reputation for classic cooking
and excellent service. *LD open to 23.30. Band plays*
until 24.00 (01.00 Sat). A.Ax.Dc.V. £££+

School Dinners   6 D5
1 Robert Adam St W1. 071-486 2724. Ex-public
schoolboys and middle-aged businessmen flock to this
book-lined headmaster's study staffed by 'schoolgirls' in
mini-skirts and gym-slips. Choose between Bunter's
menu of dishes like steak 'n' kidney pie and apple crumble, or the more sophisticated Headmaster's menu of
prawns, steak or lamb. Finish your meal or be 'spanked'
by an angry senior girl. Party atmosphere, not for the
timid. *D (last reservation 20.30) open till late. Closed*
Sun. A.Ax.Dc.V. ££

Smollensky's on the Strand   7 C6
105 Strand WC2. 071-497 2101. Big, bright and
bustling restaurant with dancing to live music on *Fri &*
Sat evenings. The menu offers grilled and barbecued
steaks done seven different ways. Also lamb, chicken
and vegetarian dishes. Rich desserts and cocktails. *D*
open to 24.00, to 00.30 Fri & Sat, to 22.30 Sun.
A.Ax.Dc.V. ££

Terrace Restaurant 10 D2
Dorchester Hotel, Park Lane W1. 071-629 8888.
Stately and grand restaurant overlooking Hyde Park.
Elegant dinner dances. Waiters in evening dress serve
quality French food. Cuisine naturelle – sweetbreads,
grouse, salade de foie gras and sole Dorchester. *D
(Reserve) open to 23.30. Dancing to 01.00. Closed Sun
& Mon.* A.Ax.Dc.V. £££+

Tiberio 10 E2
22 Queen St W1. 071-629 3561. Popular, crowded
late-night restaurant with a celebrity clientele. Excellent
varied Italian menu and exceptionally smooth and
friendly service. Dance till early morning to a resident
quartet. *D open to 02.00. Closed Sun.* A.Ax.Dc.V.
£££+

Tiddy Dols 10 E2
55 Shepherd Market, off White Horse St W1. 071-499
2357. A unique restaurant on the site of the original
May Fair in former houses dating to 1741. Low
ceilings, winding staircases, open fires and a collection
of 18thC hand-coloured caricatures add to the
atmosphere. The Tiddy Dol Players, an ensemble of
singers, actors and instrumentalists, will entertain while
you dine on English dishes like toad in the hole, angels
on horseback, roast beef, jugged hare and syllabub.
Dancing *to 01.00, to 24.00 Sun. D open to 23.30.*
A.Ax.V. ££

Villa dei Cesari 14 F2
135 Grosvenor Rd SW1. 071-828 7453. Converted
riverside warehouse with a fine view over the River
Thames. The Roman Empire lives on here with waiters
in tunics, classical decor and a latinised menu. Dancing
to resident band. *D open to 01.30. Closed Mon.*
A.Ax.Dc.V. £££+

Windows on the World 10 D2
Hilton Hotel, 22 Park Lane W1. 071-493 8000. Dine
28 floors up for an intoxicating view over London.
Tables by the window are at a premium. Two bands
and a dancefloor. French menu; smoked salmon, foie
gras, caviar, châteaubriand, pepper steak. *D (Reserve)
open to 01.00. Closed Sun. Dancing to 02.00.*
A.Ax.Dc.V. £££+

RESTAURANTS FOR PARTIES

MANY restaurants have separate rooms available for party bookings and will produce a special set menu for you. Failing that, you can simply make a group booking at one of the many restaurants that have the right atmosphere for a party venue.

Antipasto e Pasta   14 B5
511 Battersea Park Rd SW11. 071-223 9765. This cheerful pasta restaurant has a separate conservatory available for parties which seats 35. Relaxing atmosphere for a private dinner party. Tailor-made or set menu. No hire charge. *LD open to 23.30.* A.Ax.V. ££

Bombay Palace   6 B5
50 Connaught St W2. 071-723 8855. An up-market Indian restaurant with an adjoining party room seating 40. Excellent north Indian cuisine and superb service. Tailor-made or set menu. No hire charge. *LD open to 23.30, to 23.00 Sun.* A.Ax.Dc.V. ££

Break for the Border   6 F5
8 Argyll St W1. 071-734 5776. This is a real party restaurant with a lively atmosphere, loud music and a long list of cocktails. There is also a separate party room which seats 80. Tex-Mex food comes in huge portions. No hire charge. *LD open to 23.45.* A.Ax.V. ££

Chin's   13 C5
311-313 New King's Rd SW6. 071-736 8833. A luxury Chinese restaurant where your party can take over the whole restaurant or one of its elegant feature areas – the Garden Room, The Waterfall Room and the Dragon Room. Each seats up to 20. Adaptable set menus of Cantonese, Szechuan and Beijing cooking. No hire charge. *LD open to 23.45.* A.Ax.V. ££

Dan's   10 B6
119 Sydney St SW3. 071-352 2718. A bright, airy restaurant serving French cuisine. Hire the conservatory which leads out onto the garden (seats 34) or there is a smaller private room downstairs (seats 14). Set menu. No hire charge. *LD open to 22.45. Closed L Sat & LD Sun.* A.Ax.V. £££

Dôme   1 F1
38-39 Hampstead High St NW3. 071-435 4240. You
can have a completely private setting for a dinner
party or buffet at this lively brasserie. Big windows
lead out onto a private balcony and you even have
your own bar. Seats 40. No hire charge but minimum
bill £200. *LD open to 23.00, to 22.30 Sun.* A.Ax.Dc.V.
££

Mongolian Barbeque   16 B3
147 Upper Richmond Rd SW15. 081-780 9252. This
lively restaurant has a separate dining room downstairs
which seats 30 and it's a great place for a noisy group.
You help yourself to pieces of meat (turkey, chicken,
lamb, pork, beef and fish). Add raw vegetables and your
choice of sauces and the chef will barbecue your meal in
front of you. No hire charge. *D open to 24.00.* A.Ax.V.
££

Nancy Lam's Enak Enak   17 D1
56 Lavender Hill SW11. 071-924 3148. This small
Indonesian restaurant has a separate room for parties
which seats 16. Nancy Lam is very friendly and
the hospitable service makes this an ideal venue for
a party. Stir-fries and satay dishes are the mainstays.
No hire charge. *D open to 22.45. Closed Sun & Mon.*
A.V. ££

Nikita's   13 E2
65 Ifield Rd SW10. 071-352 6326. An atmospheric cavernous restaurant, exquisitely decorated in red and
gold. You can hire the whole place or one of their private rooms. There is a wonderful room for 12, hidden
away behind a decorated door, and there are also two
cosy alcove areas for six, curtained off with heavy
tapestry drapes. Russian food and a wide selection of
vodkas. No hire charge. *D open to 23.30. Closed Sun.*
A.Ax.V. £££

Paulo's   13 A2
30 Greyhound Rd W6. 071-385 9264. A lively
party atmosphere at this Brazilian restaurant which
offers a set buffet dinner. There's a separate room in the
basement which seats 20. Set menu or main course
buffet where you choose from over 20 dishes. Brazilian
cocktails. Portuguese and Brazilian wines. No hire
charge. *D open to 22.30. Closed Sun.* No credit
cards. ££

PUB RESTAURANTS

WHAT could be more congenial for a quick snack or a simple meal than the good old British pub? The pubs below have been chosen either for their excellent food or for their famous historical background, in some cases both. Most of the pubs mentioned do bar snacks and light meals such as salads, sandwiches, ploughmans, sausage and mash, lasagne, chilli con carne. Where full meals are served, a restaurant area is normally set aside. Times given in this section are for meals only.

The Albert   **10 F4**
52 Victoria St SW1. 071-222 5577. Authentic Victorian wood-panelled pub with upstairs carvery restaurant serving set price three-course lunches – prawn cocktail, roast beef, lamb or pork, sweet trolley. Packed at lunchtime with businessmen and MPs, it even has a division bell linked to the House of Commons to recall tardy diners at voting time. *LD (Reserve) open to 21.30.* A.Ax.Dc.V. ££

The Alma   **16 E2**
499 Old York Rd SW18. 081-870 2537. Large and decorative pub with a huge mahogany bar. Well-reputed French restaurant at the back. *Sunday* lunch is served upstairs. *L open to 15.00. D open to 23.00. Closed D Sun.* A.Ax.V. ££

Baker & Oven   **6 D4**
10 Paddington St W1. 071-935 5088. Small Victorian pub with a cosy basement restaurant. Traditional roasts and mouth-watering pies from 100-year-old baker's ovens. *LD (Reserve) open to 22.30. Closed L Sat & LD Sun.* Ax.V. ££

Blue Posts   10 F2
6 Bennet St, off St James's St SW1. 071-493 3350. Lord
Byron used to live next door to this charming tradition-
al pub. Upstairs restaurant serves roasts and other
English dishes. *LD open to 21.00. Closed Sat & Sun.*
A.Ax.V. ££

The Brewery Tap   16 E3
68 Wandsworth High St SW18. 081-870 2894. This
traditional pub is attached to Young's famous brewery
– with its real ale, dray horses, and geese in the backyard. Regulars are brewery staff and grooms. Carvery
food and salad bar downstairs at lunchtime. *L open to
14.00.* No credit cards. £

Canonbury Tavern   3 E3
21 Canonbury Pl N1. 071-226 1881. There has been a
tavern on this site since the 16th century, though this
building is only 200 years old. A good place to go with
children as there is a large garden at the rear with
tables, chairs and swings. Food is served at the bar; an
imaginative selection of cold salads, meats and pies,
with a few hot dishes. Barbecues in the garden *in
summer.* Traditional Sunday lunch. 'Fast food' served
in the evening. *L open to 14.30. D open to 20.00.*
A.V. £

Cheshire Cheese, Ye Olde   7 D5
Wine Office Court, off 145 Fleet St EC4. 071-353
6170. Rebuilt after the Great Fire, this rambling building has low ceilings, oak tables and sawdust on the
floor. Although new bars have been added, most of this
pub hasn't changed much since those early days. Six
bars. Traditional English fare; best roast beef, steak and
kidney pie and pudding, game pudding and traditional
desserts. *L open to 14.00* (bar food only on *Sun*). *D
(Reserve) open to 21.30. Closed D Sun.* A.Ax.Dc.V. ££

Cock Tavern, Ye Olde   7 D5
22 Fleet St EC4. 071-353 8570. Lawyers and nearby
office workers have replaced the journalists who used to
frequent this small tavern with literary and Dickensian
associations. Nell Gwynne, Pepys and Garrick once
drank here. English carvery, puddings and pies; try the
special steak, kidney and mushroom pie. *L open to
15.00. Closed Sat & Sun.* A.Ax.Dc.V. ££

The Crown   3 D5
116 Cloudesley Rd N1. 071-837 7107. Pretty, tradi-

tional Islington pub with lots of polished wood, brass and glass. Tables outside *in summer*. Wide range of salads and snacks. Home-cooked English food *Sunday lunchtimes*. *L open to 14.00. D open to 21.00*. No credit cards. £

Dirty Dick's   8 B5

202-204 Bishopsgate EC2. 071-283 5888. The original pub named after Nat Bentley, well-known 18th-century miser and Dirty Old Man: 'If I wash my hands today, they will be dirty again tomorrow'. Hot and cold snacks downstairs, à la carte restaurant upstairs. *L open to 14.00*. A.Ax.Dc.V. ££

French House Dining Room   6 G5

49 Dean St W1. 071-437 2477. Small, first-floor restaurant above the French House pub in Soho which was the London centre for the Free French during the war; De Gaulle drank here. The daily-changing menu may include such delights as guinea fowl in red wine, lamb and barley stew, or grilled pigeon with leeks. Jovial atmosphere and friendly service. *LD (Reserve) open to 23.30. Closed Sun*. A.Ax.Dc.V. ££

George Inn   11 G2

77 Borough High St SE1. 071-407 2056. Galleried 17th-century coaching inn, once patronised by Dickens and mentioned in *Little Dorrit*. Traditional draught beer and hand-pulled lager. Choice English table d'hôte; à la carte with specialities such as mushrooms George Inn (with bacon and herbs), roasts and smoked trout or salmon. Refectory-style long tables, most appropriate in this setting. *L open to 14.00. D (Reserve) open to 21.00. Closed Sat & Sun*. A.Ax.Dc.V. ££

Grapes

76 Narrow St E14. 071-987 4396. This pub was reputedly immortalised by Dickens as The Six Jolly Fellowship Porters in *Our Mutual Friend*. Amid wharves and warehouses by the Pool of London, there are good views up and down the river. Restaurant serving fine fish; oysters and lobster when in season. *L open to 14.00. D open to 22.00. Closed LD Sun & D Mon*. A.Ax.V. ££

Grenadier   10 D3

18 Wilton Row SW1. 071-235 3074. Once an officers' mess for the Duke of Wellington's soldiers. Full of military bric-à-brac – there's even a sentry box outside. English food in the restaurant; specialities are half a

roast duck in citrus sauce, steak and kidney pie, beef Wellington, pork Grand Marnier. *L open to 14.00. D open to 22.00.* A.Ax.Dc.V. £££

Grouse & Claret 10 D4
Wilton Mews SW1. 071-245 1224. A Belgravia mews pub is an unlikely location for a Thai restaurant, but above this pub is a smart wood-panelled dining room, the **Oriental Brasserie**. Excellent Thai cuisine. *L open to 15.00. D open to 24.00, to 23.00 Sun. Closed L Sun.* A.Ax.Dc.V. ££

The Guinea 10 E1
30 Bruton Pl W1. 071-409 1728. Pleasant old pub hidden away in a narrow cobbled Mayfair mews. Originally known as the One Pound One, probably because of the cattle pound that is thought to have once stood nearby. English dining room. *L open to 14.00. D open to 22.00. Closed L Sat & LD Sun.* A.Ax.V. ££

Island Queen 7 E1
87 Noel Rd N1. 071-226 5507. Restaurant: 071-226 0307. Has without doubt the most outlandish decor of any pub in London. Giant papier-mâché caricatures of politicians and famous figures are suspended from the ceiling. The upstairs restaurant is light and sunny and offers a three-course set meal where you can eat as much as you like of each course. *L (Sun only) open to 14.00. D (Fri & Sat only) open to 21.00.* A.Ax.Dc.V. ££

Jack Straw's Castle
North End Way NW3. 071-435 8885. Comfortable pub with an extensive view over Hampstead Heath. Book in advance to ensure getting a window seat. English carvery. *L open to 14.00. D (Reserve) open to 21.30.* A.Ax.Dc.V. ££

King's Head 3 E5
115 Upper St N1. 071-226 0364. Probably the best known and most widely reviewed of the theatre pubs. Order your set meal from a traditional English menu then stay at your table for the play. Lunchtime menu includes a range of vegetarian dishes, salads and burgers. *L open to 14.00. D (Reserve) open to 20.00.* A.Dc.V. £

The Orange Tree
45 Kew Rd, Richmond, Surrey. 081-940 0944. The cellar restaurant is traditional with old panelling,

brick walls and Spanish wrought-iron fittings. European food, cooked with flair and beautifully presented; poached salmon, duck à l'orange, pork in fennel, lasagne, paella, ham on the bone, curries. *L open to 14.00. D open to 23.00.* A.Ax.Dc.V. ££

Prospect of Whitby   12 F2
57 Wapping Wall E1. 071-481 1095. Historical dockland tavern dating back to the reign of Henry VIII. Samuel Pepys and Rex Whistler drank here, as did 'hanging' Judge Jeffreys and so many thieves and smugglers that it was known as the Devil's Tavern. Continental cuisine in the terrace restaurant. *L open to 14.00. D open to 21.45 (bar food to 21.30). Closed L Sat & D Sun.* A.Ax.Dc.V. £££

Queen's Head   9 A4
13 Brook Green W6. 071-603 3174. Three-hundred-year-old wayside inn. The Marquis of Queensbury, who lived nearby, is thought to have mulled over the Queensbury rules of boxing here. Beer garden at the back. Good English cooking with at least three specialities each day. *L (Reserve) open to 14.30. D open to 21.30. Closed L Sat & L Sun.* A.Ax.Dc.V. £

Red Lion   10 E2
1 Waverton St W1. 071-499 1307. A 17th-century Mayfair inn. Inside, Royal Academy prints and paintings hang in comfortable, intimate surroundings. Top quality international food; also Scotch salmon and game in season. *L open to 14.00. D (Reserve) open to 21.45.* A.Ax.Dc.V. ££

Rose & Crown   10 D2
2 Old Park Lane W1. 071-499 1980. 200-year-old pub, said to be one of the most haunted pubs in London because the doomed, en route for Tyburn gallows, were sometimes incarcerated overnight in the cellars and apparently returned later, in spirit. Five hot dishes each day and a cold buffet until *22.00. L open to 14.30.* A.Ax.V. £

Rossetti   2 A5
23 Queen's Grove NW8. 071-722 7141. Modern, attractive St John's Wood pub. Light and airy with Rossetti etchings on the walls. Thai menu in the restau-

rant; Imperial prawns, Emerald chicken. Wide variety of desserts. *L open to 14.45. D (Reserve) open to 23.00, to 22.30 Sun.* A.Ax.Dc.V. ££

Running Footman 10 E2

5 Charles St W1. 071-499 2988. Pub whose full name was once the longest in London – 'I am the only Running Footman'. The task of the running footman was to run before a carriage clearing the way and paying the tolls. A la carte restaurant serving English food. *L open to 14.30. D open to 21.30. Closed L Sat & L Sun.* A.Ax.Dc.V. ££

Sherlock Holmes 11 B2

10 Northumberland St WC2. 071-930 2644. This used to be the Northumberland Arms where Sir Arthur Conan Doyle 'arranged' the first meeting between Sir Henry Baskerville and Sherlock Holmes in *The Hound of the Baskervilles*. In 1957 it changed its name and took the fictitious detective as its theme. Upstairs is a replica of Holmes' study at 221b Baker Street. French and English cooking in the restaurant. *L open to 14.00. D open to 21.30.* A.Ax.Dc.V. ££

Spotted Dog, The Old

212 Upton Lane E7. 081-472 1794. Handsome inn dating back to the late 15th century and used by the city's merchants during the Great Plague. Dick Turpin connections, though the interior decor concentrates on the earlier Tudor theme. Oak beams, plaster whitewash. Grill menu; rump, sirloin or fillet steak, plaice. Vegetarian meals. Children's menu. *L open to 14.00. D open to 22.00. Closed L Sat.* A.Ax.V. ££

White Horse 13 D5

1-3 Parsons Green SW6. 071-736 2115. Beautiful old Victorian bar with huge windows and wooden floors. Counter food of unusual quality; roast leg of lamb, roast beef, kipper pâté, spinach soup. All salads have a unique home-made dressing. The steak and kidney pie is made with rump steak. A different home-made soup each day *in winter*. Home-made puddings or first-rate farmhouse Stilton to follow. Excellent wine list. Tables outside *in summer*. *L open to 14.00. D open to 22.00.* A.Ax.V. £

RIVERSIDE

THE Thames affords many good views from its banks, and riverside restaurants along its winding path and in developed wharves and marinas have some of the best views London has to offer. The following restaurants are either on the river or within a few minutes' walk from it.

Anchor Bankside　　　　　　　　　　　　**11 F1**
34 Park St SE1. 071-407 1577. An inn with a wealth of historical associations. The original pub was destroyed by the Great Fire of 1666; the present building, full of nooks and crannies, exposed beams and a large open fireplace, is 18th century. The restaurant is on two levels, The Upper Chart and The Lower Chart, and offers a modern British menu. *LD (Reserve) open to 22.00, to 21.00 Sun.* A.Ax.Dc.V. **££**

Angel　　　　　　　　　　　　　　　　**12 E3**
101 Bermondsey Wall East SE16. 071-237 3608. A 16th-century Thames-side tavern built on pillars, with a superb outlook over the River Thames. Views upstream of Tower Bridge and St Paul's, and downstream towards Greenwich Reach. Low ceilings, wood panelling, walls hung with prints of the area as it used to be. Modern British cuisine in the elegant restaurant. Also traditional pub grub in the downstairs bar. *LD open to 22.00. Closed L Sat & D Sun.* A.Ax.Dc.V. **£££**

Blueprint Café　　　　　　　　　　　　**12 C3**
Design Museum, Butler's Wharf SE1. 071-378 7031.

This stylish restaurant on top of the Design Museum is another Sir Terence Conran creation. It has a fabulous setting alongside the River Thames with spectacular views of Tower Bridge. The international menu places emphasis on Mediterranean dishes. Outdoor tables on the terrace. *LD (Reserve L) open to 23.00. Closed D Sun.* A.Ax.V. ££

The Canteen   13 F4
Harbour Yard, Chelsea Harbour, off Lots Rd SW10. 071-351 7330. Magnificent views of the marina from this restaurant which is owned by Michael Caine and Marco Pierre White. The varied menu includes sea bass, lobster, rump of lamb, with bisquit glacé or lemon tart for dessert. *LD (Reserve) open to 23.45, to 22.45 Sun.* A.V. £££

Compleat Angler, Valasian Restaurant
Marlow Bridge, Marlow, Bucks. (0628) 484444. A magnificent setting in an historic hotel overlooking the river. Beamed ceiling, wood panelling, open fires. Enjoyable English and French cuisine. Excellent fish dishes; gratin of salmon, brioche and pastry crust, caviar sauce. *LD (Reserve at weekends) open to 22.00.* A.Ax.Dc.V. £££+

Cutty Sark
Ballast Quay, Lassell St SE10. 081-8583146. 17th-century pub overlooking the river and wharves near the famous *Cutty Sark* in dry dock. Traditional English fare with some unusual additions like whitebait suppers. *LD open to 22.00. Closed D Sun & LD Mon.* A.V. ££

Deals   13 F4
Harbour Yard, Chelsea Harbour, off Lots Rd SW10. 071-376 3232. Lively, popular diner in the Chelsea Harbour complex decked out in bare wood and brickwork. The menu is American with Thai influences and is divided into 'Raw Deals' – salads, 'Big Deals' – ribs, steaks and burgers, and 'Hot Deals' – Thai curries. *LD open to 23.00.* A.Ax.Dc.V. ££

Dickens Inn   12 C2
St Katharine's Dock, St Katharine's Way E1. 071-488 2208. Originally an 18th-century spice warehouse which has been reconstructed in the style of a 19th-century inn. Impressive redwood beams and pillars, antique furniture and maritime relics. A choice of restaurants – Pizza on the Dock offers pizzas and pasta dishes and has verandah seating; the Pickwick Room has a modern

British menu with an imaginative selection of fresh fish and grills. *LD (Reserve) open to 22.30.* A.Ax.Dc.V. Pizza on the Dock £ Pickwick Grill ££

East of the Sun West of the Moon   **11 D2**
Gabriel's Wharf, Upper Ground SE1. 071-620 0596. Riverside location with fabulous views across the Thames to St Paul's. The interior is light and airy with windows looking out onto the river; there is also outside seating. Cuisine is a combination of east and west with a huge choice of dishes from China, South East Asia and eastern Europe. *LD open to 24.00, to 01.00 Fri & Sat.* A.Ax.Dc.V. ££

Founders Arms   **11 F1**
Bankside SE1. 071-928 1899. Restaurant adjoining a pub built on the site of the iron foundry that cast the bells for St Paul's. Views across the river. Plain, wholesome food; avocado with prawns, pan-fried trout, steak, beef Stroganoff. Busy with City trade *at lunchtime. LD (Reserve) open to 21.15. Closed L Sat & D Sun.* A.Ax.V. ££

RS Hispaniola   **11 B2**
River Thames, Victoria Embankment WC2. 071-839 3011. A floating restaurant on a steamer moored on the Embankment. International food with a French influence. Outdoor seating on the deck. Pianist plays *nightly. LD (Reserve) open to 22.00, to 22.30 Sat. Closed L Sat & LD Sun.* A.Ax.Dc.V. £££

Ken Lo's Memories of China   **13 F4**
Harbour Yard, Chelsea Harbour, off Lots Rd SW10. Stunning views of Chelsea Harbour marina from this bright modern Chinese restaurant. Ken Lo's cooking focuses on regional dishes; Szechuan crispy beef, Cantonese sea bass and crispy king prawn kebab. *LD open to 23.00, to 22.00 Sun.* A.Ax.Dc.V. £££+

London Apprentice
62 Church St, Old Isleworth, Middx. 081-560 1915. A 15th-century Thames-side pub, with fine Elizabethan and Georgian interior, decorated with prints of Hogarth's 'Apprentices'. The first-floor restaurant overlooks the river and provides excellent English fare. *LD open to 22.00, to 22.30 Fri & Sat. Closed L Sat & LD Sun.* A.V. ££

Mayflower   **12 F3**
117 Rotherhithe St SE16. 071-237 4088. A 17th-centu-

ry pub overlooking the river. It was originally called the Shippe, but changed its name when the *Mayflower*, which carried the Pilgrim Fathers from this part of the Thames, reached America. Hot and cold food available from an international menu; Cantonese beef, Cajun sausages, chicken Creole. Thirty different dishes; menu changes monthly. *LD open to 22.00.* A.Ax.Dc.V. £

Ovations 11 D2
Upper Ground, South Bank SE1. 071-928 2033. Restaurant on the first floor of the National Theatre complex. To get a good view of the river, it is necessary to book well in advance. Predominantly English menu; fennel soup, sirloin of beef, venison steaks, lemon sole fillet. Extensive wine list. Changing exhibition of paintings. *LD open to 23.00. Closed Sun.* A.Ax.Dc.V. ££

Le Pont de la Tour 12 C2
36D Shad Thames, Butler's Wharf SE1. 071-403 8403. This restaurant in Sir Terence Conran's converted Thames-side complex has spectacular views of Tower Bridge and the Thames. *In summer*, tables on the terrace provide superb open-air dining. Modern cuisine with Mediterranean influences; marinated mozzarella, roast pepper and aubergine salad, Arbroath smokies with tomato and Gruyère, saffron risotto. Much use is made of the open charcoal grill and seafood is very fresh. Extensive wine list. *LD (Reserve) open to 24.00, to 23.00 Sun. Closed L Sat.* A.Ax.Dc.V. L £££ D £££+

Princes Room 12 C2
Tower Thistle Hotel, St Katharine's Way E1. 071-481 2575. Impressive views over the Thames and Tower Bridge from the windows of this comfortable hotel restaurant and bar. International cuisine with a seasonal menu. Various set menus on offer including a menu à santé – especially designed for the health conscious. Dancing *Fri & Sat to 24.00. LD (Reserve) open to 22.30. Closed L Sat.* A.Ax.Dc.V. £££+

Le Quai 11 F1
1 Broken Wharf, off Upper Thames St EC4. 071-236 6480. Charming, light and airy restaurant between Blackfriars and Southwark bridges. Excellent views of the river through huge windows. Attracts a large business following from the City. The main menu offers creative French cuisine. There is also a modestly-priced brasserie luncheon menu. *LD (Reserve) open to 21.00. Closed Sat & Sun.* A.Ax.Dc.V. L ££ D £££+

Quayside   12 C2
World Trade Centre, St Katharine's Dock E1. 071-481
0972. The World Trader's Luncheon Club is open to
the public as a restaurant for lunch and dinner. Very
smart with excellent food. Lobster, sole, lamb en croûte,
beef, mushroom and Stilton pie, rich desserts. Extensive
wine list. Menu changes every two weeks. *LD (Reserve)
open to 22.00.* A.Ax.Dc.V. £££

Ransome's Dock Restaurant   14 B3
35-37 Parkgate Rd SW11. 071-223 1611. Located within a riverside development in Battersea, this bustling
restaurant offers contemporary British cooking.
Attractive setting; the interior is decorated in
Mediterranean blues and greens, modern jazz music
plays in the background and there is a dockside terrace
for open-air dining *in summer. LD (Reserve) open to
23.00. Closed D Sun.* A.Ax.Dc.V. ££

PS Tattershall Castle   11 B2
Victoria Embankment SW1. 071-839 6548.
Sophisticated buffet and bars on board this paddle-
steamer pub, moored near Cleopatra's Needle. Wide
range of hot and cold dishes available on the daily-
changing menu. Cream teas and coffee from *15.00-
17.00 in summer.* Restored engine room on view. *LD
open to 24.00.* A.Ax.Dc.V. £

OPEN AIR

T HE European habit of eating alfresco can be very
   pleasant on a hot summer's day. More and more
London restaurants are providing outside seating areas,
but they are often just pavement tables and are too many
to list. The restaurants around Covent Garden (**7 B6**),
Charlotte Street (**6 F4**) and Greek Street (**6 G5**) will
whip out pavement tables and chairs at the first glimmer
of sun. Those listed here have access to a garden, courtyard or terrace.

L'Artiste Assoiffé   5 C6
122 Kensington Park Rd W11. 071-727 4714.
Informal, friendly restaurant in a large town house near
Portobello Road. The small patio and garden are ideal
for summer dining. Provincial ·French cuisine; snails
with garlic, deep-fried Camembert, filet Dijon, entrecôte

au poivre. *D open to 23.00, L Sat only. Closed Sun.*
A.Ax.Dc.V. £££

Bleeding Heart Yard Restaurant   **7 D4**
Bleeding Heart Yard, Greville St EC1. 071-242 3238.
The yard features in Dickens' *Little Dorrit* and the
restaurant has a fine collection of the author's first edi-
tions. Outside seating for 30-40 in the yard itself where
you can enjoy French regional cuisine. Beware of the
ghost of murdered Lady Elizabeth Hatton who returns
to scrub clean her bloodstains from the cobbles – hence
the restaurant's name. *LD (Reserve) open to 22.30.
Closed Sat & Sun.* A.Ax.Dc.V. £££

Café La Ville   **5 G3**
453 Edgware Rd W9. 071-706 2620. A relaxed and
friendly café serving all-day breakfasts and club sandwiches. More substantial dishes range from bangers and
mash to spaghetti bolognese. You can sit outside on the
terrace overlooking the canal and watch barges passing
by. *LD open to 18.30.* No credit cards. £

East of the Sun West of the Moon   **11 D2**
Gabriel's Wharf, Upper Ground SE1. 071-620 0596.
Riverside location for this light and airy restaurant
with an international menu. Outside seating provides
fabulous views across the Thames to St Paul's. Cuisine
is a combination of east and west with a huge choice of
dishes from China, South East Asia and eastern Europe;
bangers and mash add a British influence. *LD open to
24.00, to 01.00 Fri & Sat.* A.Ax.Dc.V. ££

La Famiglia   **13 F2**
7 Langton St SW10. 071-351 0761. Warm, friendly
Italian restaurant with seating for 100 under a blue and
white awning in the garden. An emphasis on Tuscan
dishes and 14 different types of pasta. Italian wines. *LD
open to 24.00.* A.Ax.Dc.V. ££

Frederick's   **3 E5**
Camden Passage N1. 071-359 2888. A choice of
surroundings at this elegant French restaurant – the
Conservatory, the airy Garden Room at the back, or
candlelit tables at the front. Classic dishes; veal medal-
lion with crab, duck bourguignon, salmon mousse.
Innovative vegetarian dishes. *LD (Reserve) open to
23.30. Closed Sun.* A.Ax.Dc.V. £££

Glaisters   **13 F2**
4 Hollywood Rd SW10. 071-352 0352. Lively restau-

rant, popular with locals. Pretty stone-walled garden at the back with hanging greenery and a canopy in case the weather turns. Wide-ranging menu from burgers to Dover sole. *LD open to 23.30, to 22.30 Sun.* A.Ax.V. ££

Opera Terrazza! 7 B6

45 East Terrace, The Piazza, Covent Garden WC2. 071-379 0666. Sunny, informal atmosphere at this conservatory-style trattoria. The large outdoor terrace overlooks Covent Garden piazza. New-wave Italian cuisine; fresh pasta dishes, chargrilled chicken and fish. Lively bar with Happy Hour and live music. *LD open to 23.30.* A.Ax.Dc.V. ££

Le Pont de la Tour 12 C2

36D Shad Thames, Butler's Wharf SE1. 071-403 8403. Spectacular views of Tower Bridge and the river from the terrace of Sir Terence Conran's Thames-side restaurant. Modern cuisine with Mediterranean influences; marinated mozzarella, roast pepper and aubergine salad, Arbroath smokies with tomato and Gruyère, saffron risotto. Extensive wine list. *LD (Reserve) open to 24.00, to 23.00 Sun. Closed L Sat.* A.Ax.Dc.V. L £££ D £££+

Pontevecchio 13 E1

256 Old Brompton Rd SW5. 071-373 9082. Comfortable, modern restaurant with tables outside enclosed by box hedges. Brightly-coloured awnings give good protection from the occasional shower. Tuscan cooking; charcoal-grilled lamb, calamari and pollo. Traditional English roast on *Sundays. LD open to 23.30.* A.Ax.Dc.V. ££

San Lorenzo 10 B4

22 Beauchamp Pl SW3. 071-584 1074. Charming, family-run establishment, popular with a fashionable clientele. Dine in either the bright central raised area or at the more intimate surrounding tables. The roof rolls back *in summer* to make an indoor garden. Daily-changing menu of familiar Italian dishes. *LD (Reserve) open to 23.00. Closed Sun.* No credit cards. £££+

I Sardi 14 B2

112 Cheyne Walk SW10. 071-352 7534. Modern and bright Sardinian restaurant with garden seating for 40. The menu is written in Sardinian and includes specialities such as fried Sardinian cheese with spicy tomato sauce, diced lamb with wine and artichokes and Sardinian fish stew. *LD open to 23.45.* A.Ax.V. £££

RESTAURANTS FOR CHILDREN

Most restaurants in London welcome children over eight, and less expensive restaurants are happy to supply children's portions on request. We have recommended those that cater for the younger ones with children's menus or special junior helpings, and those that provide special entertainment for children. Remember that pubs and wine bars are off limits for families with children under 14 unless there is a separate family room.

Biguns Ribs   10 F4
160 Victoria St SW1. 071-630 5733. An American menu offers ribs and burgers. Good value children's menu available for under 10s. *LD open to 23.00, to 00.30 Fri & Sat.* A.V. ££

Blue Elephant   13 D3
4-6 Fulham Broadway SW6. 071-385 6595. Thai restaurant with an excellent *Sunday* brunch buffet, offering all-you-can-eat for adults, and a pricing system for kids where children under four feet tall are measured and charged £2 per foot! Clowns entertain while you eat. *LD open to 00.30, to 22.30 Sun. Closed L Sat.* A.Ax.Dc.V. £££+

Caesar's American Restaurant   11 D3
103-107 Waterloo Rd SE1. 071-928 5707. Offers American-style menu, specially for those under 10, at a very reasonable price. *LD open to 22.30.* A.Ax.Dc.V. £

Chicago Pizza Pie Factory   6 E5
17 Hanover Sq W1. 071-629 2552. Children's menu consists of either burger or pizza, with ice-cream and a soft drink. Comic sketches, face-painting and magic tricks at *13.00* and *15.00 Sun. LD open to 23.45, to 22.30 Sun.* A.Ax.V. £

Deals   13 F4
Chelsea Harbour, Harbour Yard, off Lots Rd SW10. 071-376 3232. Lively, popular diner decked out in hare wood and brickwork. On *Sunday* they have a special family day with magicians and face-painting from *12.00-15.00.* Children's menu with burgers, fish fingers and fries. *LD open to 23.00.* A.Ax.Dc.V. ££

Garfunkel's   6 E5
265 Regent St W1. 071-629 1870. Chain of family
restaurants with branches all round the West End.
American-style food with a separate menu for children.
LD open to 23.30. A.V. ££

Henry J. Bean's Bar & Grill   14 B1
195-197 King's Rd SW3. 071-352 9255. Modelled on a
typical American grill. Special children's menu of burgers, chicken, salad and ice-cream. Huge garden with a
play area. *LD open to 23.00, to 22.00 Sun. A.Ax.V. ££*

Restaurant & Arts Bar   6 D5
Jason Court, 76 Wigmore St W1. 071-224 2992.
Comfortable, spacious basement restaurant offering fine
modern British cuisine. Half-price children's portions
and lunchtime entertainment *12.00-15.00 Sun.* Puppet
shows, music, magicians, story-telling, all in a supervised
play area. *LD (Reserve) open to 23.00. A.Ax.Dc.V. £££*

Rock Island Diner   10 G1
2nd Floor, London Pavilion, Piccadilly Circus W1. 071-
287 5500. Truly American '50s and '60s diner complete
with dancing waitresses and its own radio station,
WRID. Grilled sandwiches, burgers, hot dogs, salads
and chocolate brownies with hot fudge sauce and
ice-cream. Children's menu *until 17.00.* Children
under 10 eat free from *12.00-17.00 Sat & Sun* when
accompanied by an adult who orders a main course.
Competition and prizes, DJs, *12.00-23.00 Sat & Sun.*
LD open to 23.30, to 22.30 Sun. A.Ax.Dc.V. £

Signor Zilli   6 G5
41 Dean St W1. 071-734 3924. Family *Sunday* lunches
of either Italian food or traditional roasts.
Entertainment *13.00-15.00 Sun* can be tableside
magicians, puppets, Punch & Judy shows, kids disco.
LD (Reserve) open to 23.30. A.Ax.Dc.V. ££

Smollensky's Balloon   6 E6
1 Dover St W1. 071-491 1199. Enterprising family
restaurant. Excellent menu with special junior steaks,
hamburgers, chicken nuggets, fish and chips and pasta
dishes. Try the peanut butter cheesecake. Entertainment
on *Sat & Sun afternoons* including a Punch & Judy
show, magicians, clowns, cartoons on TV, kiddies disco,
Nintendo games. Highchairs and booster seats available.
LD open to 24.00, to 22.30 Sun. A.Ax.Dc.V. ££

TGI Friday's   7 B6
6 Bedford St WC2. 071-379 0585. Part of a large

American family restaurant chain. Loud and lively and
always busy. Burgers, steaks, pasta, south-western and
Cajun specialities. Special children's menu includes
potato skins, hamburgers, hot dogs and pizza bites.
High chairs and booster seats available. *LD (no reservations) open to 23.30, to 23.00 Sun.* A.Ax.V. ££

Tootsies

115 Notting Hill Gate W11. 071-727 6562.	**9 D2**
120 Holland Park Ave W11. 071-229 8567.	**9 B2**
140 Fulham Rd SW10. 071-370 2794.	**13 F2**
177 New King's Rd SW6. 071-736 4023.	**13 F3**
148 Chiswick High Rd W4. 081-747 1865.	
216 Haverstock Hill NW3. 071-433 3896.	**2 B2**
48 High St SW19. 081-946 4135.	

Small chain of cheerful American restaurants serving
steaks, burgers, sandwiches and vegetarian dishes.
Special children's menu is cheap and healthy. Booster
seats available. *LD open to 24.00, to 23.00 Sun.* A.V. £

Uncle Ian's Deli Diner

8-10 Monkville Parade NW11. 081-458 3493. Lively
atmosphere at this busy diner serving deli-style sandwiches plus traditional European dishes. Extremely popular for family lunches. Excellent children's menu and
free lollipops. There are no reservations so expect to
queue. Unlicensed. *LD (no reservations) open to 23.30,
to 16.00 Fri.* A.V. £

UNUSUAL

IF you're looking for somewhere unusual to enjoy good
food, the following are restaurants with something
out of the ordinary to offer.

Bateaux London   7 C6

Departs from Temple Pier, Victoria Embankment WC2.
071-925 2215. The restaurant cruiser *Symphony* com-
bines fine dining in a luxurious setting with magnificent
views of London from the river as you sail past some of
London's most famous landmarks. All food is freshly
prepared on board by the ship's own chef and the international menu includes dishes such as fillet of beef with
oyster sauce and wild mushroom and asparagus
tagliatelli. Music and dancing on dinner cruises. *LD
(Reservations essential).* Lunch cruises depart *12.45,*
dinner cruises *20.00.* A.Ax.Dc.V. L £££ D £££+

Blades 16 A1
94 Lower Richmond Rd SW15. 081-789 0869. Cook your own meat on the huge grill at the front of this barbecue restaurant. Choose from steak, burgers, kebabs or fish. Also pasta and vegetarian dishes. Delicious desserts. *D open to 23.00.* A.Ax.Dc.V. ££

Caspers
6 Tenterden St W1. 071-493 7923. 6 E5
2 St Anne's Court, off Dean St W1.071-494 4941. 6 G5
Restaurant and bar with a table-to-table telephone network, so you can make contact with fellow diners without revealing your identity. The menu is varied; burgers, grilled chicken, nachos, pasta dishes, salads. Exotic cocktails. *LD open to 23.00, to 02.00 Thur-Sat. Closed L Sat & LD Sun.* A.Ax.V. ££

Chapter House 11 G2
Southwark Cathedral, Montague Close SE1. 071-378 6446. Attached to the grand cathedral, it looks like a small, Gothic church from the outside, but inside has high ceilings, stone flooring and pine furniture. Garlic bread, doughballs, a variety of interesting pizzas. Good choice for vegetarians on the menu. *L open to 16.00.* A.Ax.Dc.V. £

Le Gothique 17 A4
Royal Victoria Patriotic Building, Fitzhugh Grove, Trinity Rd SW18. 081-870 6567. Housed in a building with a chequered history. Originally an orphanage, it was then used by MI5 and MI6 as an interrogation centre – the prison cells are below the restaurant. Excellent French cuisine, with gourmet weeks held *every month* when more unusual and elaborate dishes are created. Good value set menus. Excellent and lengthy wine list. Walled garden for open-air dining. *LD open to 22.30. Closed Sun.* A.Ax.Dc.V. ££

The Jam 13 G2
289a King's Rd SW3. 071-352 8827. Friendly, relaxed restaurant with an unusual seating arrangement. The restaurant is built on different levels of scaffolding which you have to climb to get to your table. You also choose how bright or dim you want the lighting, and how loud you want the music. International menu. *D open to 24.00.* A.Ax.Dc.V. ££

Just Around the Corner
446 Finchley Rd NW2. 071-431 3300. A popular restaurant where you pay for your meal what you think

it was worth! Extensive menu; mainly French cuisine. *D
open to 24.00, to 23.00 Sun.* A.Ax.Dc.V. £?

Mongolian Barbeque   **16 B3**
147 Upper Richmond Rd SW15. 081-780 9252. Lively
restaurant where you help yourself to pieces of meat
(turkey, chicken, lamb, pork, beef and fish). Add raw
vegetables and your choice of sauces and the chef will
barbecue it in front of you. *D open to 24.00.* A.Ax.V. ££

Le Raj Avion
Le Raj Restaurant, 211 Firtree Rd, Epsom Downs,
Surrey. (0737) 371371. You meet at Le Raj Restaurant,
board a coach which takes you to the airport for a
mystery flight, and once airborne, lunch is served! Set
Indian meal with champagne. *Phone Le Raj Restaurant
for details of departures and prices.* A.Ax.Dc.V.

Suki-Yaki Joe's   **6 F6**
15-16 Kingly St W1. 071-287 1221. Lively Japanese
karaoke restaurant. The karaoke machine is turned on
at *21.00* and you can dine on authentic Japanese cuisine
throughout the evening. Chicken teriyaki, tonkatsu,
vegetable tempura, yakitori. Japanese beers. *LD
(Reserve D) open to 01.00. Closed Sun.* A.Ax.Dc.V. ££

Terrazza Est   **7 D5**
109 Fleet St EC4. 071-353 2680. A large, lively basement
restaurant known as the Spaghetti Opera because of the
opera singers from the Royal Opera House and the
English National Opera who perform while you dine.
Italian cuisine with set and à la carte menus. *D (Reserve D
Fri) open to 23.00. Closed Sat & Sun.* A.Ax.Dc.V. £££+

INEXPENSIVE

There are plenty of places in London where you can
eat without spending a small fortune. Many of the
more inexpensive restaurants are traditional cafés, often
run by Italians, who serve huge portions of hearty food
at low prices. Many budget restaurants offer set-price
meals and you can often take your own wine or beer to
keep costs down. We have not included station buffets
or 'fast food' chains as these can be found on most high
streets. At all of the restaurants listed below you can eat
a **three-course meal for under £10.**

Also look out for the single £ symbol in other
sections, especially under *Chinese, Indian* and *Italian.*

Alpino   6 D4

42 Marylebone High St W1. 071-935 4640. Pleasant atmosphere in this alpine-style Italian restaurant. Busy and crowded at all times. Service is quick and efficient. Generous portions of pasta, fish and chicken dishes. *LD open to 23.00. Closed Sun.* A.Ax.Dc.V.

Barocco   7 A5

13 Moor St, off Charing Cross Rd W1. 071-437 2324. Café serving mainly Italian dishes, but some British choices too. Tagliatelle al pesto (basil and garlic sauce), steaks, omelettes, veal, home-made gnocchi (dumplings with tomato and mushroom sauce). Dish of the day and excellent trifle for dessert. Unlicensed, but you can bring your own wine. *LD open to 22.45. Closed Sun.* No credit cards.

Bedlington Café

24 Fauconberg Rd W4. 081-994 1965. This café serves traditional fry-ups at lunchtime and is transformed into a Thai restaurant serving eastern stir-fries and curries in the evening. Relaxed atmosphere and charming service. Unlicensed, but you can bring your own wine or beer. *LD (Reserve) open to 22.00.* No credit cards or cheques.

Boggi's   7 D3

34 Topham St, off Farringdon Rd EC1. 071-837 8392. Light and airy restaurant upstairs and a sandwich bar downstairs. Offers a daily variety of specials; home-made minestrone, various pasta dishes, scampi, apple pie. *L open to 15.00. Closed Sat & Sun.* No credit cards.

Café in the Crypt   11 B1

Crypt of St Martin-in-the-Fields, Duncannon St WC2. 071-839 4342. Friendly restaurant in the large vaulted crypt of St Martin-in-the-Fields. Serves wholesome food to tourists and office workers. Beef bake, spinach and cheese pancakes, sweet and sour pork. *LD open to 20.30, to 15.30 Sun.* A.V.

Chelsea Kitchen   10 C6

98 King's Rd SW3. 071-589 1330. Part of the Stockpot group (see below), this popular restaurant offers healthy portions of home cooking at reasonable prices. Chicken chasseur, veal scaloppine or beef goulash, followed by sponge puddings, strawberry and apple pie or chocolate cheesecake. *LD open to 23.45.* No credit cards.

Chutneys   6 F2

124 Drummond St NW1. 071-388 0604. Very good

Indian vegetarian food is served in this bright restaurant behind Euston Station. *At lunchtimes* an 'eat as much as you like' buffet is available. Dinner is à la carte and more relaxed. A speciality is the deluxe thali comprising dhal soup, papadam, bhajis, four curries, pilau rice, raita, pickles, pooris and a dessert. Wine, beer, lassi or herbal teas. *LD (Reserve) open to 23.30.* A.V.

Diana's Diner   7 B5
39 Endell St WC2. 071-240 0272. Good, traditional British and Italian cuisine in a friendly restaurant, convenient for theatreland. Grills, roasts, pasta dishes and risottos. Unlicensed. *LD open to 20.30, to 17.00 Sun.* No credit cards.

Diwana Bhel Poori House   6 F2
121-123 Drummond St NW1. 071-387 5556. Great value Indian vegetarian restaurant. Try the thali, a set meal which includes a variety of delicacies. Unlicensed. Also at 50 Westbourne Grove W2 (**5 D5**). 071-221 0721. *LD open to 23.30.* A.Ax.Dc.V.

Gaby's Continental Bar   7 A5
30 Charing Cross Rd WC2. 071-836 4233. Busy Middle Eastern café serving salt beef, pastrami, houmous and baklava in generous portions. *LD open to 24.00, to 22.00 Sun.* No credit cards.

The Granary   6 F6
39 Albemarle St W1. 071-493 2978. Self-service restaurant on two levels with a fresh and lively atmosphere. Daily dishes may include lamb and mint casserole, moussaka, hot avocado pear with spinach, salad Niçoise, coronation chicken, ratatouille, some vegetarian quiches and various salads. Extensive range of desserts. Wine, lagers and fresh fruit juices. *LD open to 20.00, to 17.00 Sat & Sun.* No credit cards.

Jimmy's   6 G5
23 Frith St W1. 071-437 9521. Huge helpings of Cypriot food at very reasonable prices. Specialities include beef stew, moussaka, lamb tava, afelia or pastuchi. To follow, baklava or kateifi – very popular, sticky sweets. *LD open to 23.00. Closed Sun.* No credit cards.

Khan's   5 E5
13-15 Westbourne Grove W2. 071-727 5420. Cheap and cheerful, always busy with hurried, erratic service. The vast dining hall, with its oriental arches and palm tree pillars, was formerly a Lyons tea house. North

Indian cuisine; specialities include kofti dilruba (spiced curried meatballs) and mattar panir (white cheese with peas and herbs). No reservations, so expect to queue. *LD open to 24.00.* A.Ax.Dc.V.

Mustoe Bistro 2 C4
73 Regent's Park Rd NW1. 071-586 0901. Small, intimate bistro which has long been popular with the residents of Primrose Hill. For starters, aubergine and yoghurt, eggs Madras. Garlic or pepper steak to follow. Vegetarian dishes available. Good dessert trolley. Open for lunch on *Sun* only. *D (Reserve) open to 23.15, to 22.45 Sun.* No credit cards.

New Piccadilly 6 G6
8 Denman St, off Shaftesbury Ave W1. 071-437 2562. Nothing much has changed since this place opened in the '50s. Pasta dishes, chicken, steak and fry-ups are excellent value. Unlicensed, but you can bring your own wine. *LD open to 22.00.* No credit cards.

Pasta Fino 6 G5
27 Frith St W1. 071-439 8900. Below a shop selling fresh pasta and Italian foods is this small bright restaurant serving excellent dishes using only the freshest ingredients. Agliata (vegetables with a garlic dip) to start, five types of freshly made pasta to follow. Friendly, helpful service. *LD open to 23.30, to 24.00 Thur-Sat. Closed Sun.* A.Ax.V.

Perdoni's 11 D4
18-20 Kennington Rd SE1. 071-928 6846. Big, bustling restaurant serving Italian and English food. Basic decor – formica tables and tiled floor. Pasta, veal and beef dishes. Fresh fruit salad, crumble, apple dumplings to follow. *LD open to 19.00, to 12.00 Sat. Closed D Sat & LD Sun.* No credit cards.

Pho 6 G6
2 Lisle St WC2. 071-437 8265. Enjoy huge portions of Vietnamese food at this popular café. The decor is very basic and you just sit where you can find space at one of the round tables. Try the Vietnamese soup (pho) which contains noodles and slices of raw beef and comes with a plate of coriander, mint and onions. *LD open to 23.30.* No credit cards.

Pollo 6 G5
20 Old Compton St W1. 071-734 5917. Very busy ground floor and basement restaurant which is immensely popular so expect to queue. Huge varied

menu; pasta dishes, omelettes, fish, chicken and steaks. *LD open to 23.30. Closed Sun.* No credit cards.

Stockpot
6 Basil St SW1. 071-589 8627.   **10 C3**
LD open to 23.00, to 22.30 Sun.
40 Panton St, off Haymarket SW1. 071-839 5142.   **6 G5**
LD open to 23.30, to 22.00 Sun.
Informal, noisy restaurants with large communal pine tables and benches. Home-made soups, casseroles, pasta dishes and desserts. No credit cards.

The Three Lanterns   6 G5
5 Panton St, off Haymarket SW1. 071-839 5031. Always busy with tourists and theatre-goers. Daily-changing menu, but favourites like roast beef and Yorkshire pudding, mixed grills, moussaka and spaghetti bolognese are normally included. *LD open to 23.00, to 20.30 Sun.* No credit cards.

Tootsies
115 Notting Hill Gate W11. 071-727 6562.   **9 D2**
120 Holland Park Ave W11. 071-229 8567.   **9 B2**
140 Fulham Rd SW10. 071-370 2794.   **13 F2**
177 New King's Rd SW6. 071-736 4023.   **13 F3**
148 Chiswick High Rd W4. 081-747 1865.
216 Haverstock Hill NW3. 071-433 3896.   **2 B2**
48 High St SW19. 081-946 4135.
An American chain of attractive bistros serving steaks, burgers, sandwiches and vegetarian dishes. The atmosphere is casual and cheerful, the clientele mostly young. Children's portions. *LD open to 24.00, to 23.30 Sun.* A.V.

Wagamama   7 B4
4 Streatham St, off Bloomsbury St WC1. 071-323 9223. Immensely popular Japanese noodle bar. Huge bowls of ramen noodle soup, noodles with vegetable or seafood toppings, grilled dumplings, rice dishes and curries. All served by super-efficient waiters and waitresses wielding hand-held computer pads. No smoking. Expect to queue. *LD open to 23.00.* No credit cards.

Wong Kei   6 G6
41-43 Wardour St W1. 071-437 6833. Large, cheap and cheerful Cantonese caff on four floors. Always busy, so expect to share a table. Excellent Singapore noodles and huge servings of wun tun soup. Free pots of Chinese tea. The waiting staff are notoriously rude. *LD open to 23.30.* No credit cards or cheques.

OUT OF TOWN

THE following is a selection of restaurants within an easy drive of central London. Many are in or near historic towns or are set in picturesque countryside.

Bell Inn
Aston Clinton, nr Aylesbury, Bucks. (0296) 630252. Charming old inn with a dining room facing onto the garden. Leather seating, murals, an aura of polished comfort. High quality, imaginative French food. Game and fish are specialities. Superb wine list. Bistro menu in the smoking room and bar at *lunchtimes. LD (Reserve) open to 21.45.* A.Ax.V. £££

Boote House
Felsted, nr Great Dunmow, Essex. (0371) 820279. Elizabethan house built in 1596 by George Boote, a master builder. Now a cosy, informal family restaurant. Old-fashioned and luxurious, with exposed beams and velvet curtains. International menu; specialities are Chinese dishes. *Sunday buffet. LD (Reserve) open to 21.30, to 22.30 Sat & Sun.* £ £

Duck Inn
Pett Bottom, Canterbury, Kent. (0227) 830354. Rustic 17th-century inn. Dining room with candlelit tables. Menu changes monthly and may include scampi with pernod and fennel sauce, genuine Aberdeen Angus steaks. Greene King Abbot's ale and a distinguished wine list. *LD (Reserve) open to 21.30. Closed D Mon (bar meals available).* A.Ax.V. £ £

Elizabeth
82 St Aldates, Oxford, Oxon. (0865) 242230. 15th-century restaurant of studied distinction. Delightful panelled dining room. Interesting menu; smoked fish pâté, carré d'agneau, salmon, mussels in garlic butter, wild duck, entrecôte au poivre. Sorbet au champagne to follow. Noteworthy claret on a superior wine list. *LD (Reserve) open to 23.00, to 22.30 Sun. Closed Mon.* A.Ax.Dc.V. £££

Gravetye Manor
East Grinstead, West Sussex. (0342) 810567. Attractive Elizabethan manor house with fine gardens. Eat in the great dining room with its panels and open fire. Waiters in livery. Mostly modern European cuisine. Exceptional wine list. No smoking. *LD (Reserve) open to 21.30, to 20.30 Sun.* No credit cards. £££

Honours Mill
High St, Edenbridge, Kent. (0732) 866757. An old mill converted into a handsome restaurant with a balcony overlooking the mill pond. Predominantly French menu offers fine dishes such as ragoût d'escargots à la forestière, poulet en soupière aux ecrevisses et homard, grillade de gigot d'agneau. *LD (Reserve) open to 22.00. Closed LD Mon, L Sat & D Sun.* A.V. £££+

King's Lodge
Bridge Road, Hunton Bridge, nr Watford, King's Langley, Herts. (0923) 263506. Reservations: (0923) 268915. A delightful old hunting lodge given to Charles I in 1642. The interior is beamed and the refurbished lodge covered in original Charles I crests. Smart dining room with an informal atmosphere. International menu includes some French and Italian dishes. The lodge is also an hotel. *LD open to 22.30. Closed D Sun.* A.Ax.Dc.V. ££

Lamb Inn
Sheep St, Burford, Oxon. (0993) 823155. Comfortable, airy restaurant in a 15th-century inn built of Cotswold stone. Antiques, candles, flowers and a view of the garden make this a charming place to dine. Menu changes daily, but dishes always have a strong English flavour. Also has guest rooms. *LD open to 21.00.* A.V. ££

Lythe Hill Hotel, L'Auberge de France
Petworth Road, Haslemere, Surrey. (0428) 651251. Manor house with a splendid view over gardens and a lake. 14th-century dining room in which to enjoy French and international dishes. Specialities include salmon in pastry, carré d'agneau, roti au pot de fines herbes. *Sunday lunches. D (Reserve) open to 21.45. Closed Mon.* A.V. £££

Le Manoir aux Quat' Saisons
Church Rd, Great Milton, Oxon. (0844) 278881. Situated in a 15th-century manor house, this award-winning restaurant offers a distinctive menu. Tartar de saumon sauvage à la croque de concombres (marinated wild salmon bound with sour cream and caviar), Norfolk baby pigeon in salt crust. Vegetarian dishes on request. Extensive gardens. Set lunch menu. *LD (Reserve) open to 22.30.* £££+

L'Ortolan
The Old Vicarage, Church Lane, Shinfield, Berks. (0734) 883783. Pleasing dining room in this lovely converted vicarage. It has a well-earned reputation for producing complex, innovative English cooking with strong French overtones. Long and interesting wine list.

Set menus available. *LD (Reserve) open to 22.15. Closed D Sun & LD Mon.* A.Ax.Dc.V. £££+

Sopwell House Hotel Restaurant
Cotton Mill Lane, St Albans, Herts. (0727) 864477. Within easy reach of London, a grand Georgian house set in eleven acres of land. The elegant dining room overlooks a delightful garden. A predominantly French menu prepared from good fresh ingredients by hotel chefs. Menu changes regularly. Comprehensive wine list. *LD (Reserve) open to 22.00. Closed L Sat & D Sun.* A.Ax.Dc.V. ££

Sundial
Herstmonceaux, nr Hailsham, Sussex. (0323) 832217. A pretty, 16th-century cottage on the Sussex Downs offering Italian and French dishes. Fish, including lobster, comes from Dieppe. Outstanding set lunch. Fine clarets. *LD (Reserve) open to 22.00. Closed D Sun & LD Mon. Also closed in Jan & for the last 3 weeks in Aug.* A.Ax.Dc.V. L ££ D £££

The Thatchers
29 Lower High St, Thame, Oxon. (084421) 2146. Picturesque Elizabethan thatched hotel with a small, attractive restaurant. Traditional English lunch or French nouvelle cuisine. Menu changes frequently but may include the delicious cream of mussel soup garnished with poached snow eggs. *LD (Reserve D) open to 22.00. Closed L Sat & LD Sun.* A.V. £££

Waterside Inn
Ferry Rd, Bray-on-Thames, Berks. (0628) 20691. One of the most beautiful settings for some of the best French food outside London. French windows look out from the dining room on to the water and the willows. Faultless cuisine. Filet de lapereau grillé aux marrons, followed by tarte au citron. Some fine French wines. *LD (Reserve) open to 22.00. Closed LD Mon, L Tue (& D Sun in winter).* A.Dc.V. £££+

Wife of Bath
4 Upper Bridge St, Wye, Kent. (0233) 812540. Large period house provides civilised and comfortable dining. Imaginative cooking using first-class ingredients. Menu changes regularly and may include scallop chowder, tartlet with chicken and leeks, roasted Kent duck, loin of English lamb, paupiette of salmon, chocolate truffle cake, brown bread ice-cream. *LD (Reserve) open to 22.30. Closed Sun.* A.V. £££

BREAKFAST & BRUNCH

HOT bread and pastries can be obtained as early as 06.00 from bakeries. Continental-style cafés, brasseries and pâtisseries serve fresh croissants and coffee, plus more substantial brunches. For a traditional English breakfast splash out at one of the traditional hotels listed below.

Times in this section are given for breakfast only. Price symbols *for this section only* are:
£ – under £5; ££ – £5-£10; £££ – over £10.

CAFES, BRASSERIES & PATISSERIES

Bar Italia   6 G5
22 Frith St W1. 071-437 4520. Italian café serving croissants, pain au chocolat, fresh coffee. *Opens 07.00.* No credit cards. £

Bartholomew's   7 E4
57a West Smithfield EC1. 071-606 3903. Traditional English. *Open 07.00-11.00. Closed Sat & Sun.* A.Ax.Dc.V. £

La Brasserie   10 B5
272 Brompton Rd SW3. 071-584 1668. French-style café serving continental breakfast. *Opens 08.00.* A.Ax.Dc.V. £££

Canadian Muffin Co   7 A6
The Trocadero, 13 Coventry St W1. 071-287 3555. Healthy and delicious muffins, café au lait, almond milk. *Opens 08.00 (09.00 Sat, 10.00 Sun).* No credit cards. £

Fleur de Lys   9 F5
13a Gloucester Rd SW7. 071-589 4045. Pâtisserie where everything is baked fresh on the premises. *Opens 08.00. Closed Sun.* No credit cards. £

Fortnum & Mason   10 F1
181 Piccadilly W1. 071-734 8040. Elegant continental
or English breakfast in The Patio or The Soda Fountain.
*Opens 07.30 (The Soda Fountain), 09.30 (The Patio).
Closed Sun.* A.Ax.Dc.V. ££ (continental) £££ (English)

Gambarti   7 C3
38 Lamb's Conduit St WC1. 071-405 7950. English
and continental breakfasts. Fresh, Italian coffee. *Opens
07.00. Closed Sat & Sun.* No credit cards. £

Gate Diner   9 C1
184a Kensington Park Rd W11. 071-221 2649. American-
style restaurant serving continental breakfast and brunch.
Open 11.30-24.00 (Reserve Sun brunch). A.V. ££

Harry's   6 F6
19 Kingly St W1. 071-734 3140. All-night café serving
cooked breakfasts and snacks. *Open 22.00-09.00 Mon-
Fri, 22.00-06.00 Sat. Closed Sun.* A.V. ££

The Hermitage   7 B2
19 Leigh St WC1. 071-387 8034. Friendly, stylish café.
Traditional English breakfast or specials such as
smoked salmon and scrambled egg. Newspapers provided. *Opens 10.00 Sun only.* A.Ax.V. ££

Maison Bertaux   6 G5
28 Greek St W1. 071-437 6007. Croissants and pastries
all day. *Opens 09.00.* No credit cards. £

Maison Bouquillon   5 E6
41 Moscow Rd W2. 071-229 2107. Very French patis-
serie serving delicious croissants and marvellous coffee.
Opens 08.30. No credit cards. £

Pasticceria Cappucetto   6 G5
8-9 Moor St, off Charing Cross Rd W1. 071-437 9472.
Continental pâtisserie. *Opens 07.30 (08.30 Sun).* No
credit cards. £

Pâtisserie Valerie   6 G5
44 Old Compton St W1. 071-437 3466. Fresh
croissants and continental pâtisseries. *Opens 08.00
(10.00 Sun).* No credit cards. £

Quality Chop House   7 D3
94 Farringdon Rd EC1. 071-837 5093. *Sunday brunch.
Open 12.00-16.00.* No credit cards. £££

Le Tire Bouchon   6 F6
6 Upper James St, off Beak St W1. 071-437 5348.
Continental breakfast. *Open 08.30-21.15.* A.Ax.Dc.V. ££

WKD Café   2 E4
18 Kentish Town Rd NW1. 071-267 1869. Breakfast club;
English or continental breakfast to the accompaniment of
live jazz. *Opens midday Sat & Sun only.* A.Ax.V. ££

HOTELS

Basil Street Hotel   10 C4
Basil St SW3. 071-581 3311. English or continental. *Open 09.30-10.15.* A.Ax.Dc.V. ££ (continental) £££ (English)

Blakes Hotel   13 F1
33 Roland Gdns SW7. 071-370 6701. Elaborate breakfast menu. *Open 07.30-10.30.* A.Ax.Dc.V. £££

Brown's Hotel   6 E6
Dover St W1. 071-493 6020. English or continental. *Open 07.15-10.00 (08.00-10.00 Sun).* A.Ax.Dc.V. £££

Cadogan Hotel   10 C4
75 Sloane St SW1. 071-235 7141. English or continental. *Open 07.30-10.00.* A.Ax.Dc.V. £££

Claridge's   6 E6
Brook St W1. 071-629 8860. English, à la carte, continental or health breakfast. *Open 07.30-10.30.* A.Ax.Dc.V. £££

Hyde Park Hotel, Park Room   10 C3
66 Knightsbridge SW1. 071-235 2000. English, à la carte or continental. *Open 07.00-10.30, (08.00-11.00 Sun & B.hols).* A.Ax.Dc.V. £££

Portman Hotel   6 D5
22 Portman Sq W1. 071-486 5844. English buffet, à la carte or continental. *Open 07.00-11.00.* A.Ax.Dc.V. £££

Ritz   10 F2
Piccadilly W1. 071-493 8181. English or continental. *Open 07.00-10.00 (08.00-10.30 Sat & Sun).* A.Ax.Dc.V. £££

The Savoy   7 C6
Strand WC2. 071-836 4343. English, continental or fitness breakfast. *Open 07.00-10.30 (08.00-10.30 Sun).* A.Ax.Dc.V. £££

Tower Thistle Hotel   12 C2
St Katharine's Way E1. 071-481 2575. English or continental breakfasts. The Carvery *open 06.30-09.30.* ££. Which Way West *open 07.00-11.00.* ££. A.Ax.Dc.V.

PUBS

Albert   10 F4
52 Victoria St SW1. 071-222 5577. English breakfast cooked to order. *Open 08.00-10.30. Closed Sat & Sun.* A.Ax.Dc.V. ££

Fox & Anchor   7 E4
Charterhouse St EC1. 071-253 4838. English breakfast. *Open 07.00-10.30.* A.V. ££

Gloucester   10 C4
187 Sloane St SW1. 071-235 0298. Continental or English breakfast. *Open 08.00-11.30. No breakfast Sun.* A.Ax.Dc.V. ££

AFTERNOON TEA

AFTERNOON tea is a British institution, at one time very fashionable. Most large department stores serve afternoon tea in their restaurants, and there are many pâtisseries and tea shops in London which offer tea and cakes. However, if you want to sample afternoon tea in traditional style, go to one of the hotels listed below. Prices can vary but you should not normally expect to pay more than £14.00 for a full tea.

TEA & CAKES

Maison Sagne   **6 D4**
105 Marylebone High St W1. 071-935 6240. Traditional tea shop with its own bakery and delicious pâtisserie. *Open to 17.00, to 12.30 Sat. Closed Sun.*

The Muffin Man   **9 E4**
12 Wright's Lane W8. 071-937 6652. A range of set teas: Devon, 'Muffin Man', traditional. *Open to 17.45, to 17.30 Sat. Closed Sun.*

Pâtisserie Valerie   **6 G5**
44 Old Compton St W1. 071-437 3466. Soho pâtisserie serving excellent cream cakes and sandwiches. *Open to 20.00, to 19.00 Sat, to 17.30 Sun.*

TEA IN HOTELS

Brown's Hotel   **6 E6**
Dover St W1. 071-493 6020. Elegant country house setting for sandwiches and cakes. *15.00-18.00.*

Claridge's   **6 E6**
Brook St W1. 071-629 8860. Sandwiches, assorted pastries and home-made scones in sumptuous surroundings. *15.00-17.30.*

Dorchester   **10 D2**
Park Lane W1. 071-629 8888. Elegant surroundings in
which to enjoy sandwiches, cakes, scones and Viennese
pastries. Tea from 12 different nations. *15.00-18.00.*

Ritz   **10 F2**
Piccadilly W1. 071-493 8181. Beautiful setting for tea
in the Palm Court; sandwiches, pastries and cream
cakes. *(Reserve).* Tea served at *15.00 & 16.30.*

DEPARTMENT STORES

Fortnum & Mason   **10 F1**
181 Piccadilly W1. 071-734 8040. Afternoon tea is
available at three locations in the store *Mon-Sat.* St
James's Restaurant serves a set tea of sandwiches,
scones, cakes, tea or coffee to a piano accompaniment
15.00-17.30. The Patio Bar and Soda Fountain offer an
à la carte tea menu *14.30-17.30.*

Harrods Georgian Restaurant   **10 C4**
Knightsbridge SW1. 071-730 1234. Sandwiches, scones,
cakes and pastries served from *15.30 Mon-Sat.* Tea also
served on the Terrace from *15.00 Mon-Sat.*

THE DANSANT

Waldorf Hotel   **7 C6**
Aldwych WC2. 071-836 2400. Opulent Palm Court tea
lounge. Enjoy Edwardian elegance, dancing to the band
and full set tea *15.30-18.30 Sat & Sun. (Reserve).*

ICE-CREAM

THERE are many ice-cream parlours in London where
you can choose between American-style ice-cream in
an abundance of flavours, and traditional, creamy
Italian ices and sorbets.

Baskin-Robbins
Empire Cinema, Leicester Sq WC2. 071-734 8222. **6 G6**
Plaza Cinema, Lower Regent St W1. 071-930   **10 G1**
0144.
Delicious American ice-cream in 31 flavours. *Open
11.00-23.00.*

Criterion Ices
118 Sydenham Rd SE26. 081-778 7945. Old-fashioned
gelateria serving a large range of ices, sorbets and
sundaes. *Open 10.30-17.30, to 18.00 Sun.*

Dayvilles
264a Earl's Court Rd SW5. 071-370 0083.   **9 D5**
Open 09.00-23.00.
2 The Mall W5. 081-567 3778.
Open 11.00-24.00, to 01.00 Fri.
More than 30 flavours of delicious ice-cream.

The Fountain   **10 F1**
Fortnum & Mason, 181 Piccadilly W1. 071-734 8040.
Ice-creams, sorbets, sundaes and knickerbocker glories.
Open 08.30-23.00. Closed Sun.

Häagen-Dazs
75 Hampstead High St NW3. 071-794 0646.   **1 F1**
Open 10.00-23.00.
138a King's Rd SW3. 071-823 9326.   **10 C6**
Open 10.00-23.00.
The Piazza, Covent Garden WC2. 071-240 0436.   **7 B6**
Open 10.00-23.00.
Leicester Sq WC2. 071-287 9577.   **6 G6**
Open 10.00-24.00.
Delicous ice-cream with a huge choice of flavours;
chunky peanut crunch, raspberries and cream, peach
yoghurt. Also Belgian chocolate waffle cones, sundaes,
milk-shakes and hot and cold drinks.

Marine Ices   **2 C3**
8 Haverstock Hill NW3. 071-485 3132. Ice-cream par-
lour run by the same Italian family for over 60 years.
Italian ice-cream and water ices. *Open 10.30-23.00, to
19.00 Sun.*

BRASSERIES & CAFES

CONTINENTAL-STYLE brasseries and cafés are a welcome addition to pubs and bars in London. They
offer informal, stylish surroundings where you will find
good food (from breakfasts to three-course meals) and
alcoholic drinks (which you can consume without having to eat). Most have taken advantage of the relaxed
licensing laws which allow them to stay open all day.
The following is a selection of brasseries and cafés offering value for money and a pleasant atmosphere.

La Brasserie   **10 B5**
272 Brompton Rd SW3. 071-584 1668. Probably one of
the closest things to a real French brasserie in London.

Conventional menu; dishes of the day, omelettes, blanquette de veau, avocados stuffed with smoked salmon and celery, all competently prepared. Open for breakfast and throughout the day for coffee and pâtisseries – newspapers provided. *BLD open to 24.00.* A.Ax.Dc.V.

Brasserie du Coin   7 C3
54 Lamb's Conduit St WC1. 071-405 1717. Typical French brasserie with wooden floors and candlelit tables. You can get quick meals such as fresh filled baguettes at the counter or more leisurely classic French dishes such as moules marinières and boeuf bourguignon. *LD (Reserve L) open to 22.00, to 23.00 Sat. Closed Sun.* A.Ax.Dc.V.

Brasserie Lott   10 C4
27-31 Basil St SW3. 071-584 4484. Just behind Harrods, this attractive brasserie has a modern menu which changes monthly and a café next door serving breakfasts, light snacks, pasta dishes and steak sandwiches. *BLD open to 22.30. Closed D Sun, D Mon & D Tue.* A.V.

Brasserie du Marché aux Puces   5 B4
349 Portobello Rd W10. 081-968 5828. Trendy and minimalist, this brasserie is pleasantly light and airy due to its street-corner position. Very busy on a *Saturday* with custom from the nearby Portobello Market. International menu changes daily. Full meals, snacks and pastries available all day. *Sunday* brunch. *LD open to 23.00, to 16.00 Sun.* No credit cards.

Brasserie Rocque   8 B4
37 Broadgate Circle EC2. 071-638 7919. Smart, modern brasserie overlooking the Broadgate development. Very busy at lunchtimes with City office workers. Modern French food; lobster broth, spinach salad, tagliatelle with wild mushrooms. *LD open to 22.00. Closed Sat & Sun.* A.Ax.Dc.V.

Brompton Brasserie   13 F2
224 Fulham Rd SW10. 071-351 3956. Relaxed, friendly atmosphere and a varied menu. Anything from the special Brompton Blini (smoked salmon, sour cream and Danish caviar on a toasted muffin) to traditional bangers and mash. Also afternoon teas and Sunday brunch. *LD open to 24.00, to 23.00 Sun.* A.V.

Café des Amis du Vin   7 B5
11-14 Hanover Pl, off Long Acre WC2. 071-379 3444. This extremely popular brasserie is sandwiched between

a wine bar in the basement and the elegant Salon des Amis du Vin restaurant upstairs. The walls are adorned with photographs from the nearby Opera House. Several types of French sausage are on the reasonably priced menu. Award-winning cheeseboard. Good range of French, German, Spanish and Californian wines. *LD (Reserve) open to 23.00. Closed Sun.* A.Ax.V.Dc.

Café Bohème   6 G5
13 Old Compton St W1. 071-734 0623. Pleasantly chaotic French-style brasserie in the heart of Soho . You can have a cappuccino, a beer, snacks such as croque monsieur and omelettes, or a full meal. *BLD open to 02.45, to 23.00 Sun.* A.Ax.V.

Café Casbar   7 B5
52 Earlham St WC2. 071-379 7768. Modern, attractive café enlivened by an evening club which runs monthly exhibitions of art for viewing and sale, games nights and poetry readings. The food is café-style with an accent on healthy eating. Breakfasts, salads, sandwiches, baked potatoes, pasta dishes, hot daily specials. *BLD open to 22.00.* No credit cards.

Café Delancey   2 E5
3 Delancey St NW1. 071-387 1985. Relaxed, European-style brasserie with a sophisticated, bohemian appeal. You can have any dish you like, whatever the time of day. Breakfasts, brunches, delicious cakes and coffee, salads, steaks, unusual daily specials. *BLD open to 24.00.* A.V.

Café Flo
51 St Martin's Lane WC2. 071-836 8289.	7 B6
127 Kensington Church St W8. 071-727 8142.	9 D2
676 Fulham Rd SW6. 071-371 9673.	13 C4
205 Haverstock Hill NW3. 071-435 6744.	2 C3
334 Upper St N1. 071-226 7916.	3 E5

149 Kew Rd, Richmond, Surrey. 081-940 8298. A growing chain of chic Parisian-style cafés. Continental and English breakfasts, bistro snacks, simple set meals, French classics such as pot au feu or cassoulet. Well-selected wine list. *BLD check with individual branches for opening hours.* A.V.

Café Italien (des Amis du Vin)   6 F4
19 Charlotte St W1. 071-636 4174. Good value, classic Italian dishes in this charming brasserie which spills out onto the street *in summer.* Italian, French and Californian wines. Also a restaurant and wine bar. *LD (Reserve L) open to 23.00. Closed Sun.* A.Ax.Dc.V.

Café Météor   **13 A2**
158 Fulham Palace Rd W6. 081-741 5037. Authentic, informal brasserie/restaurant with a wide range of snacks and more substantial dishes. Interesting French menu including snails, chorizo sausage with warm potato salad, pork chop in apple and brandy sauce. Honey, cream and nut crêpes or chocolate profiteroles to follow. *LD open to 22.45.* A.V.

Café Pelican   **7 B6**
45 St Martin's Lane WC2. 071-379 0309. Lively and noisy theatreland brasserie with tables spilling onto the pavement outside. Inside is divided into two sections; you can have snacks and drinks at the front, and full meals at the back. An extensive menu covers typical French day-long dishes; croissants, croque monsieur, onion soup, plus full meals including vegetarian dishes. Jazz pianist *nightly from 21.00. LD (Reserve) open to 02.00. Snack menu only from 24.00.* A.Ax.Dc.V.

Café Rouge   **5 C6**
31 Kensington Park Rd W11. 071-221 4449. One of a chain of Parisian-style cafés with a warm and welcoming atmosphere. Breakfast, croissants and baguettes, salads and sandwiches or full brasserie meals. French wine list. *BLD open to 23.00, to 22.30 Sun.* A.V.

Camden Brasserie   **2 E5**
216 Camden High St NW1. 071-482 2114. A relaxed atmosphere at this popular brasserie near the canal. Mediterranean food; merguez sausages, pasta parcels with Gorgonzola and walnuts. Also meat or fish cooked on the charcoal grill and accompanied by excellent pommes frites. An open fire in winter adds to the relaxed ambience. *LD (Reserve) open to 23.30, to 22.30 Sun.* V.

Covent Garden Brasserie   **7 B6**
1 The Piazza, Covent Garden WC2. 071-240 6654. Parisian-style café with glassed-in seating *in winter*, opening onto the pavement *in summer*. Snacks such as nachos and mussels, plus more substantial French and Italian dishes. Also open for breakfast *(summer only)* and afternoon tea. Good wine list, mostly French. *BLD open to 23.00, to 22.30 Sun.* A.Ax.Dc.V.

Dôme
38 Long Acre WC2, 071-836 0701.   **7 D6**
34 Wellington St WC2. 071-836 7823.   **11 C1**
290-291 Regent St W1. 071-636 7006.   **6 E5**
354 King's Rd SW3. 071-352 7611.   **13 G2**

341 Upper St, Islington N1. 071-226 3414.   **3 E5**
38-39 Hampstead High St NW3. 071-435 4240.   **1 F1**
98-100 Shepherd's Bush Rd W6. 071-602 7732.
85 Strand on the Green W4. 081-995-6575.
16 Montpelier Vale SE3. 081 318 9164.
Successful chain of brasseries named after the famous
Paris Dôme with branches all over London, distinguished by their brown and cream striped canopies.
Friendly, lively atmosphere and standard brasserie fare.
BLD open to 23.00, to 22.30 Sun. A.Ax.Dc.V.

Floods Café Bar   15 D5
410 Brixton Rd SW9. 071-274 6545. Lively café/bar
serving a range of food from dim sum, sandwiches and
nachos, to a three-course meal. *LD open to 23.30, to
22.00 Sun.* A.Ax.Dc.V.

Flumbs   17 F4
67-69   Abbeville   Rd   SW4.   081-675   2201.
Brasserie/café/wine bar serving breakfasts, brunches,
pastries, bar snacks, afternoon teas and full meals from
a modern British menu. *BLD open to 23.00.* A.Ax.V.

Le Metro   10 C4
28 Basil St SW3. 071-589 6286. In the heart of fashionable Knightsbridge, Le Metro is a French country-style
brasserie with a menu that changes throughout the day.
Croque monsieur, warm goat's cheese salad, bangers
and mash. An extensive selection of wines. *LD open to
23.00, to 22.00 Sat. Closed Sun.* A.Ax.V.

Soho Brasserie   6 G5
23-25 Old Compton St W1. 071-439 9301. Pub conver-
sion with an arty French interior. Coffee, drinks and
snacks at the bar in the front which *in summer* opens on
to the pavement. Meals in the large brasserie-style dining
room. The menu may include fish soup, steak with blue
cheese, stuffed chicken breasts with wild rice. *LD open to
23.00, to 24.00 Thur-Sat.* A.Ax.Dc.V.

Soho Soho   6 G5
11-13 Frith St W1. 071-494 3491. A glass-fronted wine
bar/brasserie with a French restaurant upstairs and a
rotisserie downstairs. The atmosphere in the brasserie is
always lively and tables spill out onto the pavement.
The menu is French; salads, smoked salmon with basil
cream, duck with mango and lime dressing. Brasserie
LD open to 24.00, rotisserie *LD open to 01.00*, wine
bar *open to 23.00. All closed Sun.* A.Ax.Dc.V.

Tuttons   **11 B1**
11-12 Russell St WC2. 071-836 4141. Right on the
edge of Covent Garden Piazza, this is a large, airy
brasserie with a good, reasonably priced English/inter-
national menu. Plenty of tables outside on the piazza.
Atmospheric cellar bar. *BLD (Reserve) open to 23.30,
to 24.00 Fri & Sat.* A.Ax.Dc.V.

WKD Café   **2 E4**
18 Kentish Town Rd NW1. 071-267 1869. This popular
north London café serves simple, well-prepared food during the day. You can read the papers or play chess while
you drink cappuccinos and eat open sandwiches. The fuller
menu has salads and hot daily specials such as spicy grilled
chicken. There is also a breakfast club; enjoy English or
continental breakfast to the accompaniment of live jazz
(Sat & Sun only). In the evening the café becomes a club.
BLD open to 02.00, to 23.00 Sun. Closed Mon. A.Ax.V.

WINE BARS

WINE bars are a well-established alternative to the good
old English pub. From the vast selection in London
the following includes those establishments with good
wines and a relaxed atmosphere. They all serve food –
cheese, pâté, quiche and salads are typical wine bar fare –
although some serve more substantial food or have restaurants of their own. Most carry a range of well-known
wines, a few unusual bottles and at least one reliable house
wine. Almost all offer wine by the glass but it usually
works out cheaper to buy a bottle. Wine bars are now able
to stay open all day (except *Sun*) if they choose, though
some still close for a few hours in the afternoon.

Andrew Edmunds   **6 F6**
46 Lexington St W1. 071-437 5708. Small but charming wine bar/restaurant which serves excellent wines
and imaginative food. The menu changes daily but there
are some good staples such as the pumpkin tortellini
with wild mushroom sauce, Toulouse sausages,
couscous. Salads are inventive; warm duck salad with
radicchio and frisée. *LD (Reserve) open to 22.30.* A.V.

Archduke   **11 C2**
Concert Hall Approach SE1. 071-928 9370. Built into
two railway arches underneath Waterloo Bridge, this wine
bar serves excellent food; good salads, pâtés and cheeses,
and a restaurant upstairs specialising in sausages from all
over the world. Live jazz *nightly. LD (Reserve) open to
23.00. Closed L Sat & LD Sun.* A.Ax.Dc.V.

L'Artiste Musclé   **10 E2**
1 Shepherd Market, off White Horse St W1. 071-493
6150. French wine bar/bistro, particularly appealing in
summer when you can sit outside at the pavement tables.
Well-prepared French menu and a fine selection of
cheeses. *LD open to 23.30. Closed L Sun.* A.Ax.Dc.V.

Balls Brothers
One of the oldest wine bar chains in London with most
of its branches in the City. They share a common list of
more than 60 wines, with the occasional fine claret or
Burgundy. Food and its availability vary from bar to
bar. Most branches close early at *20.30/21.00* and are
closed on *Sat & Sun. Check with individual branches
for times.* A.Ax.Dc.V.
2 Old Change Ct, St Paul's Churchyard EC4.   **7 F5**
071-248 8697.
3 Budge Row, Cannon St EC2. 071-248 7557.   **7 G6**
42 Threadneedle St EC2. 071 628 3050.   **8 A5**
St Mary at Hill EC3. 071-626 0321.   **12 B1**
6 Cheapside EC2. 071-248 2708.   **7 F5**
5 Carey Lane, off Foster Lane EC2. 071-600 2720. **7 F5**
Moor House, London Wall EC2. 071-628 3944.   **7 F4**
Hay's Galleria, Tooley St SE1. 071-407 4301.   **12 B2**
Gows Restaurant, 81 Old Broad St EC2.   **8 A5**
071-920 9645.

Bar des Amis   **7 B5**
11-14 Hanover Pl, off Long Acre WC2. 071-379 3444.
A popular wine bar below the Café des Amis du
Vin brasserie and the elegant Salon des Amis du Vin
restaurant. Daily specials include vegetarian dishes and

delicious savoury crêpes. The wine list includes over 20 wines from the New World, plus monthly specials. *LD open to 23.00. Closed Sun.* A.Ax.V.Dc.

Le Beaujolais   **7 B6**
25 Litchfield St WC2. 071-836 2955. Lively, mixed clientele in this popular and intimate French wine bar. The wine list includes their own-label house red and white plus, of course, Beaujolais. Authentic French cooking. *LD open to 23.00. Closed Sun.* A.V.

Betjeman's   **7 E4**
44 Cloth Fair, Smithfield EC1. 071-796 4981. Housed in the Jacobean home of former Poet Laureate John Betjeman, this excellent wine bar boasts a range of bar snacks, a full restaurant menu and an extensive wine list. The Betjeman Society holds meetings here. *LD open to 23.00. Closed Sat & Sun.* A.V.

Bill Bentley's Wine Bar   **10 B4**
31 Beauchamp Pl SW3. 071-589 5080. Below a superb fish restaurant, the wine bar here is cosy and old-fashioned with a relaxed atmosphere. There's an oyster bar serving delicious and well-presented snacks including fish cakes and potted shrimps. Patio garden. *LD open to 23.00. Closed Sun.* A.Ax.V.

Bow Wine Vaults   **7 F5**
10 Bow Churchyard, off Cheapside EC4. 071-248 1121. Victorian bar within the sound of Bow Bells. Popular with City workers for its good range of hot and cold dishes, wide selection of wines and first-class cheeses. Over a hundred French, Spanish, German and Californian wines. Also fortified wines and malt whiskies. Snacks and cheeseboard from the bar until 20.00 and hot free bar snacks. *L open to 15.00. Closed Sat; Sun & B.hols.* A.Ax.Dc.V.

Brahms & Liszt   **11 B1**
19 Russell St WC2. 071-240 3661. Lively, crowded Covent Garden wine bar with live music downstairs. Hot dishes include lamb curry, chicken kiev, fresh butterfly pasta with capers, open steak sandwich. French country pâté. Wide selection of wines. Upstairs *LD open to 23.00, to 22.30 Sun.* Downstairs *LD open to 01.00, to 22.30 Sun.* A.Ax.Dc.V.

Cork & Bottle   **7 A6**
44-46 Cranbourn St WC2. 071-734 7807. Crowded cellar bar just off Leicester Square. The walls are

covered with posters of wines and champagnes. Excellent selection of wines, bar snacks and hot dishes. *LD open to 24.00.* A.Ax.Dc.V.

Crusting Pipe   **7 B6**
27 The Market, Covent Garden WC2. 071-836 1415. Popular wine bar, part of the Davy's chain (see below). Outside seating under the piazza canopy. Good food, including grills and bar snacks, and reasonably priced wines. *LD open to 23.00. Closed D Sun.* A.Ax.Dc.V.

Daniel's   **6 F6**
68 Regent St W1. 071-437 9090. At the back of the Café Royal, this pleasant, relaxed wine bar has a resident pianist, conventional bar snacks and a varied wine list. *LD open to 23.00. Closed Sat & Sun.* A.Ax.Dc.V.

Davy's
Dusty barrels, old prints and sawdust-covered floors create the Victorian image of these wine bars, the names of which date back to the wine trade of 100 years ago. The chain offers a good selection of wines and the food is excellent; ham off the bone, beef, game pie, crabs, prawns and smoked fish, usually a hot dish or two, game in season and good cheeses. Service shows old-fashioned courtesy. Port, sherry and Madeira from the wood, sound French and German wines by the glass, fine wines by the bottle. The claret list is generally stronger than the Burgundy, but both are exceptional and moderately priced. Particularly noteworthy are the blackboard special offers. These may include Grand Cru clarets or Grande Marque champagne. *The City bars close at 20.00 or 20.30 and at weekends – phone for details. All branches closed Sun.* A.Ax.Dc.V.
The following list is a selection:
Boot & Flogger   **11 F3**
10 Redcross Way SE1. 071-407 1184.
Bottlescrue   **7 E5**
Bath House, Holborn Viaduct EC1. 071-248 2157.
Bung Hole   **7 C4**
55-57 High Holborn WC1. 071-242 4318.
City Boot   **7 G4**
7 Moorfields High Walk, Moorgate EC2. 071-628 2360.
City Flogger   **8 B6**
120 Fenchurch St EC3. 071-623 3214.
Davy's   **7 E5**
10 Creed Lane, off Ludgate Hill EC4. 071-236 5861.

Davy's Wine Vaults
165 Greenwich High Rd SE10. 081-858 7204.

Gyngleboy   5 G5
27 Spring St W2. 071-723 3351.

Skinkers   12 B2
42 Tooley St SE1. 071-407 7720.

Tappit Hen   7 B6
5 William IV St WC2. 071-836 9811.

Dover Street Wine Bar   6 E6
8-9 Dover St W1. 071-629 9813. This large basement
wine bar with its arched vaults is renowned for top-
quality live music; jazz, blues and soul, played *six nights
a week from 22.00*. There is a good wine list, snack
menu and an à la carte restaurant open *at lunchtime*
and for evening meals. The food is mainly French but
there is usually a roast as well. *LD open to 02.00.
Closed Sun.* A.Ax.Dc.V.

Downs
Arch 166, Bohemia Pl E8. 081-986 4325. Reasonably
priced east London wine bar housed in a converted railway arch. Candelit tables make for an intimate atmosphere and the chargrilled dishes are particularly popular. *LD open to 22.45.* A.Ax.Dc.V.

Ebury Wine Bar   10 E5
139 Ebury St SW1. 071-730 5447. Popular wine bar
which is always crowded and lively. Comprehensive
wine list and good selection of reasonably priced food.
Various wines of the week. Also beers and spirits.
Restaurant serves daily specials, a cold table, cheeses
and English puddings. *LD open to 22.15.* A.Ax.Dc.V.

Fenchurch Colony Wine Bar   8 B6
14 New London St, off Fenchurch St EC3. 071-481 0848.
Colonial-style decor in this slick wine bar with separate
champagne bar. Popular with City office workers.
Specialises in enormous sandwiches – ham, turkey, bacon
and cranberry, avocado and bacon. More elaborate dishes
too. Wine list is predominantly French but there are also
choices from Italy, Germany, Australia and New Zealand.
L (Reserve) open to 14.30. Closed Sat & Sun. A.Ax.Dc.V.

Gordon's Wine Bar   11 B2
47 Villiers St WC2. 071-930 1408. This famous 300-
year-old wine cellar has escaped demolition on more
than one occasion. The ancient stone walls and ceilings
often drip with water but this just adds to the charm of
the place. Excellent selection of wines, ports and sher-

ries, plus wholesome buffet food. *LD open to 23.00. Closed Sat & Sun.* No credit cards.

Pitcher & Piano

214-216 Fulham Rd SW10. 071-352 9234.   **13 F2**
871-873 Fulham Rd SW6. 071-736 3910.   **13 B5**
8 Balham Hill SW12. 081-673 1107.   **17 E4**
18-20 Chiswick High Rd W4. 081-742 7731.

Pleasant and airy wine bars, the Pitchers have well-chosen wine lists and a changing menu which always includes their trademark: picker baskets – oriental savoury packets with various dips. *LD open to 23.00, to 22.30 Sun.* A.Ax.V.

Shampers   **6 F6**

4 Kingly St W1. 071-437 1692. Despite its name, wine is Shampers' most impressive feature, with over 160 different varieties from Italy, France, Germany, Australia, New Zealand, California, Chile and England. Also at least 20 champagnes, vintage port, sherries, good clarets. Downstairs brasserie serves international dishes such as sautéed lamb's kidneys, roast guinea fowl, lamb cutlets and daily fish and vegetarian specials. The menu is changed weekly. *LD open to 23.00. Closed D Sat & LD Sun.* A.Ax.Dc.V.

Smith's   **7 B5**

33 Shelton St WC2. 071-379 0310. Below Smith's Art Galleries, this comfortable cellar wine bar offers light snacks plus dishes from the excellent restaurant attached. The fish soup is delicious. *LD open to 23.00. Closed Sun.* A.Ax.Dc.V.

El Vino   **7 D5**

47 Fleet St EC4. 071-353 6786. Something of an institution; musty atmosphere and thoroughly masculine. Little seems to change here; still a regular haunt of lawyers and journalists. Women must wear a skirt, men a jacket and tie. Spirits and liqueurs are available, also a wide range of mainly French and German wines, and about ten varieties of champagne. Sandwiches upstairs, or downstairs restaurant serving soup, pâté, smoked salmon and salad, where it is essential to book. *L only. Open to 20.00. Closed Sat & Sun.* A.Ax.V.

Whittington's   **7 F6**

21 College Hill, off Cannon St EC4. 071-248 5865. Housed in vaulted cellars, claimed to have once belonged to Sir Richard. Enterprising à la carte menu which is changed regularly – fish soufflé with prawns, pan-fried carp, suprême of guinea fowl, paupiettes of

Dutch veal, orange gratin, plus daily specials. Wide-ranging wine list includes bottles from Australia, France, Germany, Spain, Italy, Portugal and Austria. *L open to 14.30. Closed Sat & Sun.* A.Ax.Dc.V.

Wine Press 6 E3
White House Hotel, Albany St NW1. 071-387 1200. Housed in the beamed cellar of a 1930s hotel. Wide range of French wines with a selection of German, Italian, Spanish and Californian bottles too. Wild boar and pheasant pâtés, soup, salad and three hot dishes a day. Packed on Friday lunchtime. *LD open to 21.00. Closed LD Sat & LD Sun; open to 10.00 for breakfast Sat & Sun only.* A.Ax.Dc.V.

OPEN LATE

THE following restaurants and cafés keep serving until at least *02.00;* some are open *all night.* Also note that hotel coffee shops are often open *24 hrs* and serve light meals to non-residents.

Bar Italia 6 G5
22 Frith St W1. 071-437 4520. The most authentic Italian café in Soho, always lively and vibrant. The decor and atmosphere have changed little since the 1950s. Pizza, panettone, parma ham sandwiches. Unlicensed, but this does not seem to detract from its popularity. *Open to 04.00, 24 hrs Sat & Sun.* No credit cards. £

Café Bohème 6 G5
13 Old Compton St W1. 071-734 0623. Popular French-style brasserie in the heart of Soho which attracts a young crowd. You can have a cappuccino, a beer, snacks such as croque monsieur and omelettes, or steak and chips, right through to the small hours. *Open to 02.45, to 23.00 Sun.* A.Ax.V. ££

Calamitees
104 Heath St NW3. 071-435 2396. American-style restaurant serving hamburgers and pizzas into the early hours. *Open to 02.00, to 03.00 Fri & Sat.* A.V. ££

Canton   6 G6
11 Newport Pl WC2. 071-437 6220. Ever popular Chinese restaurant serving authentic Cantonese dishes. *Open to 02.00.* Ax.Dc.V. £

Cuba Libre   3 E5
72 Upper St N1. 071-354 9998. This bar/restaurant, decorated in Cuban style, has live music *most evenings*. Try the aperitivos 'Cuba Libre', a mixture including dips and fried plantain. Good choice of main courses and desserts. *Open to 02.00 Tue-Sat, to 24.00 Sun & Mon.* A.Ax.V. ££

Dover Street Wine Bar & Restaurant   6 E6
8-9 Dover St W1. 071-629 9813. Traditional French cuisine, live music and partying into the small hours. The wine list is mainly French, with some Italian additions. *Open to 02.00. Closed Sun.* A.Ax.Dc.V. ££

Gallipoli   8 B5
8 Bishopsgate Churchyard, off Bishopsgate EC2. 071-588 1922. Turkish cuisine and *twice nightly* belly-dancing cabaret act. *Open to 02.00. Closed Sun.* A.Ax.Dc.V. £££

Harry's   6 F6
19 Kingly St W1. 071-434 0309. Food all through the night; the breakfasts are popular with the night-clubbing set. *Open to 06.00.* A.V. ££ (breakfast £)

Hodja Nasreddin   3 G2
53 Newington Green Rd N1. 071-226 7757. A family-run Turkish restaurant with a homely atmosphere. The boreks (cheese samosas) are excellent and the feta cheese salad is massive. *Open to 01.30, to 03.30 Fri & Sat.* A.Ax.V. £

Istanbul Iskembecisi   4 C1
9 Stoke Newington Rd N16. 071-254 7291. This popular Turkish restaurant serves food practically right through the night, as is customary in Turkish tripe houses. Unusual offal dishes are the speciality here. Also conventional Turkish fare for the less strong-stomached! *Open to 05.00.* No credit cards. £

Lido   6 G6
41 Gerrard St W1. 071-437 4431. Large and busy

Chinese restaurant on two floors. *Open to 05.00.* A.Ax.Dc.V. £

Los Locos
24 Russell St WC2. 071-379 0220. **11 B1**
14 Soho St, off Oxford St W1.071-287 0005. **6 G5**
Lively Mexican bar and restaurant with lots of Tex-Mex specials. Mexican beer and cocktails. Disco from *23.30 every night. Open to 03.00 (for bar food only).* A.Ax.Dc.V. £

Marquee Café **6 G5**
20 Greek St W1. 071-287 3346. Owned by the Marquee Club which is situated directly behind, this café is popular with clubbers. Decorated with musical instruments and graffiti. Live bands play *every night.* Burgers, barbecued dishes, bangers and mash. *Open to 03.00.* A.Ax.Dc.V. ££

Mayflower **6 G6**
68-70 Shaftesbury Ave W1. 071-734 9207. Open into the early hours, this fashionable Cantonese restaurant has specialities such as stir-fried crab, steamed scallops with garlic, yam-stuffed fried spiced duck. *Open to 04.00.* A.Ax.Dc.V. ££

New Diamond **6 G6**
23 Lisle St WC2. 071-437 2517. Elegant Chinese restaurant serving seafood specialities. *Open to 03.00.* A.Dc.V. ££

Paradise Cottage **8 D2**
477 Bethnal Green Rd E2. 071-729 6119. Middle Eastern restaurant; prints of old Istanbul adorn the walls. Try crisp borek (flat baked pastry filled with soft cheese and parsley). *Open to 03.30.* A.V. ££

Rocky's **6 F6**
3 New Burlington St W1. 071-494 3955. Light snacks and salads until *03.00.* Pop videos to accompany cocktails until *03.00.* Steaks, omelettes and burgers through the night. *Open to 06.00.* No credit cards. £

Up All Night **13 G1**
325 Fulham Rd SW10. 071-352 1996. Steaks, burgers and spaghetti through the night. *Open to 06.00.* A.Ax.V. ££

Yung's **6 G6**
23 Wardour St W1. 071-437 4986. Small, comfortable Chinese restaurant on three floors. Fish dishes are their speciality; try shark's fin and chicken soup or fried noodles and prawns. *Open to 04.30.* A.Ax.Dc.V. ££

INDEX

MAPPED AREA INDEX

PRE-THEATRE MENU INDEX

AFTER-THEATRE & LATE-NIGHT EATING INDEX

(last orders after 23.00)

SUNDAY EATING INDEX

NICHOLSON

MAPS

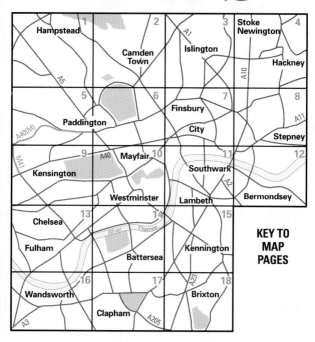

KEY TO MAP PAGES

Hampstead **1**	Camden Town **2**	Islington **3** A1	Stoke Newington **4** Hackney
Paddington **5** A5 A40(M)	**6**	Finsbury **7** City	Stepney **8** A11
Kensington **9** A40 M41	Mayfair **10** Westminster	Southwark **11** Lambeth A2	Bermondsey **12**
Chelsea **13** Fulham	Battersea **14** River Thames	Kennington **15**	
Wandsworth **16** A3	Clapham **17** A205 A23	Brixton **18**	

A10

KEY TO MAP SYMBOLS

M41	Motorway	⇄ ⇄	British Rail Station
Dual A4	Primary Route	⊖	Underground Station
Dual A40	'A' Road	⊖	Docklands LR Station
B504	'B' Road	⊕	Bus/Coach Station
	Pedestrian Street	P	Car Park

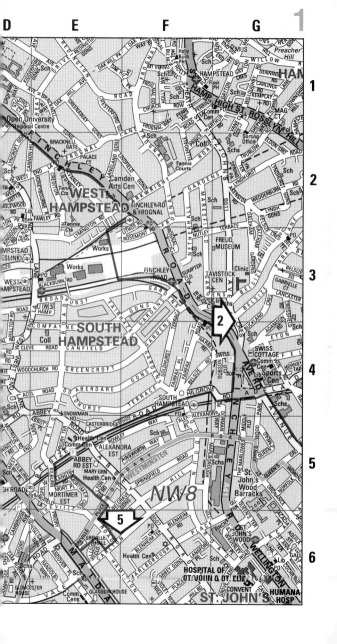

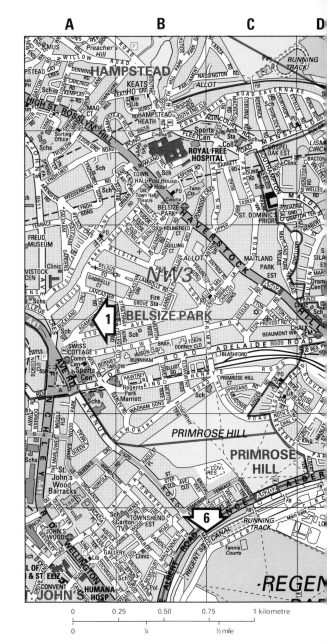

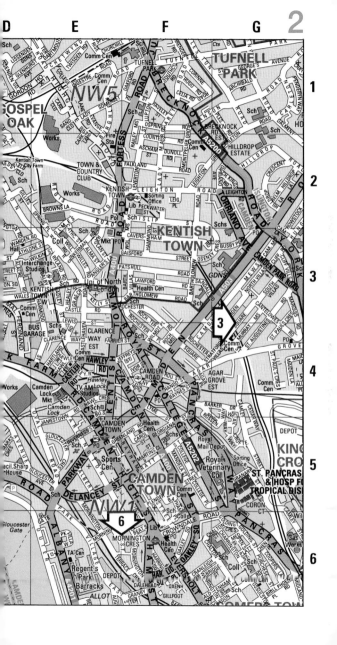

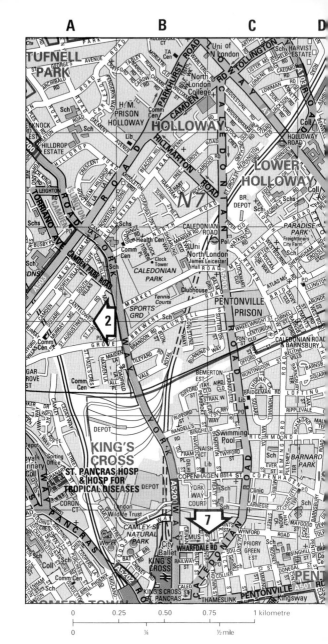

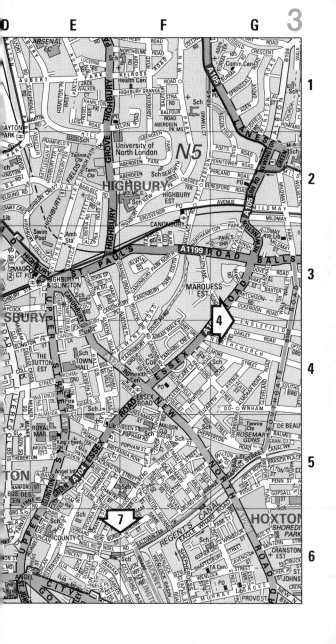

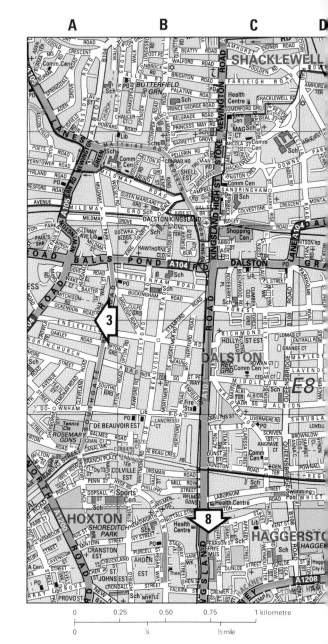

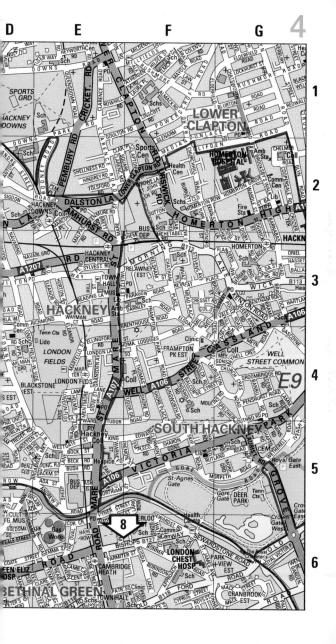

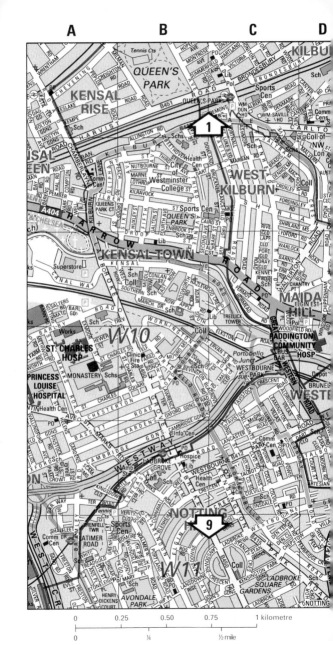

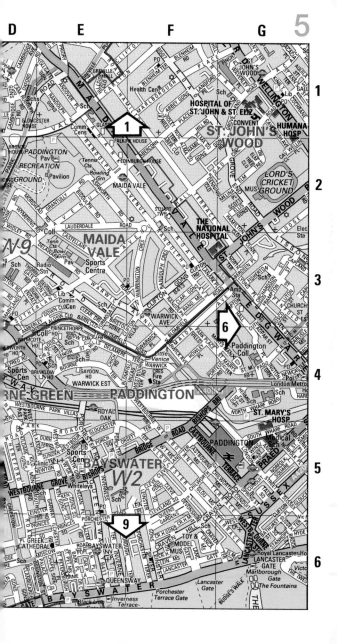

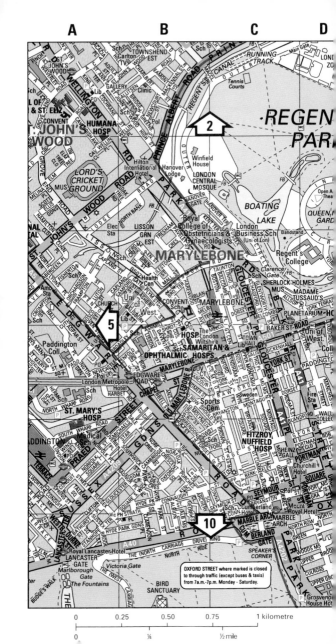

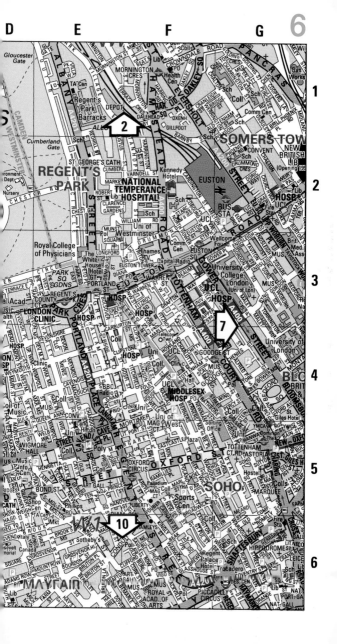

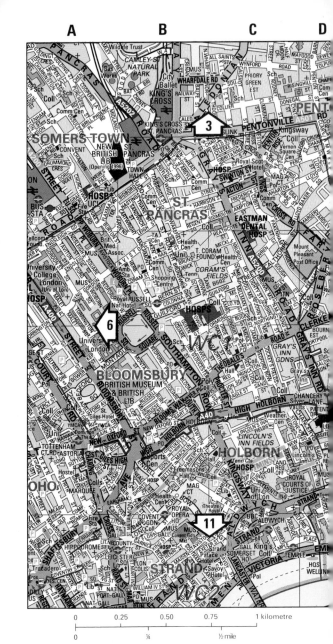

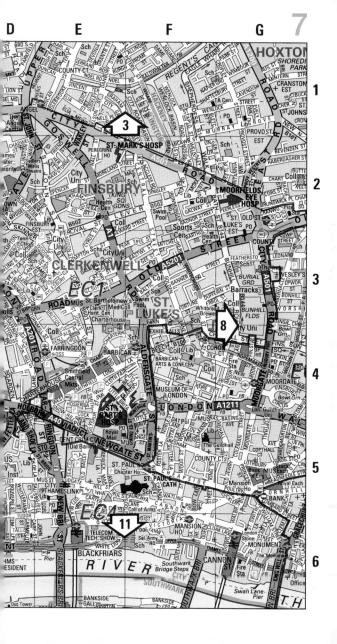

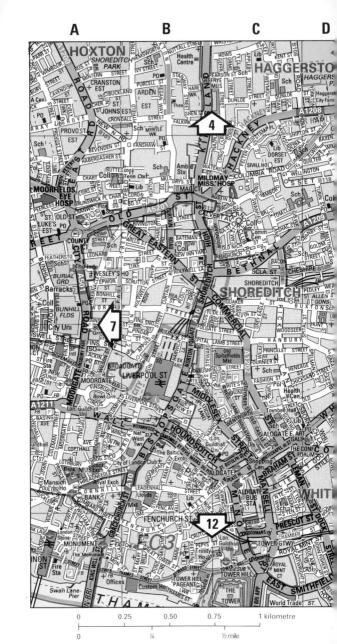

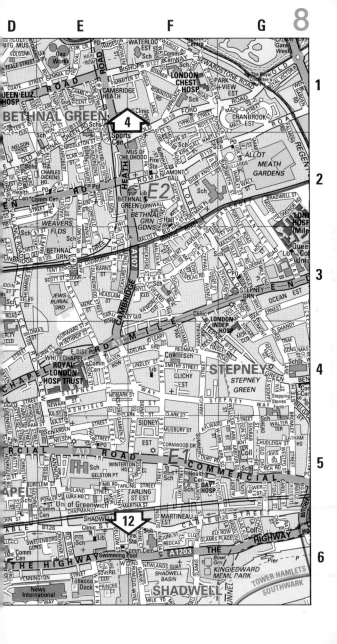

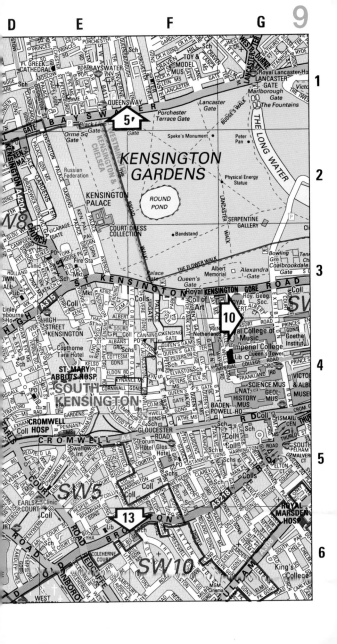

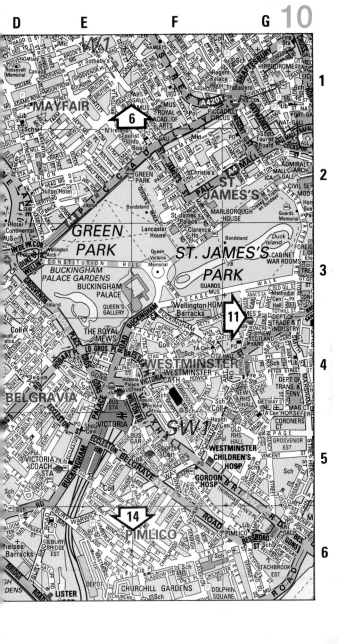

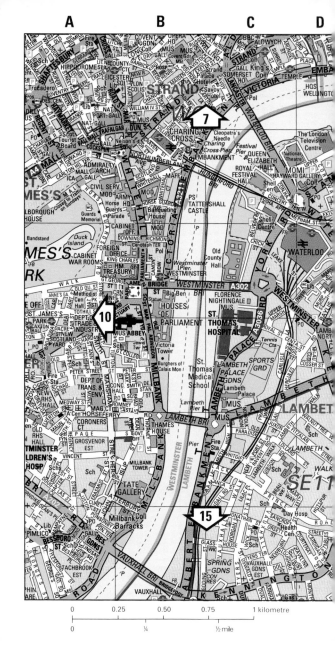

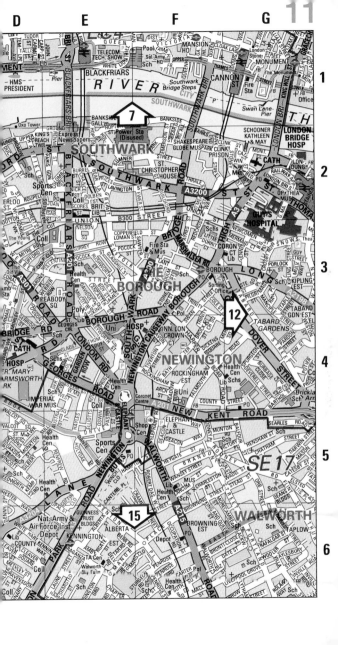

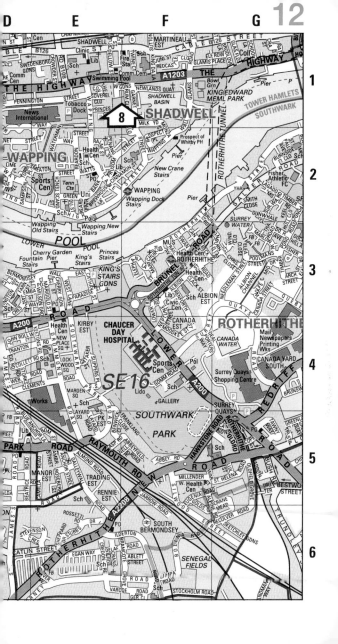

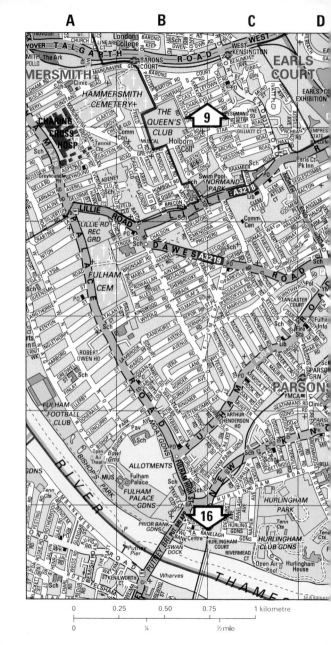

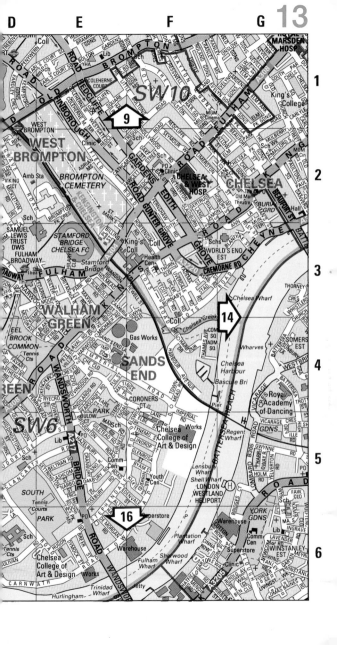

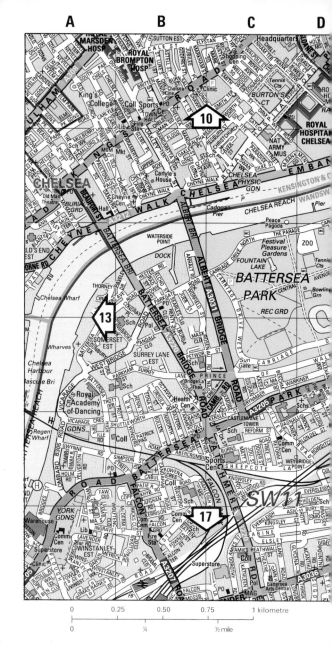

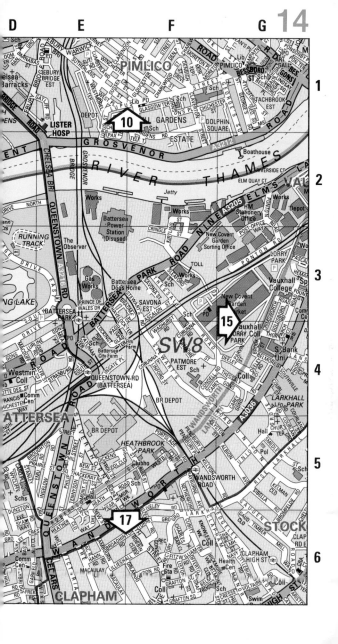

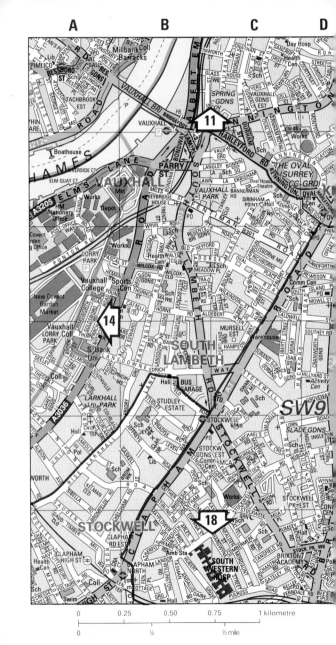

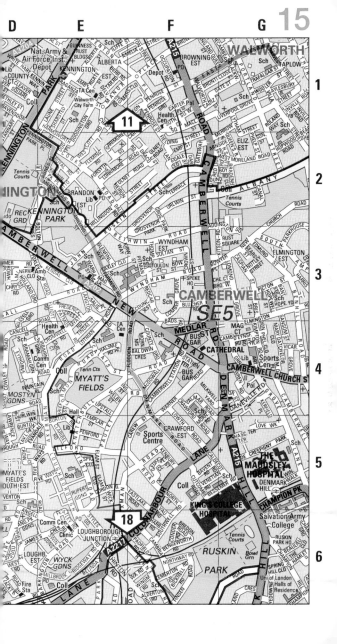

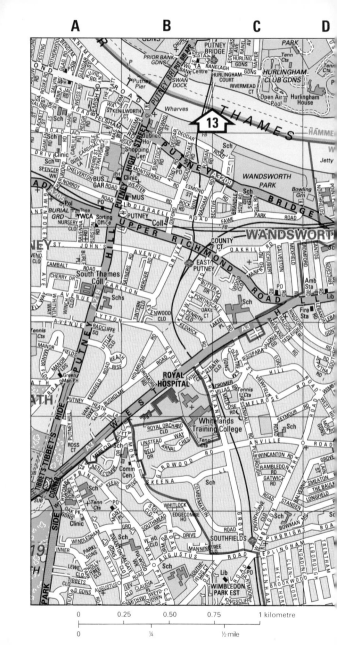

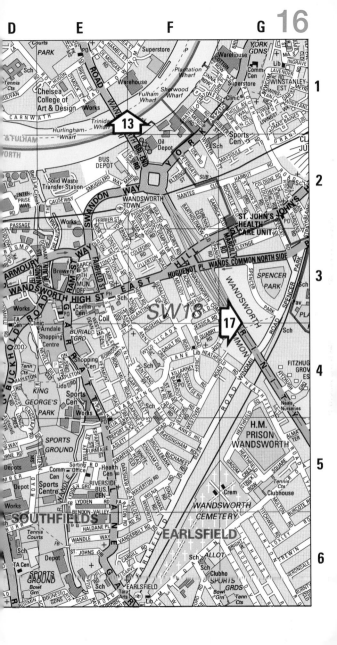

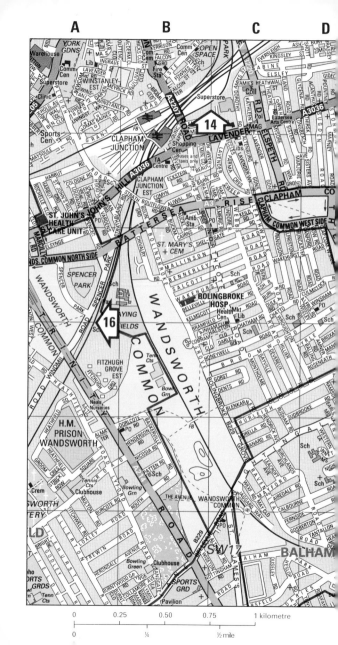

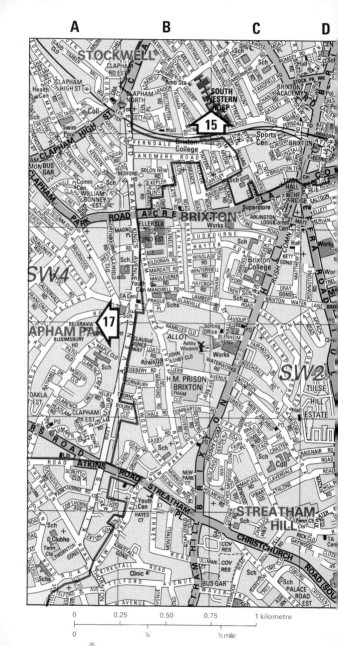

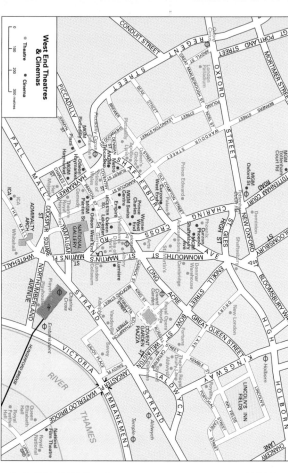

West End Theatres & Cinemas

0 100 200 300 metres

● Theatre
● Cinemas

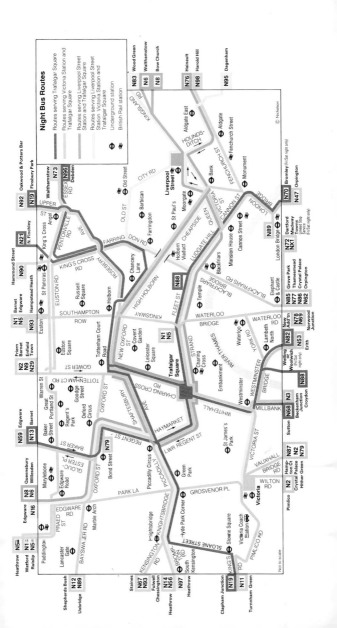

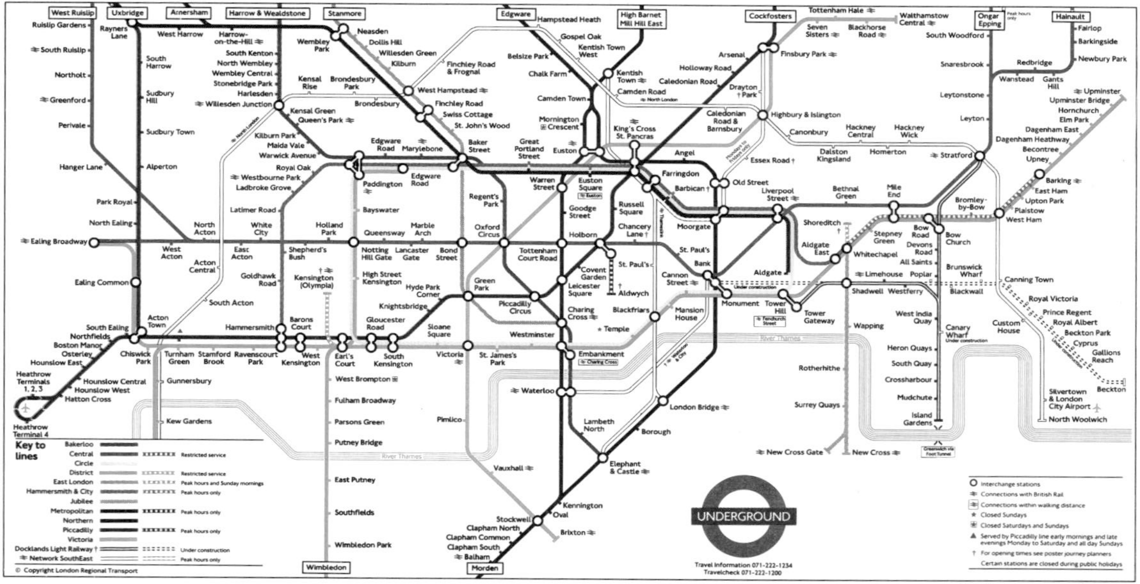

LRT Registered User No 94/1496